BRAHMANANDA SWAMI SIVAYOGI *and* HIS SELECTED WORKS

P.V. Gopalakrishnan

PUBLICATIONS

KALPAZ PUBLICATIONS

DELHI - 110052

Brahmananda Swami Sivayogi and His Selected Works
[*Religion*]

Rs. 790

ISBN: 81-7835-101-3

Published in 2002 in India by
Kalpaz Publications
C-30, Satyawati Nagar
Delhi-110052
e-mail: kalpaz@hotmail.com

Laser Typeset at: Alphabet, Delhi
Printed at: Chawla Offset Press, Delhi

Contents

PART - II
SELECTED WORKS OF SIVAYOGI

Preface

Every organisms in this world long for bliss and freedom. This shows that every human beings should work for others' bliss also as he should work for his bliss. It clears the matter that the true and natural religion is the 'Religion of Bliss'. All the other religions are created by religious founders. Even the famous scholars are following their religious teachings without any testing and questioning. Such religious believes do not comply with science, logic and experience. On the matters of God they have different and contradictory believes. This difference leads to religious conflicts and even to war.

Every human beings accept only good things after proper testing and experiments. But people do not test or experiment religious teachings. Each person argue that his religion is the best in the world and all other religions are false. For the benefit of the mankind this argument or belief do nothing. They should make the mind clean from all evil thoughts and make it firm. This is the teaching of Sivayogi. In order to spread Sivayogi's ideal (Anandadarsan), he wrote, published and distributed many books in the vernacular language, Malayalam. Those books were widely circulated among Malayalees. His two books *Mokshapradeepam* and *Ananda Sutra* were translated to English. It was Sivayogi's desire that his ideals should cross the country and reach among the minds of foreigners. Now I am very happy on account of the matter that Kalpaz Publications is going to publish a book on Brahmananda Swami Sivayogi and his ideals. I am grateful to the publisher and the author, Mr. P.V. Gopalakrishnan.

Sivayogi's ideals are culturally and logically far better than that of the other philosophies in India.

Uncontrolled mind is the root cause of all problems in this world. Calamities like suicide, murder and war are caused by uncontrolled and uncultured mind.

This earth is our mother. We all are children of that mother. We are all brothers and sisters. We have to develop this concept of universal humanism. Sidhasramam, through Sivayogi's ideals is trying to make people humanistic, people of different nations began to think of 'all for one and one for all'. Sidhasramam is a non-profit seeking organisation which has been trying to make a cultured and welfare society.

This book deals with all about Sidhasramam and Sivayogi. In addition to it three small books of Sivayogi are also appended. I presume that all men and women of logic would appreciate the ideals of Sivayogi and his contributions described in this book.

Nirmalananda Yogi
President

Brahmananda Swami Sivayogi Sidhasramam,
P.O. Alathur,
Palakkad, Kerala, India - 678541.

Part One

Literary and Cultural Contributions of Brahmananda Swami Sivayogi

[This part of the book is the final project report of junior fellowship awarded by Department of Culture, Ministry of Human Resource Development, Government of India during 1998-2000]

One

His Life

The greatest rationalist yogi, Brahmananda Swami Sivayogı, after Brahaspati and Carvaka, was born on August 26th 1852 in an aristocratic family as the 9th son of Smt. Nani Amma of Karat Nair family and Sri Kunjikrishna Menon of Vallengi Ravanyaram at Nemmara in the Palakkad district of Kerala. In his childhood he was called Govindankutty.

It will be worthy to mention into which social condition this child was born. Social discrimination was on the peak in those days in Kerala. As he was born in a Nair family, he had to see, from his early childhood, so many irrational things going on in his own family in the name of faith and religion. Sacrifices, vows, temple visitings, idol worships, fastings, etc. were day to day activities in his surroundings. There were inferior Gods such as Muthappan, Parakkutti, Chovva, Kuttichathan, etc. besides superior Gods such as Krishna, Shiva, Vishnu, Subrahmania, Ganpati, Brahma, etc. The inferior Gods eats and drinks, it is believed by devotees, flesh and arrack. One sensible man cannot take them models or worship them as they are far away from morals. Another important thing which worth mentioning is the social discrimination. People of Kerala were divided into several groups according to the caste system. If Namboothiris, were the upper class Menon and Nair comes just below the upper class and Ezhavas another inferior level of people. All the other Harijans are considered to be 'avarnas'.

If a new born child does not possess extraordinary courage in his heart and humanity in his mind, he would not have been a great personality but a mere drop in the flow. Such a pathetic social condition existed in Kerala. But this child was rational, scientific, and above all sympathetic and hence he began to question what he found irrational.

As per the custom which was prevalent in the Nair families in those days, Nani Amma stayed in her own house. Her husband, Kunji Krishna Menon occasionally visited Govindan Kutty spent his childhood in his mother's house at Kollankode.

Govindankutty was brought up in an orthodox way. According to the wishes of his parents and other elderly persons in the family, he used to take bath early in the morning and used to go to the worship chamber in his house for worshipping Gods. However, he was unaware of what was he doing or what is the benefit of such doings.

One day he noticed some persons stand far away from temple. They were come to worship God. But stayed back. He asked his mother why they do not go to temple as he and his mother did and worship the God. His mother told that those people were untouchables and so they were not permitted to go near temples. This seemed uncomprehesible to him. He asked himself if all creatures are made by the God how some become untouchables? This question rooted in him toubling his mind. It was an incident from which his rational life began.

His parents showed every care to give him good education. A home tutor taught him alphabets. After this he was sent to a nearby primary school.

When he completed 5th standard, his parents decided to teach him Sanskrit. Accordingly they sent him to Padmanabha Sastri at Aalampallam for learning Sanskrit. It was from there he began to write simple but meaningful poems. His ability to write poems made him popular among fellow students.

One day, by this time he was near Koodalloor Sastri for doing higher course in Sanskrit Kavya, he asked his teacher whether it is right to worship different types of Gods, if God is everywhere and in every object and especially He has no quality. It was the time in which his teacher recited a sloka which ran as follows:

"Brahmanadam Paramasukhadam kevalam Jnanamoorthim
Viswãtheetham Gagana Sathrsam thathvasyathilakshyam,
Ekam Nithyam Vimalamachalam Sarvadheesakshibhrutham,
Bhavãtheetham thrigunarahitham Sathgurumthvam Namami."

His teacher said nothing. Koodalloor Sastri must have been

understood that his pupil has reached a highest spiritual level in which mere a personal God has no place but an idea of an universal God has full power. Govindan Kutty's skeptic mind began to question everything. Earlier his parents, teachers, friends, neighbours, etc. were his victims. By this time he became well-versed in Hindu scriptures and Tamil language.

Knowing the brilliance of Govindankutty, Kunjikrishna Menon sent his son to Ernakulam for getting his son English education. It was a turning point in his life. His native place was a little village. He could get no world experience from there. But from a big town like Ernakulam, he could acquire a vast world of experience.

At Ernakulam he could see a lot of people having different culture, social life, language, life style and habit. He could learn about Christianity, Muhammedanism, Jainism, etc. This forced him to compare Hindu ideals with that of other religions. In a village like that of his, there were no chances of logic thinking, but Ernakulam was different. There were many people who dared to question irrational things found in religion. It was a place suitable to grow for a skeptic mind. So Govindan Kutty's skeptic mind had undergone rapid growth.

His main aim for going to Ernakulam was to study English, when he realised that he got a minimum knowledge in that language, he himself ceased English learning and turned his attention to philosophical learning. During the remaining days he found himself among fat texts of Vedas, Upanishads, Puranas, Gita, Mahabharata, Smritis, Sutras, etc. All the study forced him to realise a fact that God is non-qualitative; such a God will not be pleased by worship.

Returning home, Govindan Kutty continued his critical study on the scriptures. By that time wealth of his family mansion was partitioned. Nani Amma, the mother of Govindan Kutty, had to live in another house. People began to call the grown up Govindan Kutty Govinda Menon, when the family mansion was partitioned, he had to look after his own nuclear family. Agriculture, village matters, family matters, etc. began to engulf a large portion of his time. This disturbed him. But there were no other choices. However, he found time to continue his study.

His introvert nature was greatly mistaken by his parents. They thought that he had some psychological problem and that such gloomy attitude will be over when he is get married. Thinking so his innocent parents made arrangements for his marriage. Accordingly he married a 17-year old girl named Thavukutty Amma of Mukkil Marunthoor family at Vadavannor. Later Thavukkuty Amma became his disciple and got the title Yogini Matha.

A village officer's profession was considered high in those days. Though the profession demanded risky jobs such as survey and revenue collection, it is confined only to aristocratic families. Considering Govinda Menon's family history, British government appointed Govindan Kutty as a village officer. He accepted it and worked for a short period. But he felt hard to obey greed and selfishness. Hence, he resigned from the post.

Then he turned his attention to teach Sanskrit to nearby young men. From that period he put aside much of his time to distribute the wealth of knowledge.

Spending some years in that way, he found himself in the post of a Sanskrit teacher in the Native school at Kozhikode, when one of his friends brought about the news of the new post. If he was an introvert when he was at Ernakulam, his nature changed much when he went to Kozhikode. At Kozhikode he could find a lot of like minded persons. He discussed with them the questions that budded in his mind.

During this period a branch of Brahma Samaj was started at Kozhikode. It was an organisation of reformers. Govinda Menon participated in the discussion classes of Brahma Samaj organised under the leadership of Sri Ayyathan Gopalan. Before long the learned men of the Brahma Samaj realised that Govinda Menon was a genius in spiritual matters and logic. When he wrote a book called *Brahma Sangeerthanam* for the need of Brahma Samaj, the learned men of that organisation gave him the title 'Brahmananda Swami' knowing his knowledge both in spiritual matters, logic and literary ability. From there he began to practise Rajayoga. As he was away from family knots, he had enough time to do *dhyana* and *upasana*. Getting the title 'Brahmananda Swami', he thought of giving up worldly happiness. According to him it is transitory. So as Mahatma Gandhi did, he discussed the matter with his wife and with her consent, he took the Brahmacharya vow. Knowing that his service should get to his villagers, he gave up his job at Kozhikode and left for his native place.

In 1899 he joined as a Sanskrit teacher in the Alathur Board School at Alathur in the Palakkad district of Kerala. In the school he was known as 'Brahmananda Swami'. As a practitioner of Rajayoga he was also known as a 'Yogi'.

His habit of free thinking increased the number of his disciples. They do not confined in the school only. For practising the yoga and giving advices to his devotes, he built a small ashram at Vanoor in the Palakkad district and named it 'Vanoor Sidhasramam'.

Realising that animal sacrifices are against all moral aspects he protested against it. Orthodox people thought that he was a rationalist, learned men thought that he was a revolutionary. But he was neither. He was a free thinker, a scientist seeing the truth.

Later he shifted his ashram to Alathur in the same district. People began to visit the Sidhasramam in scores. Like a new Socrates he preached what he found true. People, till that day, was not able to distinguish real religion from that of the religion taught by the priests. Brahmananda Swami separated irrational things and superstition from false religion and gave people real and pure religion. This work made him popular, people from all parts of Kerala, visited him; got enlighted and left with a happy mind.

In 1905, he stopped his teaching profession and became a full time yogi. He believed that man is not mere material. His mind is important. One should control the mind, otherwise his life would be miserable.

His two speeches one at Kozhikode in 1910 and the other at Guruvayur in 1912 attracted the attention of many learnt men. Some became his disciples, others adored him. A few orthodox people stood against him. This protestation did not shake him. He preached again and again that Hindu religion is full of superstition. And all the religion should be rebuilt. His sole aim was to reform this religion and to make it rational and scientific. Then only it would do good to mankind. He stormed against minor Gods of Hindus who eat flesh and drink arrack. He proclaimed that only by learning, Hindu ladies will get more status and better living.

He explained his ideas with examples and proofs through his literature, speeches, letters, meetings and advices.

His literary career lasts from 1893 to 1928. During this period he wrote 13 books. They all are superb in contents. From his works, one thing can be easily understood that from 1893 to 1928 he had a restless period of writing and writing. His literature varies from poetry to supreme spiritual thoughts. He wrote and published *Sivayoga Rahasyam* in 1893, *Sthree Vidya Poshini* in 1899, *Sidhanbhuthi* in 1903, *Aananda Kalpa drumam* in 1905, *Mokshapradeepam* in 1905, *Ananda Sutram* in 1910, *Aananda Sopanam* in 1913, *Rajayoga Parasyam* in 1914, *Vigraharadhana Gandhanam* in 1916, *Aananda Vimanam* in 1916, *Aananda Motha Parasyam* in 1919, *Aananda Kummi* in 1920, *Aanandadarsam* in 1927, and *Aanandadarsamsam* in 1928. *Aananda Sopanam* is an edited work. His master piece is *Mokshapradeepam*. Thousands of copies of *Mokshapradeepam* were sold in all parts of Kerala. It was interesting to note that he never distributed his books through book sellers or through agents but sold all of the copies by direct, i.e., by post. Hindi and English versions of some books were also published considering the demand from north India and abroad. From 1905 he confined to his ashram. He never went far off places. Twice only he took long journeys. One to Kozhikode for a speech and the other to Kannur for the inauguration of Yogasala. He spent his time to practice Rajayoga, write replies to letters of devotees, discussions and counselling.

He was a spokesman of Rajayoga. He believed that Rajayoga was supreme, when compared to the other branches of yoga like Karmayoga, Jnanayoga and Sanyasayoga. It was his belief that our body and mind are the most important things and one can get salvation by cleaning and controlling our own body and mind. He advocated universal harmony and an universal religion which was none other than Aananda religion. He strongly opposed distinctions. According to him there is no Hindu, no Muslim, no Christian, no Brahmin, no Kshatriya, no Vaisya, no Sudra. The following words of Swami Vivekananda must have been in his mind and it must have been made him compassionate.

"Each Soul is potentially divine. The goal is to manifest the divinity within by controlling nature, external and internal.

Do this by work, or worship or psychic control, or philosophy— by one, or more, or all of these—and be free.

This is the whole of religion. Doctrines, or dogmas, or rituals or books or temples, or forms are but secondary details".

He advocated that all human beings, all organisms stand for the bliss eternal. So there is only one religion which is the bliss eternal, i.e., Aananda. The differences are external. But internally all are alike. He wondered on thinking that why people make distinctions and discriminations. He couldn't understand and compromise with all the follies which were part of religions. Hence, his sword of pen fell upon the neck of many orthodox people. They had no equal sword of logic. This fight of Sivayogi was a rescue for poor, neglected and suppressed people.

But people of Kerala did not get that shelter for ever. On 10-9-1929, at the age of 77, the great rationalist Yogi of Kerala, not, of the world, left this world, leaving the burden of continuing his reformational work to his wife, Yogini Matha.

References

1. Asathyathilninnu Sathyathilekku-Brahmananda Swami Jeevacharithram-Bhiman Guruji, published by Sidhasramam, Alathur.
2. *Brahmananda Swami Sivayogi— Pavanan*, published by the Publications Division, Cultural Department, Government of Kerala.
3. *Manasse Enna Daivam* — Dr. M.S. Nair, Distributed by Current Books, Kottayam.
4. *Saragrahi magazine*, pp. 6-11, July-August-1999 issue, published by Sidhasraman, Alathur.
5. *Sri Sivayogi Souvenir 1952*, pages 65-67, published by Sri Sivayogi Souvenir Committee, Sidhasramam, Alathur.
6. *Ananda Maha Sabha Souvenir*, 1961, pp. 5-11, published by Sidhasramam, Alathur.
7. *The Vedanta Kesari*, Vol. 80, March 1993 issue, published by Sri Ramakrishna Math, Madras.

Two

Contemporary Social Reformers of Brahmananda Swami Sivayogi

Social condition in Kerala during the later part of 19th century and first part of 20th century were so pathetic. Untouchability, social discrimination, superstition, irrational customs, social injustices, etc. were taking an upper hand in those days. To make the condition right social reformers like Ayyankali, Vakkom Abduk Kader Moulavi, Brahmananda Swami Sivayogi, Chattambi Swami, Sree Narayana Guru and Vagbhadanandan were in the scene. Ayyankali and Vakkom Abdul Kader Moulavi were only social reformers, where as Brahmananda Swami Sivayogi, Chattambi Swami, Sri Narayana Guru and Vagbhadanandan were spiritual leaders cum social reformers. Their work was mainly on religious reformation. Apart from Sivayogi, a brief study of the other three reformers are given below, because of the identity of work with that of Sivayogi.

1. Chattambi Swami

Another social reformer, apart from Sivayogi, who lived in the renaissant period is Chattambi Swami. He was born on August 25th of 1853 at a little village called Kollur near Thiruvananthapuram. His father's name was Ananda Sarma and mother's was Thirunankamma. His name was Ayyapan. But he was called in his childhood days, Kunhan. Kunhan learnt alphabets from his neighbours. Later he learnt Sanskrit from a Sastri. Then he joined in the school of Raman Pillai in Petta. He learnt Mathematics, Tamil and music from the school. As he was smart, school teachers made him class leader to control students at spare time. So students called him Chattambi. He kept this title till his death.

Poverty did not permit him to go for higher studies. Situations forced him to do labour works to look after the family. Later he became a document writer. It was in this period that he became interested in yoga. Accordingly, he discipled himself to Thykkave Ayyave, a great yogi. Stopping yoga practice for a short period, he learnt Vedas from Subbha Jada Padhi. When he realised that he became well-versed in Vedas and Vedanta, he decided to undergo a long pilgrimage. During this period he completed yoga.

His life message was love, nonviolence and brotherhood. He opposed animal sacrifice and caste system. He advocated that low caste people have the right to temple worship. He proclaimed that priesthood is not limited to Brahmin caste only.

His books are evidence to his scholastic knowledge in Indian Philosophy. On 5-5-1924 at Panmana, a place in the Thiruvananthapuram district, he went to the other world.

2. Sree Narayana Guru

Sree Narayana Guru was born in 1855 at Chembazhanthy in the Thiruvananthapuram District. His first name was Narayanan. He learnt alphabets from Madanasan , his own father. Then learnt Sanskrit from Raman Pillai of Karunagappally. After this he spent his time by teaching students of his village. During this period he was known as 'Nanu Asan'. The name 'Narayana Guru' was contributed to him later by the native people.

It was a period of superstition and social injustices, people suffered a lot by this. Seeing people's difficulties he grieved. The gloomy Sree Narayana Guru increased the sorrow of his parents. They conducted his marriage. But his destiny was another one. For a yogi, worldly pleasure is nothing. Hence he gave up sexual life. Like a new Buddha he left his abode seeking a way to smash the miseries of people, wandering many places he reached 'Maruthua Mala'. There he spent some months enjoying yogic pleasure. After a long period he reached near Neyyar river. He built a new temple and stayed there.

Sree Narayana Guru was a man of Ezhava folk. In those days people of Ezhava caste were not permitted to temple worshipping. So they worshipped inferior Gods such as Chathan, Chamundi, Madan, Poothathan, Chudala Madan, etc. Those inferior Gods were drunkards and meat eaters. Sree Narayana Guru advocated that worshipping such Gods was wrong because they were far from morals. He persuaded people to worship superior Gods such as Siva and Subrahmanya. For this purpose he built a Siva temple at Aruvippuram. Upon the temple wall he wrote.

"Jathi bhetham matha dvesham
Ethumillathe Sarvarum
Sodharathvena Vazhunna
Mathrka Sthana Manithu."

[This is an ideal place where people live together like brothers irrespective of evils like caste and religion].

Seeing it a success several temples were built at different places in his leadership. Truth, justice, sympathy, love, etc. were idols there. By this time he had realized that humanity is the greatest virtue and virtues like truth, justice, sympathy, love, etc. are to be worshipped.

In fact, it created revolutionary results. Ezhava caste was the largest caste in the Hindu community in Kerala. Many evil customs were spread among Ezhavas. He decided to wipe off all the evils and irrational customs spreaded among the people. In 1920 he gave an advice to his people to stop toddy tapping which were the caste-profession of Ezhavas. He said, "toddy is poison. Do not make it, do not sell it, do not drink it".

In 1924 he called religious leaders of all religion for a religious summit. It was to put an end to the controversies among religions. In the summit he preached about the importance of education and knowledge. He strongly opposed irrational customs such as 'Thalikettu Kalyanam' (a type of child marriage) Therandukuli (a custom usually conducted using a large sum at the first menstruation of girls). He advised people to conduct simple marriages. In 1928, he passed away. The organisation called Sree Narayana Darma Paripalana Yogam (S.N.D.P. Yogam) continues the reformational work started by Sree Narayana Guru.

3. Vag Bhadanandan

Vag Bhadanandan, one of the contemporary social reformers of Sivayogi, was born on April 27th of 1887 at Padyam in the

Koothuparam be in Kerala as the first child of Koran Gurukal of Vayaleri Vazhavalappil, Thankandiyil, Padyam and Vayaleri Cheeruvamma. Koran Gurukal was a respectable man. Vag Bhadanandan's earlier name was Kunjikannan. As Koran Gurukal was well-versed in Sanskrit and Ayurveda, Kunjikannan did not seek a teacher outside of his abode. In his twelveth year, after acquiring preliminary knowledge from his own father, Kunjikannan began to go through Puranas and epics. In those days, in many parts of Kerala, Ezhava community were not permitted to go to school. As a result of this he did not get school education especially English education. Though he had accepted his father as teacher, he accepted Mr. A.K. Gurukal as his guide and home tutor.

During his boyhood days he was interested in epics and Puranas. Because of this interest he began to read scriptures. On reading the scriptures, his mind declined to spiritual matters and he turned his attention to Advaida and Vedanta.

When he was grown up, he decided to impart his knowledge to people through teaching and speech. At this period he went to Kozhikode for a speech. His speech was a great success. People insisted him not to leave Kozhikode. Accordingly he stayed at West Hill, Kozhikode and started a Sanskrit school in 1906, at Karapparambe in the Kozhike district to impart knowledge. Students were admitted to his school irrespective of caste, creed and wealth.

It was during this period that, he was attracted to the ideals of Sri Brahmanada Swami Sivayogi. Kunjikannan was known by this period, V.K. Gurukal. Sivayogi's 'Mukshapradeepam' attracted him deeply. Later he saw Sri Brahmananda Swami Sivayogi renamed him as 'Vag Bhadanandan', seeing his ability to speech and his knowledge in logic. Vag Bhadanandan started spreading of the ideals of Sivayogi. In order to spread Rajayoga he founded 'Rajayogananda koumudi Yogasala' at Kallai, Kozhikode. The ideals of 'Moksha pradeepam' and 'Vigraharadhana Gandhanam', two famous works of Sivayogi, attracted him very much.

Complying with the ethics of Bharthru Hari, he made

elaborate descriptions on Asam Chindhi (destroy the desire), Bhaja Kshamam (adhere to forgiveness), Jahi Madham (discard the ego), pāpe Mathim Makrtha (do not think of evil) Sathya Bhruhi (tell truth), Manyan Manaya (respect the respectable persons), Vidhisho pyanunaya (comply even with enemies), Nayahyu Sadhu padavim (do not follow the evil path), Devaswa vidhwajjanam (depend the learnt men), prakhyapaya prasrayam (expand obedience), keerthim palaya (keep greatness), dhukhithe kurudhayam (show sympathy to depressed). Like Sivayogi he also believed that mind is the root cause of all evils and all virtues.

He was against temple visiting and idol worship. According to him God is Nirguna and He is pervaded everywhere.

He advocated the importance of knowledge. He was not a mere spiritual leader, but he was a social reformer who come in the category of Sree Narayana Guru, Chattambi Swami and Brahmananda Swami Sivayogi.

On 1922 April 23rd he married Vag Devi. In order to spread his ideals, he founded an institution called 'Atma Vidya Sangh'. Its headquarter was at Kozhikode.

Besides usual speech and direct advices, he used his pen to spread his ideals. In 1925 he wrote a book called *Atma Vidya*. It is a book which stands against superstitions and fanatical religious customs and beliefs. Another popular book of Vag Bhadananda was published in 1934. Its name is 'Atmavidya Lekhamala'. It is dedicated to the practicability of Advaita and it contains a detailed critical note on Gita.

On March 30th, 1937, he died.

References

1. *Sree Narayana Guru Swamikal Navodhananthinte Pravachakan* - P. Parameshwaran, published by Poorna Publications, Kozhikode.
2. *Sree Narayana Guru* - K. Ramachandran, Kairali Children's Book Trust, Kottayam.
3. *Keralathinte Samskarika charithram* - P. K. Gopalakrishnan, State Institute of Languages, Thiruvananthapuram.
4. *Sri Chattambi Swamikal* - Dr. K.P.K. Menon.
5. *Vag Bhadananda Guru Vum, Samboohika Navodhanavum* - Dr. M.S. Nair, Department of Cultural Publications, Government of Kerala, Thiruvananthapuram.

was published in 1934. Its name is 'Atmavidya Lekhamala'. It is dedicated to the practicability of Advaita and it contains a detailed critical note on Gita.

On March 30th, 1937, he died.

References

1. *Sree Narayana Guru Swamikal Navodhananthinte Pravachakan* - P. Parameshwaran, published by Poorna Publications, Kozhikode.
2. *Sree Narayana Guru* - K. Ramachandran, Kairali Children's Book Trust, Kottayam.
3. *Keralathinte Samskarika charithram* - P. K. Gopalakrishnan, State Institute of Languages, Thiruvananthapuram.
4. *Sri Chattambi Swamikal* - Dr. K.P.K. Menon.
5. *Vag Bhadananda Guru Vum, Samboohika Navodhanavum* - Dr. M.S. Nair, Department of Cultural Publications, Government of Kerala, Thiruvananthapuram.

Three

Sivayogi's Position in the Indian Philosophy

Ancient Indian philosophy was built upon the strong base of the Vedas. The Vedic tradition is classified into two aspects such as Jhana Kanda (knowledge aspect) and Karma Kanda (ritualistic aspect). Later Buddha, Charvaka and Mahavir expressed their disbelief in the testimony of the Vedas. So their system of philosophy is called 'Nastik'. The word 'Nastik' means one who do not believe in God and rebirth. But in the Indian context the expression 'Nastik School of Philosophy' means the system of philosophy which do not believe in the testimony of the Vedas. The 'Astik' class is divided into two schools of philosophies; one based on Vedas and the other having independent origin. The Veda school has two branches mentioned earlier, i.e., Karma Kanda and Jhana Kanda.

Brahmananda Swami Sivayogi's philosophy 'Anandadarsan' can be considered to be one in the category of 'Nastik class'. The place of 'Anandadarsan' in the Indian philosophical system can be easily understood from the following chart.

Indian Philosophical Systems

Astik	Nastik
↓	↓
1. Based on Vedas (emphasizing karma philosophy) 2. Philosophies having independent origin such as Sankhya, Yoga, Nyaya and Vaishesika.	Charvaka, Buddha, Jain and Brahmananda Swami Sivayogi

Anandadarsan and the other philosophies in the Nastik class

Charvaka one of the great leader of the Nastik philosophy in the ancient India antagonized against the Vedas. According to him the Vedic ritualism is useless. Likewise Brahmananda Swami Sivayogi also refutes the Vedas. He says, "Those who taking up the path of ritualism, do not know the way to salvation, and are immersed in darkness or ignorance. They delude others by their preaching and get them introduced to their ignorant path of sacrifice, vows and the like, and lead them astray from the path of salvation or eternal bliss."

Charvaka believed that pleasure is the ultimate end of life. Sivayogi was also in the same thought. According to him 'Bliss alone reigns supreme.'

According to Buddha desire is the root cause of all pain and sufferings. In another word jumping of mind from one matter to other is desire. Brahmananda Swami Sivayogi, also had the same opinion. He says, "The meaning of sense control is the gaining of such a control over the senses that they can be directed to the right path as intended by the yogi. If that does not become possible, the result is harm to oneself and others too. The goal of eternal bliss cannot also be attained."

References

1. *Indian Philosophy* - Dr. Vatsyayan, Kedarnath Ramnath, Meerut.
2. *Moksha pradeepam - Brahmananda Swami Sivayogi*, Sidhasramam, Alathur.
3. *Anandadarsam - Brahmananda Swami Sivayogi*, Sidhasramam, Alathur.

Four

Sidhasramam

Sidhasramam at Alathur, Kerala is a great cultural institution founded by Sri Brahmananda Swami Sivayogi. Its messages for the world are non-violence, manly effort, Rajayoga, rational thinking and right knowledge - these are the five pillars of Anandadarsam.

The contribution of the Ashram can be understood from the words of S. Nijalingappa, former A.I.C.C. President; "Rationality and true thinking like salt need to be applied to all walks of life. Salt itself may not be liked by people, but it gives tastes to all dishes. Out thoughts also must stand to rationality. There are the enemies of progress. They spread dead belief and benefit out of that. Many a thoughtless homely creature might fall easy pray to them. Brahmananda Swami Sivayogi and Sidhasramam of Alathur have been trying to rescue such men."

From its very beginning to the date, the Ashram is doing great works like spreading of skepticism, humanism and thereby dispelling the ongoing irrationalities, superstitions and customs performing in the name of religion.

Sivayogi

Sri Brahmananda Swami Sivayogi was born in the 'Karate' family as the dear son of Kunhukrishna Menon on 26th of August, 1852.

As his family and surroundings were highly religious, he had to see so many irrational things practised in the name of religion in his own family and in the surroundings also. As an owner of skeptic mind, the boy's first question were to himself. He could see many things false and useless in religion. Seeing that the existing religions do not make man happy, he tried to evolve his own philosophy. At last he could find that the greatest God and the greatest devil of man is his own mind. He preached that there is no God but mind. According to him, the temples, prayers, the Vedas, etc. are all worthless. The only thing to get *mukthi* (liberation from sorrow) is to keep the mind clean. He added in his preaching that *moksha* is not the *jivatman's* identification with the *paramatman*, but freedom from sorrow and happiness through psychological stability.

Sri Brahamananda Swami Sivayogi was the founder of a new school of thought having revolutionary aspects among devotees. His era (1852-1929) was characterised by the other social reformers such as Sri Narayana Guru (1854-1925) and Chattambi Swami (1853-1924). What distinguishes him from other social reformers is his consideration of mind as the God which is acceptable even to the rationalists. During his period, he advised his disciples to reject all that stand against common sense and rationalism.

In the month of September 1929 he died leaving his Ashram of rationalist thought in the hands of Yogini Devi, his wife.

Yogini Matha

Yogini Devi, the second President of Sidhasramam was born at Vadavannoor in Palakkad district of Kerala on 27th April 1867. She was known as Thavukutty Amma in her early years. In her 17th year she was married to Sri Brahmananda Swami Sivayogi. As she could get an eminent person as her husband, she could learn more about rationalism, religion and right way of thinking in her early twenties. As a result of this she took the Brahmacharya vow and became a sanyasini. By the death of Sri Brahmananda Swami Sivayogi on the 10th of September 1929, she took up the responsibility to continue the reformational work started by Sivayogi. This transformation of an ordinary woman to the head of a spiritual institution gave her a new name Yogini Devi. Devotees called her 'Yogini Matha' considering her as their own mother. Performing the duties of the President of Sidhasramam and Ananda Maha Sabha was not so easy. There were heavy administrative works. Besides these there were other duties like conducting Rajayoga camps and writing replies to devotees and receiving media workers and other visitors. The other duties of the President of Sidhasramam were editing the 'Saragrahi', official journal of Sidhasramam, and edit, publish and distribute literature on and of Sivayogi. Though she was forced to take up all these responsibilities in an unexpected day, she could discharge her duty as if she was born to it and could lead the life of human beings to prosperity who could get a chance to contact with the Ashram.

Nirmalananda Yogi

Niramalananda Yogi, the present President of Sidhasramam, was born at Kollankode in Palakkad district of Kerala in 1925. His previous name was Sukumaran. Sukumaran was very brilliant. He learned Sanskrit and used to practice Rajayoga from his very boyhood. The more he grew, the more his quest for truth increased and he felt discomfortable at home.

Like in the case of Swami Vivekananda, he began to search for a guru who can quench his spiritual thirst. As a result of this he reached at Sidhasramam as a disciple of Sivayogi and took the brahmacharya vow and became a sanyasi. From there he learned spiritual texts and well versed in Sanskrit. When Yogini Matha died on 15th of February 1956, he had to take up the responsibilities of the Ashram. Nirmalananda Yogi was the man who could popularize the ideals of Sivayogi.

He believed in the all round development of men. So he started a school named 'Brahmananda Swami Sivayogi (B.S.S.) Gurukulam High School in 1971. Later he added 'Dhatri Girls' High School' and Rajas High School and a parallel college to his educational endeavour. His book called *Happy Life* was a great success. It deals with the psychological and spiritual problems of people. He is popular in foreign countries also. His speech delivered at Moscow in 1984 on the subject of world peace was appreciated by many world leaders. He still continues the reformational works of the Ashram though he is at his 77th year.

References

1. *A Passage to the Bliss Supreme* - P.V. Gopalakrishnan, Sidhasramam, Alathur.
2. *Asathyathil Ninnu Sathyathilekku* - K. Bheeman, Sidhasramam, Alathur.
3. 'Indian skeptic' dated 15-5-1998, Podanur.

Five

Ananda Maha Sabha, Ananda Samajas, Ananda Yogasalas and Ananda Pracharana Samities

It is stated earlier that the present Sidhasramam at Alathur, in Palakkad district of Kerala was started functioning at Vanoor. Sitting there in the abode, Sivayogi preached logic, humanism, ethics and a scientific and blissful way of living. As he was an introvert, he never approached people or addressed huge masses of people. His way of reforming people was that of a 'rishi' who sits at the bottom of a banyan tree and imparting knowledge and advises to those who approach him disturbed mind. This created many limitations. In those days mind of Keralites were full of superstitions and irrational things. Sivayogi's work against these evil forces was limited to Vanoor only. Hence on 1918, April 21st and 22nd a meeting of devotees of Sivayogi was held in Sidhasramam to strengthen and to spread the work of Sivayogi and his ideals. Mr. Sivarama Krishna Ayyar, G. Krishna Ayyar, Adv. G. Ramapanikker, K.P. Ananda Yogi, C. Kannan Nair, Kunjunni Vaidyar, Padmanabha Menon, Yoganandan, etc. were prominent figures attended the meeting. With the consent of Sivayogi an apex body called 'Ananda Maha Sabha' was formed in order to watch and guide the work of 'Ananda Samajas', local institutions which will spread the ideals of Sivayogi. The sole aim of Ananda Samajas is to mingle with local people, understand their problems and guiding them to lead a rational scientific and blissful life. It should also expose the superstitions and irrational customs spread in the society. In the meeting of 'Ananda Maha Sabha' held in 1919, Sivayogi presided the function and adviced the devotees that; (a) they should not mingle with violent religious customs, (b) they do not conduct 'thalikettu kalyanam', a type of child marriage, (c) funerals should be done using least money, (d) 'Pulakuli', a post-funeral custom, is unnecessary, and (e) conducting marriages at temples like at Guruvayur Sree Krishna temple is ignorance increasing actions.

Later Sivayogi written himself the role and duties of Ananda Samajas. They are:

(a) Impart knowledge to all that everybody irrespective of knowledge and by practising Rajayoga and by doing work such as agriculture, business, other professions one can get the bliss supreme.
(b) Prove that the scriptures which teach vows, holy bath, temple visiting, idol worship, etc. are ways leading to salvation, are false.
(c) Prove all irrational things whoever told them.
(d) Help people to stop over expenses in the name of religious customs and to help them overcome sorrows.
(e) Prove with examples and evidences that sacred places like Kasi, Chidambaram, Rameswaram, etc. are not external but internal.
(f) Help people to live in peacefully and harmoniously by understanding that all the people and other organisms in this world are after bliss and so there is no, internally distinctions such as man, animal, plants, Brahmins, Ezavas, Pulayas, Hindus, Christians, Muslims, natives, exotics, etc. among them.
(g) Help people to discard self love towards same caste, religion, etc. and teach them to keep non-violence and also to help all creatures in this world for getting salvation.
(h) Make people non-violent.
(i) Spread among people the importance of virtues like respect towards teachers, respect towards parents, manly efforts, truthfulness and peace.
(j) Teach people that the only way to salvation is the observation of Ananda way of living.

Ananda Samajas were soon proved a success though there were only the 'Ananda Maha Sabha' in the beginning, about twenty four Ananda Samajas were started at different places in an instance.

They were at: Kannur (Chirakkal), Azhikode (Chirakkal), Kalyassery (Chirakkal), Maloor (Kottayam), Shornur (Valluvanad), Thiruvazhiyode (Valluvanad), Pavukonam (Valluvanad), Gosree (Kochi), Peringottukara (Kochi), Iraviperur (Kochi), Venganoor (Travancore), Thanneermukkam (Travancore), Perihad (Travancore), Kodungallur (Kochi), Ernakulam (Kochi), Injamudi (Kochi), Ettumanoor (Travancore), Chavara (Travancore), Thalavady (Travancore), Royaranelloor (Valluvanad) Ayinikad (Palakkad), Perunnormangalam (Travancore), Maravanchery (Kochi), and Othara (Travancore).

Besides these twenty four centres in Kerala one centre at Colombo (Cylone) was also started.

Under the leadership of direct disciples of Sivayogi like M. Govindanandan, P.A. Anandan, K.P. Ananda Yogi, Sivarama Krishna Ayyer, Soorya Narayana Sharma, Vagbhadanandan, Ananda Brandan, V.K. Kombi Achan, Sekharathu Kunjunni Ezhuthachan, Sankutharakan, N.K. Anandan, G. Ramappanicker, R. Eechara Menon, Jadabharadan, Ramavarier, people rose to a highest level of thinking and they started spreading of Sivayogi's ideals.

Not before long (in 1928) one disciple of Sivayogi, Nishkalananda, translated Sivayogi's 'Moksha Pradeepam' into Hindi language and published it in Dehradun. This incident shows that reformational works of Sivayogi were applicable to all parts of India because the social condition in the other states of India was not better than that of Kerala. By the later 1940's, there were enough of Ananda Samajas in all over Kerala. Though Sivayogi died on 1929 September 10 handing over charges of the institutions to Yogni Matha, his wife, the work of Ananda Samajas did not cease but increased. Ananda Maha Sabha , the apex body failed often in handling all the matters of Ananda Samajas. Hence three regional centres of Ananda Maha Sabha were started. One was at Travancore called 'Akhila Travancore Ananda Samaja Union', another at Kochi called 'Kochi Ananda Samaja Union' and the third at North Malabar called 'Vadake Malabar Ananda Samaja Union'. These unions looked after the matters of Ananda Samajas in their jurisdiction and guided them.

Sivayogi's books are thought provoking. They lead humanity to prosperity and high standard of culture. These are proved things. So some devotees decided to build a reading room for the literature of Sivayogi and read and discussed his books with other fellows in their locality. The aim of it is not only to spread his ideals but also to find the real value of his teachings by critical discussions. In this connection a reading room was built in 1909 on January first at Thalap in the Kannur district of Kerala. It was named 'Ananda ChandrodayaYoga Sala'. This was the first Yoga Sala ever built to discuss the ideals of Sivayogi. Pamban Ambu, Chirakkayil Raman, Cherukada Kelu, Iruvankai Chandu, Thannippanthal Kannan, Panji Kayil Raman, Puthiyandi Kunjambu, Chevidichi Achuthan, Morankandy Raman, M.V. Albert, Koombayil Mukri Ramunni, Kandothankandy Pampan Kunjikannan, Pathalambeth Ramotty, Mundachali Korambeth Govindan, Kanjarangandi Kunjipaithal and Thachandi Kannur were the founder members of Ananda Chandrodaya Yoga Sala.

Taking this a model and seeing its success several devotees started Yogasalas in their locality.

Another institution called 'Ananda Pracharana Samity' is also started during this period to popularize 'Aanandadarsam' the ideals of Sivayogi. By early 1960s almost all important parts of Kerala saw any one of the institution started there. Ananda Chandrodaya Yogasala, Thalap, Kannur; Kalyassery Yogasala, Kannur; Azhikode Ananda Samaja, Kannur; Kannapuram Yogasala, Kannur; Maloor Yogasala, Kannur; Chavassery Ananda Samaja, Kannur; Nayattupara Ananda Samaja, Kannur; Alankode Ananda Pracharana Samiti, Kannur; Kozhikode Ananda Samaja, Kozhikode; Kalpathur Ananda Pracharana Samiti, Kozhikode; Thiruvazhiyode Ananda Yogasala, Palakad; Pulassery Ananda Samaja, Palakad; Thirunavaya Anand Samaja, Palakkad; Ramavarmapuram Ananda Samaja, Trichur; Injamusi Ananda Yoga Sala, Trichur; Perinchery Ananda Yogasala, Trichur; Pookode Ananda Yogasala , Trichur; Maravanchery Ananda Samaja, Trichur; Manaloor Ananda Samaja, Trichur; Thazhekode Ananda Samaja, Trichur; Kuruvilassery Ananda Samaja, Trichur; Kodakara Ananda Pracharana Samiti, Trichur; Kattakambal Ananda Pracharana Samiti, Trichur; Ekandiyur Ananda Pracharana Samiti, Trichur; Ernakulam Ananda Samaja, Ernakulum; Alappuzha Ananda Yogasala, Alappuzha; Perunnor Mangalam Ananda Yogasala,

Alappuzha; Thalavadi Ananda Yoga Sala, Allappuzha; Kizhakkanothara Ananda Yoga Sala, Alappuzha; Vallikode Ananda Yoga Sala, Kottayam; Kuzhimattom Ananda Yoga Sala, Kottayam; Panachikade Ananda Yoga Sala, Kottayam; Kadanade Ananda Yoga Sala, Kottayam; Idanad Ananda Yoga Sala, Kottayam; Chenappadi Vadake Ananda Yoga Sala, Kottayam; Chenappadi Thekke Ananda Yoga Sala, Kottayam; Erumeli Ananda Samajam, Kottayam; Kanjirappalli Ananda Samiti, Kottayam; Chavara Ananda Yoga Sala, Kollam; Adoor Ananda Samaja, Kollam and Nemam Ananda Pracharana Samiti were prominent among them. In 1963 Ananda Maha Sabha was registered under societies act (XXIst act of 1860) and got the registration number S. No. 24 of 1963.

As the social condition of Kerala had much changed since the renaissance, and as people are busy nowadays many Yoga Salas, all the pracharana samitis and a few Ananda Samajas saw their end. Apart from the Sidhasramam located at Alathur there are only eight extension centres exists in Kerala at present. They are; Kannapuram Ananda Yoga Sala, Kannur; Kalyasseri Ananda Yoga Sala, Kannur; Maloor Ananda Yoga Sala, Kannur; Thiruvazhiyode Ananda Yoga Sala, Palakkad; Perunnor Mangalam Ananda Yoga Sala, Alappuzha; Ananda Chandrodaya Yoga Sala, Thalap, Kannur; Thiruvananthapuram Ananda Samaja, Manacande, Thiruvananthapuram; Kuruvilassery Ananda Samaja, Mala, Thrissur; Kozhikode Ananda Samaja, Kozhikode. Contributions of these Yoga Salas, Ananda Samajas and Ananda Pracharana Samities to the making of a cultural Kerala is immeasurable.

References

1. *Sri Sivayogi Souvenir 1952*, pp. 67-68, 71, 72, 129-33; published by Sri Sivayogi Souvenir Committee, Sidhasramam, Alathur.
2. *Ananda Maha Sabha Souvenir*, 1961, p. 5, published by Brahmananda Swami Sivayogi Sidhasramam, Alathur.
3. Ananda Maha Sabha-Sabhayude Memorandavam, Niyamangalum, Chattangalum; published by Sidhasramam, Alathur.
4. Ananda Maha Sabha Golden jublee Sovernier, 1968, pp. 49-53; published by Sidhasramam, Alathur.
5. 'Ananda Maha Sabha Register' kept in Sidhasramam, Alathur.

Six

Cultural Contributions of Brahmananda Swami Sivayogi

When Brahmananda Swami Sivayogi came on the scene about a century back, Kerala was in a state of utter stupor. He sought light and enlightenment in the pursuit of truth. Different people reacted differently to the inspiring call of the bold reformer. They were unprepared to welcome fresh ideas. They were unwilling to think for themselves. By his clarion call and inspiring message, Swamiji infused new blood into Keralite society. Some of his contemporaries were wonder-struck, many ridiculed him, many others admired him. Nonetheless, the quest for truth continued vigorously. He never faltered in argument nor bowed his head in submission. People who were in deep slumber were awakened. He showed them the right path to happiness. The maisma of superstitious and religious malpractices vanished at the touch of his valiant call. His teachings brought new light to many fumbling in the darkness. During the last three quarters of the century, many who did not know their way about were filled with knowledge and enlightenment.

Swamiji had to wage a war against the bastions of blind faith, out worn ideas about God and religion which have been strongly entrenched in the Indian psyche. By insisting ceaselessly that it was the human mind which was basic to one's enlightenment and salvation, he succeeded in getting people discard ritualistic activities like temple worship, organized prayers which were carried out by men, causing much pain to themselves. To Swamiji the pivot of all purposeful activities was the human mind. He argued that searching for God and the soul was as futile as searching for black cat in pitch darkness. No teacher in the past, except Sri Buddha two thousand years ago had the courage to declaim against established concepts like God, Soul, worship, etc.

Enlightened persons have been devoting serious thought to this important question. Improvement of the self is, in the view of some, the best path to attain bliss; others regard progress on the materialistic front as the better path. Both these thought processes originated from man only. It is, therefore, important to realise that it is man who has to be set aright. The varied concepts which many thinking persons evolved down the edges revolved round 'God' and ritualistic practice of religion to please God. In the result, superstitions and religious malpractices grew. Through many religious reformers attempted to rectify matters, it was given to Brahmananda Swami Sivayogi who made a bold attempt to reform the human mind and remove the dross there from. He realised and sought to teach his fellow-beings that the community can attain bliss only if the human mind is kept pure. He founded the cult of 'Anandadarshan' which required man not so much to hark back to God about whom little was known as to realise the latent divinity in himself through the process of detached meditation. Swamiji unfolded this royal path for any aspirant to bliss and happiness. He was a brilliant intellectual who led a great movement and sought thereby to uplift a society steeped in darkness, superstition, lethargy and near-slavery. What exactly is this 'Anandadarshan'? Why should one follow its teachings? For ages past, all the 'Acharyas' propogated the view that this world is a myth and an illusion, that there is nothing but sorrow in this world and that man can assuage his sorrow only by worshipping God, and this God-worship led to blind faith and meaningless superstitions making man a slave of these. Sivayogi came on the scene with a breath of fresh air. He cleared the cobwebs in man's minds by holding before them a new vision of life founded on self confidence, courage, capacity and rational thinking and most importantly on control of the mind. His voice was stentorian, his message not merely loud and clear but substantiated by appropriate quotations from Vedas and Upanishads and created a revolution in the minds of the Keralites and others.

He started by making it abundantly clear that there is no need to observe two water-tight systems—the worldly life and spiritual life. His central teaching was that man should improve the quality of his worldly life and thereby derive happiness. He relied on smrithis and sruthis in support of this contention man is great, not the religion he practices. Personal experiences are more important than unquestioning religious beliefs.

It is mind that should be kept pleased not God. The happiness experienced by the mind destroys all sorrows. Only by keeping the mind at rest and in repose, one can hope for success in one's life. Such control of the mind is not, as it were, the prerogative or monopoly of the sanyasins. It should be the privilege and duty of every human being—only then by strengthening the mind he can face boldly all trying situations in life. Such a thought is not so much religion-oriented as idealism-oriented. It is by practising such high ideals that man becomes cultured and peace loving.

Even in the so-called civilized countries, people continue to be the clutches of outdated beliefs and superstitions which are about all what organized religions can offer. These stand in the way of community's progress. Freedom to think for oneself is as important as political freedom or economic freedom. Organized religions have always posed a great danger to this precious freedom of thought. But for the intrepid scientists of the west who stormed the bastions of superstitions and blind religious (mal) practices, man would have continued to stagnate and not made the phenomenal progress he has made all round during the last two centuries.

We in India can doubtless claim a long spiritual tradition established by universally respected thinkers and philosophers which India has produced. Has this tradition done us any good? The answer is a dismal 'No'. It is a sad fact that in the name of religion and religious beliefs, we have built round ourselves cobwebs, out of which we are unable to steer clear, despite intellectual and scientific achievements of which we may well be proud. The priesthood in the country have, alas! been able to justify stupid superstitions and despicable malpractices in the name of religion.

All the established religions have talked and preached about a God or Gods, attributing to the God forms, shapes and even attitudes. The Gods were misused by the practitioners of these religions to achieve their own selfish ends. In the name of God, man started hurting or even killing his fellow-being, without any compunction. To please the Gods, animal sacrifices or even human sacrifices were made. Swamiji preached the language of love and non-violence. Thanks to his incessant campaign, animal sacrifice which was rampant in many places was discontinued. In the name of religion, women were often forced to perform 'Sathi' and extinguish themselves on the funeral pyres of their husbands. Untouchability and unapproachability were widely rampant in Kerala which forced Swami Vivekananda to call Kerala a 'lunatic asylum'. When Kerala was river with such malpractices in the name of religion, Brahmananda Swami came on the scene with his refreshing message of love and non-violence, of pure reason untainted by any evil thought or superstition. He challenged on the basis of his own experiences and sharp reasoning the degradation to which organized religion has reduced mankind. He stood against the ritualistic practices of animal sacrifices, extravagant ceremonies and festivals at temples, all of which obscured man's capacity for rational thinking.

Swamiji realised that man resorted to brute physical force when he lacked reasoning power. By his trend setting works 'Sivayoga Rahasya', 'Moksha Pradeepa', 'Sidhanubhoothi' and 'Anandadarsan', he sought to establish the primacy of yuktha or Reasoning as the only guide for man.

It is only the power of reasoning, the capacity to think rationally that makes man master of himself and that makes him really strong, happy and free from all worries. It is this capacity to think for himself that has proved to be man's most precious asset and it is on this Swamiji laid the most emphasis. Swamiji who protected this rational thinking by vigorous practice of Dhyana could not naturally tolerate the atrocious malpractices perpetuated in the name of religion and idol-worship. The very first chapter of Anandadarsan sets out the panacea to correct this serious imbalance in man's vision.

While professing all sympathy for those deluded by blind faith in worship and rituals and forsake their duty, he exhorted them to realise for themselves by experience the greatness and glory which lay hidden within themselves. Blind faith in anything had absolutely no place in his teaching. He deplored that even scholars were deluded by misleading Sastras.

He wanted faith to be substituted by reason and experience. Swamiji's 'atheism' if it may be so-called was neither first stop to 'nihilism' nor was it a repudiation of the well established doctrines of justice. He envisioned for every man a sweet life full of happiness and all his teachings showed the right royal road to attain this happiness. He regarded 'Ahimsa' or non-violence as the supreme virtue the virtue—which breeds other human virtues and values. The votary of ahimsa is the worshipper of truth. Down the ages, a life based on truth, non-violence and good character has been held out as the ideal goal for a human being. Swamiji stood for that kind of world order where man would discard all blind beliefs regarding God and life in the 'other world', and practice love, non-violence, reasoned thinking free from prejudices.

Swamiji's stress on the importance of the power of reasoning quite naturally. Postulated that it is the human mind which is the all-important factor - it shapes all man's actions and therefore, his life. It is the mind which makes life happy or sorrowful or a hell or heaven of life. Swamiji's recipe for making a heaven of one's own life is the doctrine of 'Ananda'.

Seven

Other Contributions of Brahmananda Swami Sivayogi

Brahmananda Swami Sivayogi was the founder of 'Ananda Matha', a scientific, social and cultural organisation, which was a part and parcel of the renaissance flourished in the 19th century at each and every corner of India.

Among the many works of Sivayogi 'Anandadarsan' contains Sivayogi's ideals meant for fighting against irrational customs, superstitions and social discrimination which were prevailed in the society in which he lived.

In those days people were blindly following Puranas, religious leaders and scriptures without a word of question. But Sivayogi taught them to think and find the logic of others' savings especially that of scriptures and religious leaders. His Ananda

Matha stands for logic. His motto was 'Matham pareekshya Sweekaryam Vakthyananda matham Hitham.'

He advised his people accept the good qualities of all religions. This provoked the fundamental religious leaders who were in the thought that the only way to salvation is the ideals of their religion. In order to confirm his attitude he quoted Vasishta's saying; "Yukthiyukha mupadeyam Vachanam balakadapi, Anyathrinamiva thyajyamavyuktham padmajanmana".

He discovered that the existing religions give only ignorance, sorrow, material loss, etc. to all beings including human beings. Not only that, the religions existing now in this world encourage evils like killing of animals and even abusing of God! Understanding these adverse results of religions, Sivayogi put aside a large portion of 'Anandadarsam' to enlighten people. He wrote:

"Ajnanadukhadweshamscha dravyana - Samcha thadrasam,
Kayaklesamcha Himsamcha pasoonam jnaninamapi
Eesanindamcha kurvandi vividhani mathanyaho
Thanniroopananapoorvam thadwoshan pariharamyaham".

Govindankutty (Sivayogi's earlier name) started his social service in his youth by teaching Sanskrit to his neighbourhood children. His aim was to enable his pupils to comprehend the scriptures which were in the Sanskrit language. But his mind did not persist upon the matter. He turned his mind to philosophy. His philosophical mind was roused when he was able to go through the following verses in Sanskrit.

"Brahmanandam Paramasukhadam Kevalajnana moorthim
Viswatheetham gagansathrsam thathwa masyadhi lakshyam
Ekam hithyam Vimalamachalam Sarvadee Sakshibhootham
Bhavatheedam thrigunarahitham Sadgurumtham namami"

From then he started examining the Hindu scriptures critically. His critical study of the scriptures made him realize that the ongoing customs and rituals are not a part of the original religion. Understanding the fact that the present religion differs in a great deal with that of the original religion, he wrote:

"Anubhoothi prama neneivanandamatha mathra nrn.
Pourushalochanayukthakarmabiryo Jayathyalam.
Adhapathanayanthrani mathanyanyani dehinam
Udharana mahayandramannda mathamandaram".

In his philosophical work called 'Anandadarsam', he wrote that great was the ignorance that religions spread, it is because of this ignorance that people worship a attributive God and waste time in that way. In his endeavour to prove this fact he wrote:

"Naivedei payasadyeicha poojayandeeswaram Jana
Kshulpipasa peeditha kim Sampoorno Yush madeeswara?
Snapayanthee Sankalpal prathimam thasya Manava
Asudha Kim yushmadeeso visudha Ithiva Sruthi?
Vadya Chamara deepadeiruthsave shyarchayanthi tham.
Vadyadambara Kamshi Kimdabiko yushma deeswara?
Madhyamamse Samarpyapi poojayanthee Swaram Jana.
Madhyapayee Savasee kim yushmadeeso gunakara?
Dhanabyupayananee Sayarppayantheeha Manava
Upayanabimanee Kim nrupavabyushma dweeswara?
Evamajnanapadan Ha padayanthi Sisoonapi
Ajnanasala Sasthyeva bimbalaya Samabhoovi"

His Sanskrit verses like that of this is so simple and meaningful that even a layman who has a little knowledge in Sanskrit can comprehend the ideals of the verses.

He explained that 'Samnyasa' is the cleaning up of the mind and keeping it pure. According to him it is not leading a solitary life avoiding all worldly pleasures as some Vedantins interpret. Criticizing the age old idea of samnyasa, he wrote:

"Sarvathyagartha majnathwa Sarvathyaga parayana
Paranna Sangadam bokthum Sradhadana ahoaho
Sarvathyago manodoshathyaga eva Sukhayasa
Sukhahethu danathyaga Swaparaklesa Karanam"

Likewise he strongly criticised Sanyasin's begging of alms. According to him begging of alms leads the Sanyasi to disease on account of the lack of nutritious food and it would be a disturbance to the other fellows of the society on account of the untimely begging of the Sanyasins. It will be interesting to note his opinion on this matter which ran as:

"Sarvasya Swasasandyagath Swaparadrohakaraga
Bavanthi bikshaya thasmath sa thyagassamatho na na
Alasascha daridrascha Budhiheenascha bikshaya
Lokakshamam vardhayanthi drushtwa beikshabujo guroon
Yadiswam nasthi Sakthischa yaknaya nahi chethada

Bikshamadanthu Sarvaswam thyakthwa bikshadanam thudik
Yoginam Sa mahananda padavikwa mahathmanam
Yachana dukha vrithi kwa janan beiksham charethkimu."

While going through his thought provoking verses, we can get a glimpse of his talent and can grasp his eagerness to enlighten the society. He was a great social reformer. Apart from following and preaching the age old ideals, he found out a practical way of religion. It was humanistic, rational and above all simple.

His motto was non-violence. For a total socialism there is no way but non-violence. In order to praise non-violence he says;

"Yage pasuvada karya ithi vedepradarsitha
Mamsapriyei rahimseiva madrusam paramamatha
Himsa kale dukha bhaya prakambartha swaran paso
Pasyan Srunwan krupalu kassahathe rakshasadruthe
Dayadiguna Sampanna kaschideesokthi Chethada
Himsakanwara yethinan palayeth praninassada."

According to Sivayogi bliss is supreme. Every creature longs for bliss. So there is only one religion in this world which is 'Ananda (bliss)'

"Sarve byo vyathmaniprema thamavyananda Samkshaye
Nasayanthiyatho marthya Anandassarvatho mahan
Ajnavaya ma sasthjna ithi ma kuruth vyatham
Manomathra jaya neijam mahananda mavavnutha."

Sivayogi emphasised that there is no God in this universe who pleases when you worship. Warning people of the false teachings of religious leaders Sivayogi says;

"Eeswara Sarva Saktheschanna Karothi Janan Kutha
Sukhina Punyakaramscha ragadweshaviva rijjithan
Sarvajna ithi yushmathi kathamjnathassa eeswara
Pareekshitha kim Sarveshta vishayeshta budothama
Bhakthabeeshta pradascheth sa kasmabyacchithino hitham
Bhaktha daridraruk dukha deinya bajo bavanthi kim
Eeswaram nirgunam vakthi nishkriyam prabala sruthi
Kadam srushtyadikatherthathi vadanthi madavadina
Srushta Santhana handarameeswaram mathavadina
Daya varinidhim prahuraho mohamadandhatha
Aroope nirgune roopakalpanam bramakaranam
Thadroopadyana poojadi Sramayeiva na mukthaye!!

What makes him unique from the other social and religious reformers is that his logics are so simple that can be understood even by the layman. In order to reinforce his sayings he quotes verses from popular scriptures.

He was strongly against idol-worship. Idol-worship only increases ignorance. For salvation, according to him, mind control is the best way. Idol-worshippers think, while on worshipping, that the God almighty will surely solve their problems. Their false expectation prevent them from solving their problems themselves. As a result of this they do not use their manly efforts. Condemning idol worship he says:

"Sathyoktheradi marge kim midya durbashanam baveth
Jnanabyassyathi marge kathamajnan seelanam?
Eesasevadi Karmani Yogajnanadi Karanam
Ithi bruvano na jnani, ha yogi, Karmadagrani
Yogabyasasyadi margo Viyogabyasanam hukim?
Oordhagandhu radoyathra thwadi margo bavennu Kim?
Yogajnanasyathi marge karmethi Kathayennu kim?
Ksheera panasyathi karyam vishapanam bavennu kim?"

Sivayogi's strong criticism was against caste system. As he was born and brought up in a society where were all the evils of the caste system, he could realise, from his early years, that caste system is the only one phenomenon which stands as the prominent stumbling block in the path of the progress of the Keralites.

In his opinion caste system is not planned by the God. It is man made. He says:

"Mathu Pithur jathi matha bedacharanu varthanath
Suthanamapi thajjathya by a bimana pravardhathe
Nanajathi mathachara bedhacharanuvarthanath
Sikshanthe Chedeikamathya Sukham rajyeshta Sambaveth
Balyath prabhruti Samsartha dwathesham mathabishta
Abimanascha bavathi Sa hi Sadarana ghalu
Jathyabinna Yathinara Soodraya Viprasamgame
Na raso nanuragascha Suthothpathischa no bhaveth
Adagruthanam jathina muthkrshta sthree samagamath
Sukhasoonwadayo nasyooryadhithe bhinnajathaya
Nikrishtothkrishta jathyathi Spardhamana nara api
Milandyanandasidhyartham thasmadananda jathaya
Yasmin Syootham jeevajalam Soothre manigana iva

Ananda Soothram thath dhrthwa thanthu Soothram thyajejjana
Madasidhandinassarve Yathrananda Ssulabhyathe
Mathabhimanam thyakthwathe thathra gachandi Sadaram
Nijananda matheikathwam hitwa bhoorimatheiriha
Ghidhyanthe kalahayanthe balavath Sudhiyovi ha
Mathacharya pramanebhyo vismrtham thannijam matham
Kincha nanamatha bhranthir bhoova cha maheethale"

He had a panacea for all the sufferings of man. It is nothing but controlling of the mind (Rajayoga). According to him by the control of mind not only the individual but the society will also improve. For him all the distinctions are force. For one world, one religion, one custom, one aim, one people practice of Rajayoga is enough. He aimed individual's inner refinement. If the minds of men are purified, there will be no room for evils in this world. So individual refinement is the best way for social reformation.

Praising Rajayoga he says:

"He jana nijamanogathim Sada Swanugam kurutha Soukyamasnutha Poojanadhi
Chalanathmakarmmabhiryojanam nijasukhapanodanam
Manolayo nijanando yoga ithyabheedheeyathe
Advaidam rajayogascha Swathmala bhascha nethara
Drsyedantha Sushumnayam jyothirlingam mahatbudam
Vasamethi manasthasmath dhiklingam mrchilabhikam
Bhrumadye Sukhasamsparso thalumoole rasasruthi
Divyagandascha nasayam Samjayeran kathambruve
Eekeikaka mapyatma chihnam manoharana Sakthimath
Anbhooya manasthathannijanande praleeyathe"

Distinctions like costume, colour, language, nationality, caste, creed, etc. always make deep gulf between man and man. When these distinctions find no way into man's thoughts, he will become innocent and divine. Sivayogi's 'Ananda Matha' is the only one scientifically proved method that helps all people to be pure discarding the awareness of distinctions.

Reference

1. *Anandadarsam* - Brahmananda Swami Sivayogi, Sidhasramam, P.O. Alathur.

Eight

Cultural Contributions of Ananda Yoga Salas and Ananda Samajas

Kalyassery Ananda Yoga Sala, Kalyassery, Kannur

Kalyassery Ananda Yoga Sala was built during 1920-1922. Brahmananda Swami Sivayogi's disciples like T.O. Narayananandan, Uruvadanandan, Thoonoli Kunjappanandan, C.P. Chattukkutti Anandan, Thoothi Othenandan, P.M. Parvathi Anandini, Pallippurath Ambu Anandan, P. Sankaranandan, Chundakaran Kunjambu Anandan, P. Ramanandan, Sidhananda Yogi, Parammal Ramanandan and P. Pokayi Ananda were the founder members of Kalyassery Ananda Yoga Sala. Initially there were 55-60 members. Mr. T.O. Narayanandan, the first president of the Yoga Sala donated the land necessary for the Yoga Sala.

There were full of social discrimination in the name of caste, creed and religion in those days in Kannur. Members of the Kalyassery Ananda Yoga Sala decided to respond against this. Brahmananda Swami Sivayogi gave them enough encouragement and instructions.

At Keechery, a place near Kalyassery there were a temple called 'Swamigopuram'. The main offering in the temple was fowl sacrifice. Thousands of the fowls were slaughtered every year. Workers of the Yoga Sala and followers of Brahmananda Swami Sivayogi like A. Ramachandran, M. Narayanan, P.V. Achuthan, Uruvadanandan etc., requested the temple authority to cease that cruelty performed in the name of religion and show mercy towards innocent fowls. But the temple authority did not comply with their request. Seeing that there is no other way Mr. A. Ramachandran and Mr. M. Narayanan lodged a complaint at 'Pranidroha Nivarana Sangh', an organisation founded for the welfare of animals and birds, on 18 March,

1958. Fowl slaughter was fixed to conduct on 24th of March. Pranidroha Nivarana Sangh complained at Valapattanam Police Station and the police came on time and prevented the temple authority from killing of fowls. From the date that cruel custom did not find way into the programmes of the temple. If the Yoga Sala did not acted on time and did not enlighted people, there will be no end to this cruel custom. Though fundamentalists and superstitious people threatened the Yoga Sala authority, they did not discontinue their work to enlighten people and thereby wipe off the irrational cruelties. Kalyassery Yoga Sala still continues its reformational work by organising opinions against caste, creed, temple worship, pilgrimage, vows and animal sacrifice. The Yoga Sala also gives great importance to science and logic.

Perunnormangalam Ananda Yoga Sala, Kanichukulangara, Alappuzha District

Perunnormangalam Ananda Yoga Sala was founded about 84 years ago. Twenty-four people under the leadership of Sri. A.N. Govinda Kurup assembled at Panakunnath Kalari Palace and decided to establish a Ananda Yoga Sala for spreading the ideals of Brahmananda Swami Sivayogi in their locality. M.E. Padmanabha Kurup, M.E. Vasudeva Kurup, M.E. Parameswara Kurup, V.K. Neelakanda Kurup, V.E. Kunjan Kurup, Brahmasree Narayana Swami, M.N. Rama Kurup, M.E. Kochuneelakanda Kurup, K.N. Velayudha Kurup, M.N. Ayyappu Kurup, M.K. Kesava Kurup, A.N. Gopala Kurup, M.S. Gopala Panicker, M.N. Kochuneelakanda Kurup, M.N. Govinda Kurup, M.K. Parvathi Amma, C.K. Kochuparvathi Amma, V.K. Kutti Amma, V.K. Kunji Kavamma, M.K. Lakshmi Amma, M.E. Neelakanda Kurup, Y.D. Sankaran Kartha, M.M. Madhavi Amma and M.E. Kochukrishna Kurup were the people actively participated in the formation of the Ananda Yoga Sala. Two years later the Yoga Sala was shifted to a new building. Reading the great works of Brahmananda Swami Sivayogi learned people at the Perunnormangalam Swarmed at the newly established Yoga Sala and actively participated in its endeavour to create a scientific temper among people.

Perunnormangalam Ananda Yoga Sala

There was an Ezhava temple (a temple built by and for Ezhava community) called Kanichukulangara Badrakali Temple one or two kilometres away from the Perunnormangalam Ananda Yoga Sala. It was a Kali temple, on every Tuesday and Friday there were animal and fowl sacrifice at the temple. People used to come from very far places to participate in the function. People believed that had they not conducted the animal sacrifice, they will die of small pox. Four leaders of the Perunnormangalam Ananda Yoga Sala met temple authority and described them that animal sacrifice is a vulgar evil. In order to establish their points they quoted some sentences from *Mokshapradeepam*, a book written by Brahmananda Swami Sivayogi. The temple authority agreed to stop that cruelty. But they had to pacify the illiterate devotees who were in the belief that if the animal sacrifice was discontinued people will die of small pox. So the temple authority put forward two demands. One was to find out a new and harmless mode of sacrifice in lieu of animal sacrifice. The other was a proclamation of those four leaders of Ananda Yoga Sala that they will accept the punishment of Kali if she get angry. The four leaders agreed. They proclaimed as the temple authority instructed. A new offering was also found out. It was the sacrifice of tender coconut in lieu of animal sacrifice. Hence that vulgar evil custom was discontinued and people also began to think of non-violence as a great virtue.

This Yoga Sala interfered when there broke out a political conflict between RSS and CPM when the Yoga Sala members taught them the importance of being peaceful, they signed a contract of non-violence.

The members of the new governing body of the Yoga Sala are M.N. Ananda Kurup, M.K. Saseedharan, T.C. Ananda Vally Amma, K. Bhaskaran, K. Soothappan, M.P. Vijayakumar, K. Anilkumar, M.K. Ambikamma, M.R. Udayakumar, Venugopalappanicker and G. Sukumara Kartha.

Besides spreading of the ideals of Sivayogi, the Yoga Sala now started a nature cure centre, Yoga centre and occasional meetings of eminent and good natured people.

Ananda Chandrodaya Yoga Sala, Kannur

Ananda Chandrodaya Yoga Sala at Thalap, Kannur was established in 1908. Even before that, people of Kannur district were accustomed to Brahmananda Swami Sivayogi and his ideals. During the last part of the 19th century and early years of the 20th century there were many disciples of Sivayogi at Kannur. Knowing the greatness of 'Anandadarsan', the philosophy of Sivayogi, they decided to start a Ananda Yoga Sala and spread the ideals of Sivayogi, when Sivayogi called on the Yoga Sala on 26th of December 1909, he was very much pleased with its workings and named it 'Ananda Chandrodaya Yoga Sala'. Mundachalil Govindan Master, Pamban Ambu, A.K. Nayar, C. Achuthan, Mundachalil Kunjiraman Vaidyar, C.K. Kumaran and M. Govindan were the founder members of Ananda Chandrodaya Yoga Sala. Besides those eminent persons C. Kelu, Chirakkal Raman, P. Ramotty, Thachondy Kannan, Koombayil Kunjambu, Kottayi Kunjikrishnan etc. were also participated later in the great works of Ananda Chandrodaya Yoga Sala.

Workers of Ananda Chandrodaya Yoga Sala at Kannur, as directed by Brahmananda Swami Sivayogi, fought against superstition, irrational customs in the name of religion and caste system. In order to spread the ideals of Sivayogi, Ananda Chandrodaya Yoga Sala started a monthly named *Saragrahi* in

1948. Mr. A.K. Nayar was the all in all of *Saragrahi* from its beginning till his death in 1969. Later the place of publication of *Saragrahi* was shifted from Kannur to Alathur.

Ananda Chandrodaya Yoga Sala

Ananda Chandrodaya Yoga Sala conducts Sat sang (meeting for virtuous people) second Sunday of every month. It also conducts Rajayoga classes, seminars and speeches. Though the Yoga Sala spreads the light of knowledge since 1908, its greatest achievement is the peace campaign organised at Kannur. The occasion was when Kannur found itself as the centre of political conflict between CPM and RSS seeing the tears of the people of Kannur on the death of dear and near persons when the political conflict broke out Nirmalananda Yogi, the present president of Sidhasramam, an institution founded by Brahmananda Swami Sivayogi, left for Kannur on 19th of January, 2000 with his 150 disciples. On reaching at Kannur he conducted a peace procession with his disciples. It was a new chapter in the minds of the inhabitants of Kannur for they had been seeing only political processions for a few months which soon turn out to be conflicts. Seeing that people were interested in his peace procession he conducted a long speech on 'ahimsa'. It made marvellous influence in the minds of people. Politicians who were the root cause of the conflicts and assassinations felt shame on their wrong doings. Later

Nirmalananda Yogi visited the houses of persons killed in the political conflict. There is no doubt in the matter that this peace project of Nirmalananda Yogi showed good results.

Kuruvilassery Ananda Samajam, Thrissur

Kuruvilassery Ananda Samajam was started in 1951. Sivayogi's disciple Mr. Adiyath Yayanandan was the founder of this Samajam. As there had no own building for this Samajam the day to day works of the Samajam was conducted in the house of Adiyath Yayanandan. Initially there were 76 families which actively participated in the functions of this Samajam. Apart from taking initiation for external reformation this Samajam tried to purify the minds of people lived there. Taking Sivayogi's teaching that the real revolution should be happened in the minds of man as life span, Adiyath Yayanandan, P.A. Velayudhan, K.V. Karappanandan took a new mode of reformational work. They visited houses one by one and studied all the superstitions, irrational customs spreaded in those houses. Then they took classes pointing out the teachings of Sivayogi. Their classes influenced people very much and they gradually moved from ignorance to knowledge. This mode of reformational works of Kuruvilassery Ananda Samajam, created a cultural revolution in and around Kuruvilassery. In order to keep-up the scientific temper and discuss progressive matters, members of this Samajam assemble once in every month. They do not forget to teach the ideals of Sivayogi to new members when they get in touch with the Samajam.

Thiruvanandapuram Ananda Samajam, Thiruvanandapuram

Thiruvanandapuram Ananda Samajam was established in 1994 under the leadership of V.K. Narayanan, P.V. Anandan, P. Ananda Menon, Smt. Nisa Khadar, Vasudevan, K.A. Khadar, R. Anil Kumar, K.P. Balan, M.K. Krishnapilla, Chandramathi. But before the establishment of this Samajam, there were Ananda Yoga Salas and Ananda Samajams in many parts of Travancore such as Chavara, Othara, Iraviperur, Cherthala, Attukal, Venganoor, Vallikode, Kulathoor, Panachikkad, Kuzhimattom, Pala. They are not existing now. Their cultural contributions were mainly by distribution of books of Sivayogi and fighting against superstitions and caste system and religious superstitions. It was by their great work that fowl slaughter was discontinued in the Attukal Temple.

The Thiruvanandapuram Ananda Samajam existing now spreads Sivayogi's ideals by seminars, study classes, publishing of books and pamphlets.

Book release function organised by Thiruvanandapuram Ananda Samajam

In north Kerala there was a custom of compulsory donation as and when temple festivals arrive.

Thiruvanandapuram Ananda Samajam brought out a notice against the acceptance of this compulsory donations. According to the workers of the Ananda Samajam all the temples and its workings only increase ignorance. The pamphlet distributed by the contribution collectors is a typical example for this. In the pamphlet they says that there needed a offering for God to minimize or demolish the effects of evil forces. People knowing nothing about Hinduism do not know that there is no evil forces in the Hinduism.

The pamphlet distributed by Ananda Samajam workers showed good results. People objected to give donations. Though the pamphlet made a great fuss, people in and around Thiruvanandapuram city got enlighted and they started to protest against irrational customs in the name of religion.

References

1. Documents kept in Kalyassery Ananda Yoga Sala, Kannur.
2. Documents kept in Perunnormangalam Ananda Yoga Sala, Kanichukulangara, Alappuzha.
3. Documents kept in Ananda Chandrodaya Yoga Sala, Kannur.
4. Documents kept in Kuruvilassery Ananda Samajam, Thrissur.
5. Documents kept in Thiruvanandapuram Ananda Samajam, Thiruvanandapuram.

Nine

Rajayoga Preached by Sivayogi

Sivayogi's tirade against all organised religious and ritualistic practices notwithstanding, Swamiji was the foremost among the religious leaders in the true sense of the word. While he was prepared to agree with the basic principles of every religion, provided these were derivable from truth, justice and Dharma, he subjected them all to sharp scrutiny and only such of these as satisfied the tests he laid down by virtue of his sharp intelligence and relentless reasoning where accepted by him. 'Raja Yoga' was the doctrine which applied to him most. Sivayogi's Rajayoga was quite different from the one which is elaborated in Gita or Vasitam and preached by modern yoga teachers. To the Raja Yogi of Swamiji's conception, mind is the most important factor in fact the only important factor. The Rajayogi attains the state of 'Samadhi' keeping his thoughts calm, pure and serene and by constant meditation. The doctrine of Ananda which Swamiji preached would have man discover his own shortcomings and feelings and to take steps himself to rectify them. He would banish all evil thoughts and designs and would not be prey to vices and mal-practices. He will endear himself to his fellow beings with strong ties of brotherhood. The self-introspection which Raja Yoga envisages brings about a remarkable improvement over man and society. The essence of Swamiji's teaching is that perennial bliss is the birth right of all — that there is no need for man to get lost in whirlpools of sorrow and despair. He wanted everyone to realise that it is the human mind which produces excellent human beings. It is time that our Governments at the centre and states included in the syllabus of educational institutions the principles of Swamiji's doctrine of Ananda. The basic tenets of this religion of bliss will no doubt help the promotion of not only material prosperity but also secularism, peace and tranquillity, and what is more, everlasting bliss.

Sivayogi gives a elaborate description of the eight-fold yoga in his book *Mokshapradeepam*. According to him, as that of Patanjali, the eight-folds of yoga are Yama, Niyama, Asana, Pranayama, Pratyahara, Dharana, Dhyana and Samadhi.

1. *Yama*

Yama or restraint includes Ahimsa, Satya, Asteya, Brahmacharya and Aparigraha.

Ahimsa is not giving the least pain, at any time, to any being by word, mind or deed. Satyam (truthfulness) is not Satyam, wherein there is the seed for harm. Falsehood is verily Satyam, when it is accompanied by compassion or pity. That is indeed Satyam or truthfulness, which turns out to the good of mankind, and not what, which is contrary in effect.

Astheya (non-stealing) is non-covetousness by word, mind or deed of another's wealth.

Brahmacharya or chastity is the renunciation of all carnal desires by word, mind or deed, always, at all places and in all conditions.

Aparigraha (non-acceptance of anything) is defined as the non-acceptance of anything pleasurable other than what is necessary for the maintenance of the body.

2. *Niyamas*

Niyama or habitual observance consists of the followings: (1) Soucha (2) Santosha (3) Tapas (4) Swadhyaya (5) Iswara-pranidhana.

Soucha (purity of the mind) can be attained when the mental impurities, such as, jealousy and the like are washed away.

Santhosha (contentment) means calm and happy condition of the mind. It can be attained by discarding evil thoughts.

Tapas (penance) is equality of mind both in pleasure and pain. These two opposite forces should not be allowed to have any effect on the mind.

Swadhayaya (Good Study) is the study of the Sastras on Salvation.

Ishwara pranidhana (dedication to God) is the dedication of one's all actions to the supreme preceptor, viz. God.

Sivayogi pointing out the yogavartika says that Yamas alone are very essential for Yogis, but not Niyamas. Since they are a hindrance to yoga. Further he says that one should avoid the practices that tend to cause fatigue of the body, like fasting, early bath and the like. In his view Soucha (purity) is needed only for the mind. Likewise Tapas (penance) is not fasting as some Yoga masters interpret.

3. *Asana (Posture)*

It is a steady and comfortable mode of sitting. Some of the different kinds of postures mentioned are Swastikasana, Veerasana, Padmasana and Siddhasana. Among the eighty-four kinds of postures one should always practice the posture Siddhasana when Siddhasana is mastered, the three bandhas are easily had. The three bandhas referred to are:

(a) Uddiyana bandha: drawing up of the intestines above and below the naval.
(b) Jalandhara bandha: Contract the throat and press the chin firmly against the breast.
(c) Mulabandha: Pressing the yoni with the ankle, contract the anus and draw the apana upwards.

4. *Pranayama*

Pranayama is the inhaling of the air through the left nostril, keeping it stationary within as long as possible and again exhaling it through the right nostril.

5. *Pratyahara*

The restraining of the mind from the worldly objects of the senses is called Pratyahara.

6. *Dharana*

The location of the mind to a particular place is Dharana. The places referred to above are the plexuses of the navel, the heart lotus, the tip of the nose and the like. The concentration of the mind in those plexuses is Dharana.

7. Dhyana

Seeing the signs that are located in the plexus, such as moon, sun, fire, lightning sound, soft touch, bliss, divine pleasure and so forth. The mind becomes engaged in that continuous sole function of concentration on them, undiluted with any other function. This is known as Dhyana. Dhyana destroys the wavering attitude of the mind.

8. Samadhi

The forgetfulness of Dhyana itself is Samadhi. In Dhyana we experience the existence of three entities, viz. the meditator, the meditation and the meditated. In Samadhi there is no such experience of these three entities.

Dhyana is said to be of several kinds. So also are Pratyahara and Dharana. But none of them is so easy to practise. When we meditate upon the forms of man whom we have seen, sometimes we got a conception of that form, and sometimes not. By the time we try to fix our attention of the mind on the shank, after having fixed that on the feet, we miss the impression of the form of the feet. Likewise as we concentrate our attention, on the limbs, one by one, the already experienced impressions of some of those vanish, and the mind is worried at the failure of a complete grasp of all the limbs simultaneously. Then how is it possible for us to get fixed in our minds those form of Vishnu, Siva and others whom we have not seen physically. When we try to conceive in our mind the form of the feet of Vishnu or Siva, how are we to conceive of it, as unto whose feet we have seen? Is it right to think of them as unto my feet or your feet or those of somebody else? If in truth they have a form, are we not to see verily that form? If we wish to see the form of the sun or the moon, we can see that, if we but look up to the sky, can we get a vision of the sun if we look downwards with closed eyes, conceiving in the mind that the sun is round like a circle? No, without any conception of the mind, as to the form of the sun and the like, if we but look up to the sky, we get a vision of them. Likewise if we look up to the sky, with our mind, instead of the physical eye, we can get a view or vision of the light of the Atmah. Do not get confounded by hearing the names of the plexuses, such as Muladhara, Swadhistana, Manipura,

Anahata, Visuddhi and Ajna, or of their nature and the mode of meditation pertaining to each of these six plexuses. Do not be worried that you have not known the sixteen props or Adharas like the toe and the like, nor should you be sorry that you are ignorant of the fourteen nerves like Ida, Pingala and so forth, of their location and their characteristics. Nor should you get uneasy that you have not studied about the ten vital airs, such as prana and the like, their location and their functions. Yoga itself is said to be of several kinds like Mantra Yoga, Hatayoga, Layayoga, Nadayoga, Sivayoga, Brahmayoga, Jnanayoga, Adwaitayoga, Niralambana Yoga, Nirabhasayoga, Ashtangayoga and Rajayoga. Samadhi also is likewise of several kinds, namely Samprajnata Samadhi, Asamprajnata Samadhi, Sabeeja Samadhi, Nirbeeja Samadhi, Savikalpaka Samadhi, Nirvikalpaka Samadhi and so on. There are also the seven Bhumis or sources of knowledge, viz. Subhechha, Vicharana, Tanumanasi, Sattwapatthi, Asamsakti, Pararthabhavini and Turyabhumi. Jhanis are classified by some of four kinds, viz. Brahmavid, Brahmavidvara, Brahmavidvareeya and Brahmavidvarishta and by some others as of six kinds viz. Kuteechaka, Bahudaka, Hamsa Paramahamsa, Turyateeta and Avadhuta. If the time taken to grasp all these things and that spent on reading books on philosophy and holding discussions about them, were devoted to the attempt to get the mind absorbed in the Atmah, it will surely be of great use. The above divisions of Samadhi, the classification of Jhanis and the different seats of knowledge, and all, are made by the authors of Sastras, in accordance with their own temperament, inclinations and working of the mind, just as the calculation of the different time limits of pranayama and processes of pratyahara down to Samadhi, have been differentiated. Hence it is enough if one take care of the one principle, the mind.

Ten

Ananda Matha - The Universal Religion

Brahmananda Swami Sivayogi was not just a preacher of a particular religion. His preachings contained all the good qualities of world religions. His philosophy, ethics, logic, etc. do not fall in the category of a religion in the fundamental sense. If we take the definition of Sigmund Freud and accepts his religious concept, which run as; "Religion is an attempt to get control over the sensory world, in which we are placed, by means of the wish—world which we have developed inside us as a result of biological and psychological necessities. If one attempts to assign to religion its place in mans evolution. It seems not to be a lasting acquisition, as a parallel to the neurosis which the civilized individual must pass through on his way from childhood to maturity," for a typical religion, one can easily say that Sivayogi was a spokesman of a scientific religion - The Ananda Matha.

He never stood for a particular class of people. His religion was both for human beings and all the creatures of the world. Hence one may call it a scientific and universal religion.

Sivayogi's Ananda Matha, the religion of bliss, is acceptable to atheists who negate the existence of God and adhere to science and rationalism on the following grounds:

(a) Sivayogi's morals are based on the needs of this world not for the need of the other world as the orthodox religions say.

(b) His ethics are based on conscience or reason. He never believed in a Saguna God.

(c) His teachings are rational.

(d) In Ananda Matha, violence is treated as wrong or unlawful. He never used the words 'Sin' and an outer 'Hell'.

(e) His teachings influenced social relations.

All the other good qualities of a religion such as service, education, benevolence, non-violence and alms-giving are strictly observed in the Ananda Matha.

A religion which according to Sivayogi should not stand for a particular class of people. It should be for not only the entire humanity but also for the entire organisms. In such a condition, all the other distinctions such as caste, creed, nationality, language, birth status, colour of the skin, etc. will be vanished. Only that religion can be called scientific and universal.

A synthetic approach to the world religions will reveal that all the religions in the world have some common features. It is because of this unity, world leaders like Ramakrishna, M.K. Gandhi, Tagore, etc. respected every religion. The common features that they found in the religions are:

(a) Every religion holds non-violence truth, self sacrifice and self control.
(b) Every religion advocates an amicable attitude to other religions.
(c) Every religion advocates to be strong and courageous.
(d) Every religion stands for progress, peace and unity of humanity.
(e) Every religion advocates to show charity, love, service to others.
(f) Every religion believes that religion is essential for man.
(g) Every religion increases a feeling of brotherhood.
(h) Every religion accepts the existence of God.
(i) Irrespective of the difference in texts, mode and place of worship, Saints, every religion upholds the purity and truthfulness of the devotee as great.
(j) Every religion advocates that its deities should be held true.

If we go through the texts written by Sivayogi, we can easily see that all the points, except the 8th one, which have just given above are there in his texts. According to Sivayogi there is no Saguna God. His concept of God is nothing but that of Yoga Philosophers.

If we go through the 'Mahavakyas' or the great utterances of Ananda Matha and compare it with the Mahavakyas of other religions we can see, in that also, the essence of the other Mahavakyas are included in the Mahavakya of Ananda Matha.

Ananda Matha

"Ananda Eva Vijayathe
Ahimsaiva Paramo Darma."

(Bliss alone reigns supreme not to do harm is verily the greatest virtue)

Buddhism

"Buddham Saranam Gacchami
Dharmmam Saranam Gacchami
Sangham Saranam Gacchami."

Christianity

"I and my father are one".

Confucianism

"The three secrets of happiness are to see no evil, to hear no evil, and to do no evil."

Hinduism

"Tat Twam Asi" (That thou Art)

Jainism

"Ahimsa Paramo Dharma"
(Non-injury is the highest religion)

Judaism

"Be still and know that I am God."

Mohamadanism

"La-Illaha - Mohamed Rasulla-llah"

(There is no God but Allah and Mohamed is the messenger of Allah)

Sikhism

"Ek Omkar, Satnam."
(There is but one God, His name is Truth).

Sufism

"Anal Haq"

(I am God.)

Shintotoism

"Prayer is of the foremost importance in appealing for the Divine Grace".

Taoism

"Tao is everywhere, it is priceless treasure. It is the Guardian and Saviour. It is the sanctuary where all beings find refuge".

Zorashtrianism

"He is but the same one God, but men give Him diverse names, Homka, Hookta, Havareshta, Mansni, Gavasni, Kunasni-pure thought, pure words, pure deeds.

The doctrine of Ananda holds out no promise of pleasure in the other world or re-birth, or a seat in the Heaven. It holds out no temptations, but outlines a practical solution for achieving happiness only by purifying the mind, can man meet the world's manifold challenges with courage, valour and eternal vigilance; Swamiji postulated this doctrine in simple language.

'Goal of human life is to attain Ananda or happiness
Ananda is the absolute serenity or calmness of the mind;
Conquest of the mind is the greatest victory;
Non-violence constitutes the Supreme Dharma in life;
Ritualistic deeds and practices only breed ignorance and misery.

The more one ponders deeply over these five fundamental tenets, the more one stands to gain happiness and enlightenment.

The pleasure derived from worldly things is not Ananda, because even while we experience such pleasures we are not happy. Our mind is always disturbed and dissatisfied. The source of bliss surely lies elsewhere. It is the mind which is the source of bliss. The mind has to be controlled and kept calm if one is to attain eternal bliss. Swamiji's message is, therefore, very significant.

"Ananda is verily the calmness or serenity of the mind."

Mind is fickle. It has to be controlled. This is possible only through incessant meditation, without allowing it to dwell on fleeting worldly pleasures when it is free from thoughts about such pleasures, it becomes pure and can its own inherent glory. This state of mind is called 'Samadhi'. It is not that easy to attain this state, stead fast determination and constant practice of meditation alone can take one to this Summit of happiness. This is also the goal of Raja Yoga of which Sivayogi was the most innovative exponent.

"Conquest of the fickle mind is the Supreme Victory".

References

1. *Philosophy of Religion (World Religions),* Dr. Vatsyayan, Kedar Nath Ram Nath Publishers, Meerut.
2. *Brahmananda Swami Sivayogi Souvenir* -1978, pp. 4, 6-8, Sidhasramam, Alathur.
3. *Anandadarsam,* Brahmananda Swami Sivayogi, Sidhasramam, Alathur.
4. *Twelve Religions and Modern Life,* Har Dayal, Kalyani Publishers, New Delhi.

Eleven

Selections from Sivayogi

On Caste Distinction

- If the distinction of castes and creeds are made by God, what natural physical features, like the trunk for the elephant, wing for the bird or four legs for the four-footed animals, do we find man endowed with in creation, so as to differentiating him as belonging to a particular caste or creed? Since we do not find any such differentiating features and since we find that followers of all religions are after happiness. The natural religion of man is but the one Religion of Bliss.

- The soul is neither Hindu nor Christian nor Islamic and the body knows no distinction of caste. As such, is it not but due to rank ignorance that we break our heads on the score of the existence of unreal castes and creeds which are misunderstood to be real owing to our long standing and deep rooted belief in them, accustomed as we are to them from our very cradle? Is it right to attribute name and form or caste and creed, or community and race to that indescribable Supreme Power of Bliss, which is radiant always in all beings?

- None of us, mortals, are of different castes as Brahmins or non-Brahmins, Naidus or Nairs, Reddy or Chetty or Cheruman or Pulayans or Bhangis. Nor are we of different religions as observed and followed under various names as Hinduism, Christianity or Muhamadanism. We are not of different nationalities too to take a false pride as nationals opposed to aliens. These distinctions as Hindu, Buddhist, Christian, Muhamadan and so forth have been brought into existence by the ancient teachers of religion.

- Proselytism of all kinds is to be stopped by law. A Hindu converts himself as a Muhamadan, a Muslim as a Hindu as a Christian and so forth, and no new feature is seen in him on account of such conversion. On the other hand, it leads to untold untoward calamities. In countries like India, wherein exist several castes and creeds, conversion tends but to increase such calamities. As such, it ought to be put a stop to and made punishable by law. What is required is a conversion of the mind to grasp whatever is good wherever it is to be found and thus to make oneself good and useful to oneself and to society.

- It is only when the evils of religion are removed, one gets a chance to enjoy the happiness of freedom, released from the bondage of misery. If not, there is no chance at all at any time be relieved of the misery born of mutual dissension and quarrels on the score of diverse castes and creeds.

- The fundamental basis and the goal of human life are verily Bliss. If observances of castes and creeds and the systems of administration are regulated on that basic principle, it will pave the way for the cessation of all tensions, communal or otherwise, and lead to harmony, peace and happiness in society.

- Every religion undergoes difference in accordance with the scale of mental purity and knowledge of the founder of that religion. All religions were not recorded in writing at one and the same time. At first it was recorded in one way. In course of time, it was found to be wanting, and had to be rewritten according to the changing needs of the time. Likewise, religious teachings had to undergo several changes with the onward march of time. Thus in course of time, several differences crept into religions. Those religious works, which were written by authors who had attained a high level of mental purity, a sense of equality towards all beings, power of knowledge and logical reasoning, are all faultless; while those which were not so inspired, were lacking in merits, and became the cause for religious differences and wranglings. This is the very reason why a same individual is found to be an adherent of Ritualism, yet an author too of the treatise of jnana or spiritual knowledge. In accordance with the development of the intellect of the authors of religious works, religions also are evn now found to attain a high or low level.

- Caste distinction is but man-made. There is no reason whatsoever to think of it as God-ordained. We see from Nature that a lizard is not like a leach, nor a squirrel like a lizard, nor the poisonous lizard (Arana) like a squirrel; no sheep is like a poisonous lizard, nor elephant is like a sheep; Neither horse is like an elephant, nor man is like a horse. Further, paddy is not like grass, the teak tree is not like the coconut tree. Neither water is like earth, nor fire like water; neither air is like fire, nor the sky like air. Thus we see that all objects, movable and immovable, in this universe, have been created with particular differentiating forms and natures that could be easily distinguished even by boys. Can that Power, which can thus create, be incapable of creating the necessary marks of distinction in men too, to show that He has ordained several castes in the human race as, Brahma, Kshatriya, Vaisya and Sudra? Alas! a great pity! The sheep does not beget on the elephant, nor vice versa, nor do they feel any desire as between them for any mutual sexual union, nor have they the symmetry of generative organs as is seen among those of the same species. On the other hand, we do not see thus in mankind. The high caste may feel a desire for sexual union with the low, and vice versa. They have the symmetry of generative organs that pertain to those of the same species. There is for them pleasure in sexual union and they beget issue too. Hence all mankind is but of one caste. If it were of different castes, there could not be that symmetry of generative organs, nor could they beget issue. Squirrels and other beings could not beget on sheep or the like. Nor has God endowed men with distinctive marks to differentiate them, one from the other, unlike other beings of His own creation. Just as a man taking but a part in a dumb show, exults that he is a green painted figure, or a black painted figure, or a bearded one, or that he is a Rama, or a Ravana or a Surpanakha or a Khara and so forth, it is false and meaningless for men to exult in the pride of their being a Brahmin, Kshatriya and so forth. If it is not false but real, then they ought to have at their very birth the distinctive marks of the sacred thread and the like. The babies of all these men who pride in the difference of caste, look uniform at their birth. Hence the caste distinction that we see among men is verily man-made. Further, when a Brahmin becomes a convert to Muhamadanism or to Christianity, he becomes a Muhamadan or a Christian. If Brahmin is of a superior caste and others are of low castes, how can he thus change his caste? When the elephant gets into a flock of sheep, it does not turn out to be a sheep. Hence also, the intelligent could understand that caste distinctions among men are but man-made. Further, if we look into the etymology of the words denoting castes, it will be seen that such distinctions, as Brahmin, Kshatriya and the like, are based on their respective functions in life, and not on the distinctions of any caste as such.

ON GOD

- The wicked enemies of Jesus Christ caught hold of him, spat him face, smote him on his cheeks and gave for drink vinegar mixed with gall. Did God help him yet?

- If we think of the fact that God.was heartless and did not show any mercy at all unto Jesus, though he was nailed to the cross and though he cried aloud in distress, 'O my God, my God, Hast thou forsaken me', will that God, the creator of the universe, be imbued with mercy towards the believers in Jesus?

- O Ye advocates of religion! Since you and your religions advocate that God is the Creator, Protector and Destroyer, it becomes clear on the strength of your own tenet that God is a wicked being, really fastidious, and all your rituals to gain His favour are of no avail. To explain. It turns out that creation, protection and destruction are the natural functions of God.

How can God give up those His natural functions? A farmer sows the seeds, protects the crops and eventually harvests them. Will he show any mercy in the harvesting of the crops? No. Since God's cultivation is of the nature of creation, protection and destruction. He cannot but destroy you, however fervently you pray or bitterly cry out to be saved of such destruction. The dealer in flesh rears up goats and fowls; eventually he slaughters them, feeds upon them and trades in their flesh too. However bitterly the fowls and goats may cry out in agony, does he spare them out of mercy without slaughtering them? No. Likewise God also has no go to show any mercy and save them from destruction, for, what you advocate is that destruction also is the natural function of God. Will God give up that duty even if you entreat Him to desist from that duty of destruction? Will the sun ever desist from emitting heat, and keep everything cool even if he is entreated, saluted, or worshipped, not to do so? Will fire however much we may attempt to propitiate it with hymns of praise and worship and entreaty, ever cease to burn us and keep us cool? Fire burns the very hand of its votary who consecrates and maintains the sacred fire and worships it daily. If he were to touch fire, overcome with excessive devotion to his favourite deity with the soothing words 'He is my own God of Fire, my beloved deity', he is sure to have his fingers burnt. If he approaches that fire too close, that fire will reduce that devotee to ashes. None can stop or alter the course of nature. As such, all your ritualistic practices of prayer and the like to desist God from his natural duty of destruction and bless you with His favour are of no avail. Look at the life of Jesus Christ. He was a great devotee of God, whoever prayed unto him, "O creator, O creator" What a noble and virtuous soul was he whoever preached about God and made many others too to sing his praise and pray unto Him? How supremely moral he was! Such a Christ was caught hold of by his enemies who spat him in his face, smote him on his cheeks, laughed at him, set a vessel of vinegar mixed with gall before him to drink, tied him to the cross, nailed him on the breast and crucified him. Unable to bear the agony, he cried out in a loud voice saying. 'My God, my God! Why hast thou forsaken me' and yielded up the ghost. God did not give him any relief whatsoever. Where was the mercy of the Creator then? If God is of a type to be please dat His devotees, He ought to have showered His mercy of Christ. But Christ was not blessed by God even with the insight to know whether he had been accepted or not by God. If he had really known, would he have cried aloud saying. 'O my God! O my God! Why hast thou forsaken me?' When such is the state of Christ himself, what is the lot of those who believe that belief in Christ would ensure the grace of God and open the gate of Paradise for them? Surely their lot is that of pitiable Arjuna who, in the sincere belief in the words of Bhagawad Gita, the teachings of Sri Krishna, was ever devoted to the performance of action in a spirit disinterestedness, yet without gaining that knowledge of self, was afraid of the impending advent of Kali, the presiding deity of the Iron age, fled the country out of that fear, and perished on the way. The words of Christians that God created Christ and offered him in sacrifice to redeem mankind of their original sin, do not turn out to be a satisfactory explanation, but turns out only to a blasphemy that God is wicked being, who curses His own created children and kills by crucifying in the cross. These people preach that He is All-Powerful and is the seat of mercy ! What is not the Omnipotent capable of accomplishing! Adam and Eve, the first creation, had become sinners and become the object of His curse. Could He not absolve them of their sins by blessing them? Is it the characteristic of that One who is the seat of mercy, to curse His own created children and destroy them? Is it reasonable to think that He would show that mercy towards those heartless cruel, who kill and feed upon the innocent goats and fowls without showing His mercy towards them, in spite of hearing their piteous groans shaking their legs when they are slaughtered by men and of seeing their last agonies of death, unable to put up with the pain of their last moments? Is there anything more foolish than the thought that God would show His mercy towards those men who indulge more in the taste of the flesh and blood of the innocent beings like goats and fowls than in the sentiment of compassion and extreme devotional love to God? The Vedas, Sastras and the like proclaim that there is no virtue equal to pity and no sin equal to injury, and all religions in join on the virtue of pity. As such, if men give up this noble virtue of pity and indulge in doing harm to innocent beings, and if there is a God who would show His mercy towards them, who is there is the world more wicked than such a God?

There is not a God who is thus partial towards men. If there is, to which religionist has he shown such a mercy or has shown His favour? We see among those, who propitiate God in extreme devotion, many a calamity like fell disease, dire poverty, premature death, loss of beloved sons, friends, wife and the like, which are not the lot of even those ignorant who do not propitiate any God at all. Is this the grace of Gods towards His devotees? What religions teach is that they will be saved and blessed with happiness in heaven. Is it not unreasonable to say that God who will not bless His devotees with any happiness here in this world, will bless them with the same in heaven? Have those religionists been witness at any time to the fact that God had blessed any one thus? Is it not reasonable and proper that He should bless them here in this world? Should not one be fed when one is hungry? Should not one be given relief when one is afflicted with misery? O Ye men! If God is, as you advocate, the creator, protector and destroyer, then it has been shown here that He could not be pleased at you in any way and grant you salvation. By granting you salvation, God runs the risk of a great loss and a dereliction of His own inherent duty. To explain. If God is pleased and grant salvation to beings, His cultivation in the form of creation, protection and destruction would entirely fail, and He will fail in the discharge of His natural duty too. Without seeds how will the farmer sow? How will he reap the harvest? If all beings are granted salvation, how can creation continue? How can there be destruction? As seeds to the farmer, is not the aggregate of lives, the seeds for God? As devotees are being granted salvation in pursuance of their prayers and so forth, the aggregate of lives should gradually get dwindled, and the cultivation of crops in the form of worldly life must have come to an end long-long ago. According to the tenets of your religion, there is no scope too for any increase in the primeval aggregate of lives. The following facts and authorities would show that when the aggregate of lives gets dwindled in consequence of its individual constituents gradually getting salvation, there is no chance to make up the deficit by the creation of new lives. It is the very water that rises up to the sky as vapour owing to the heat of the sun that comes down as rain. The very water that falls as rain over mountains and plains, flows through streams and rivers and enters the ocean. Again in season, the same process continues. To make up the deficit of the water evaporated as vapour, no new supply of water is resorted to. If the water that has risen up above as vapour were not to come down as rain, oceans, lakes and wells would have all dried up long ago. That it does not so happen even after the lapse of a long period of time is due to the fact that water, thus gone up as vapour, comes down in due course as rain. Likewise, lives or souls also are going up and coming down, and thus it is that the ocean of worldly existence continues to exist for ever. If on the other hand, it is argued that the deficit caused by the gradual emancipation of the constituent individual souls, is made up by the creation of fresh souls, and thus it is that the ocean of worldly existence ever remains unaffected, without any change, this very argument strikes at the root of the scriptural text which says:

"Boothagrama sa evayam
bhuthwa bhuthwa praleeyathe"

which means that the same original aggregate of lives come and go revolvingly. Further it is contradictory to the scriptural text *"Aho nithya shaswathoyam puranha:"*, which means that the soul is unborn, constant, eternal and indestructible. Further, the above argument necessitates the creation of new heavens and abodes of salvation too. If not, will not the earlier emancipated and the later ones, get gradually crowded in the existing heaven, exposed to the unpleasant impact of daily increasing rush? So many are the souls that were and are being given passports to heaven by the various religions in the course of time. This is but what is revealed by these very religions too. Many are the ways enjoined in religions whereby many souls are liberated in a moment. Yet God's work of creation, protection and destruction, has not in the least been affected by it. As we think over this state of nature on the strength of experience, those religions which advocate that by the grace of God or of His incarnations or of His sons, if any, many can be and have been emancipated, lose their very stand, and the nature of the Vedas which say *"Na sa punaravarthathe na sa punaravarthathe"* which means that the emancipated do not take birth again, is exposed in all its naked reality. O Ye Founders of religions! As we proceed to comment upon the tenet that God is the creator, protector and destroyer, it becomes clear that God is heartless and is the seat of all evil virtues, who teases His own created children, that He is of a type fastidious in all ways, that He is despicable, ever bent upon doing base and wicked actions, which would not be resorted to even by the wild beasts like lions and tigers or by the wicked demons and ghosts, and as such, He ought to be punished by the united governments of the world, since He destroys all His children, as any government would punish a father who destroys his own children. O Ye Founders of religions! It was indeed harsh and rash of you to have made your God such a being. As such, have you any justification to lay down the several rituals to gain the favour of God, or to perform or to have them performed? Can you with any reason describe that your God is the seat of mercy, the friend of the distressed and the bestower of the desired objects of His devotees, and so forth? Is there any greater mistake or inconsistency than saying that God is the seat of all vices and also at the same time that He is the seat of all virtues, as one would blow hot and cold at the same breath, when one says that fire is hot and at the same time cold too? Were the Vedas and the like of Hinduism or of any other religion ever capable of producing those uncommon powers of knowledge and reason and so forth, as have been produced by our Sidha works of Anandavimana and others, to introduce into the world the religion of Ananda which detects and points out to the world this absurd inconsistency, weans them off from the several ritualistic practices of misery, and keeps them ever in the rapture of ecstasy born of Yoga? O Ye Aspirants after bliss! Those religions which advocate that Iswara (God, known as Brahma) is the Seat of mercy, Friend of the distressed, Bestower of the desired objects of His devotees, the Creator, Protector and Destroyer of the universe, and so forth are of a nature wafted away like chaff and the light cotton, when the wind of reason blows over them. If these religions, which are reduced to ashes like rags or moths in the fire of the knowledge of experience, are believed in, neither man has, nor had he, at any time any chance to experience real knowledge, mental steadfastness or bliss supreme, but his lot is only to fall a victim to fear, to get deluded and lead a miserable life, engaged in the performance of several ritualistic practices. If, on the other hand, they had a chance to experience the same, people embracing the one religion of Hinduism, would never go down, fighting on the score of caste distinctions. They would neither be quarrelling on the score of the distinctions of Saivaism. Vaishnavaism and so forth, installing several idols of stone and the like, without knowing the idol of bliss supreme. They would neither be seduced by the glamour of the muttering of mantras, like Gayatri, nor by the Tantric modes of worship, and so on. Nor would the worshippers of God wrangle on the score of the distinctions of religion, without knowing that the whole world is of the one religion of Ananda. Nor would they describe in glowing terms, that heaven would, be had after death, without giving expression to the experience of bliss or salvation, while alive here in this world. For the sake of alleviation of misery and the attainment of desired objects, they would never cry out to a God and pray unto Him, as children cry out to their father. In spite of such profuse shedding of tears, God, their Father, has not blessed them with anything, not even with the knowledge that His children should not take to quarrel and that there is neither any distinction of caste or creed, nor has He stopped their crying. On the other hand, the delusion of religion and the crying out to God, are daily on the increase in the world. Alas! Are ignorance, calamity and tears, the result of propitiation of God. Hence neither traditional customs nor textual authorities should ever be accepted as guides to salvation, on the belief that they are enjoined by the Vedas, or they are created by God, or they are approved by all, or that they have been practised from time immemorial by the followers of all religions, and none has a dissenting voice in the matter. If they are found to go against experience and reason, they are to be discarded as unto the outer rind and joint of the sugarcane, supposed to be created by God. Then alone bliss can be realised.

ON MANLY EFFORT

- Without sufficient effort, desires are not accomplished. It is only the cowards that will cling to the saying, 'what is to happen, must happen'. This means that only cowards will remain inactive, in the hope that God will bless them with all their desired objects.

- When the field is ploughed well and sown, and proper care taken of later with sufficient effort, it yields crops. Will it yield crop if you remain inactive in the hope that what is fated cannot but come to pass. When you exert yourself in your studies, you master them. You pass high examinations. If you remain idle in the belief that what is fated must happen, will you acquire learning? Thus whatever objects have to be achieved, those very objects, we see, have been achieved by the wise, verily through manly effort, and they have become worthy of this worldly happiness here and eternal bliss too. यद्भाव्यं तद्भविष्यति This means that what is to happen cannot but happen. It is said by Bhartrihari:
  "Remain quiet (inactive), for God or Fate is verily the cause for one's rise and fall."

  With implict faith in authorities like these, many give up the necessary manly effort, and in the hope that God will bless them with all their desired objects, remain lazy and become ruined in the long run. On the other hand, you should not give up your manly effort seeing such authorities or texts proclaiming, 'what is fated cannot but take place,' or 'what is fated cannot be blotted' or 'God will give us' and so on. God Himself advises us that we should exert according to our capacity. We see around us many a thing like grass and so forth, spontaneously growing on the earth, but not paddy and other food grains. They can be raised only after great effort, such as, ploughing the field several times over and again, adding sufficient manure like ash, cow dung and the like, then sowing the seed in season and taking due care in its protection. If like grass and other things, paddy and other food grains were to grow spontaneously without any manly exertion, we could remain completely inactive without taking to any exertion at all. If paddy and other foodgrains were created by God without husk and other unedible parts, we are saved of the exertion of husking the paddy too. In the place of the ocean of salt water, if God has created but half of it to be of milk, how very greatly useful it would have been ! Instead of having to dive for pearl and other precious things in the deep ocean, if God had but created them like stones and pebbles on the surface of the earth everywhere, how easily all could have become rich without any effort at all! We cannot think that God is powerless to create paddy and other foodgrains with a spontaneous growth like grass, or to create them without the undesirable parts of husk and the like, that we may thereby use them without any manly effort in preparing the food as we do now. He has created some roots and fruits too that could be eaten as they are without any further exertion. Since the Almighty has not dealt with in the same way as regards all objects, we are to conclude that He has, by His own mode of creation, shown us the way that we should exert. If we hold the belief in the texts स्वस्थास्तिषृत ('Be quiet or inactive') or यद्भाव्यं etc. (what is to happen must happen), then there is no necessity for guru or preceptor nor for the Sastras, nor for any sort of advice. No manly effort whatsoever is needed where it is needed now. In such a state, man tends to be but beastly in nature and become degenerated. We should not turn out thus.

ON MIND

- The mind is in itself the cause for one's happiness and misery. That mind which is possessed of wisdom, manliness and cheer is a friend, while that which is otherwise is a foe. The mind that is sullied by the passions of attachment and hatred gives rise to misery and several other painful experiences. Hence one should wash off these impurities of the mind with one's own wisdom and manliness and make it crystal pure. To get rid of human misery, it is the mind and not God that is to be pleased. Without purity of mind no salvation is possible.
- Motionlessness of the mind is itself salvation, while its motion is worldly bondage. Get the mind absorbed in itself and it will then merge in ecstatic Bliss. That is indeed the cessation of all misery and the attainment of final beatitude.

- All actions tending to cause pain to the mind are sins. It is he who has conquered the mind that is indeed Free, that is Great, that is Happy. Conquer the mind. It is the greatest conquest. Keep the mind steady and motionless and get it absorbed in itself. That is verily Bliss.

- Are those religious teachers, who advocate or assert the attainment of a heaven after death, real witnesses of such a heaven? Have they visited that region? The blissful state of the mind is the real heaven, while its miserable state is the veritable hell. It is to be experienced not after death, but verily while one is alive.

- O mind! Don't run after the external objects. Go to the light within, and be always exulting in bliss. Don't waste your time in vain. O mind! Give up all the evils of love, hatred and the like, completely.

- O mind! Love, hatred and the like will make you run, will take you to the well of worldly misery. Never keep company, O mind! with love, hatred and the like. Be united unto bliss.

ON POSSESSION

- All happiness is born of the soundness of the body, and this is a truth accepted by all religions too. Thus it is clear on the strength of authority, reason and experience, that the best means to ward off hunger, thirst and the like, to keep up a sound body free from all diseases, to remain undisturbed in steadfastness, to cause no harm to oneself or to others, is verily to keep up one's body with the fortune one has in one's possession, and take up to stead fastness in yogic knowledge. If one has no such fortune, one should work hard, and thus keep up one's body sound, and one's steadfastness undisturbed. That is the reason why I am in the profession. Did not, O Disciple, the lord Vasishta take up the preceptorship of Raghu's Royal house? Some take to alms. Some are seated in one place and live upon what is offered by anybody. Some are maintained by their disciples. Some take up to some kind of work. Some depend on royal favour and bounty, some who have property, do not depend on anybody. Thus in many such ways the great seers of yore, steadfast in realisation, have passed their life. It is only the ignorant that would think that one is not steadfast in one's self realisation, because one has not taken up to begging, nor accepted Sanyasihood, or one has taken up to some work that does not cause any harm to others for the sake of merely keeping up the body, or because one remains at home. Should any one go to the forest to see the lines in his own palm or should he go about begging alms, or take up to any guise? No. He could see those lines of his palm wherever he might be if he has but eyes to see them. Likewise is had the realisation of the Supreme too, if only the mind is directed properly. At times and in some places, it might be difficult to see the lines in the palm. We cannot see them in darkness. But for the realisation of the Supreme, there is no such hindrance at all. Is not the Atman verily self refulgent? Should we light a lamp or a torch to see the sun? Those who do not know the right path cannot see the light of Atman, whether they accept the pose of a yogi or resort to forest, or do anything else. Those who know that path do, undoubtedly, realise the Atman whether they remain in the house or live in the forest. Chudala had the realisation of bliss eternal, though she was a female, was living in the palace in the capital and was in the midst of royal pleasures. But her husband, the king Sikhidhwaja by name, betook himself to forest, lived upon roots and fruits there, and underwent several troubles, and yet had not the realisation of what should be realised. At last, his wife Chudala approached him in the forest in the guise of a sage, and gave him spiritual advice, whereby he gained the experience of realisation. His eyes were then opened to the view that there was not harm or hindrance to realisation in remaining in his own palace. Thus he came back to his capital, ruled over his subjects justly, in the full enjoyment of the realisation of the Atman. This story is narrated in Vasishta. To the same effect we find several other stories too.

On Ritualism

- Take the case of ritualists. They worship God, observing vows like Ekadasi and so forth, keeping fasts and long vigils, spending large sums of money in the construction of temples and in the worship of idols, and roaming about by way of pilgrimages to distant places like Kasi, Rameshwaram and so forth. Some worship God, becoming great devotees, yogis and jnanis, giving up as trash all worldly objects and possessions, not so easily possible of renunciation. All these their activities are not in their desire for misery, but for happiness alone. If worship of god is eventually to turn out as misery, few will dream of taking to such a worship, or even if they have the knowledge that worship of God will not conduce to happiness, none will ever worship God.

- Many are the mantras. Whatever a man desires, they declare, such as the enticing of a woman or influence over a king, or a great prosperity, or the begetting of issue, nay, even kingship or destruction of enemy, or cure of disease, and so forth, all these can be achieved by the performance of rituals, such as the muttering of mantras, sacrifices, penance, pilgrimage, idol-worship and the like Karma. Many a work is seen composed wherein we find narratives to show that many have accomplished their desires by taking up to this kind of ritualistic practices. Following implicitly the texts thus laid down, many a Brahmin and Hindu Ruler, and almost all Hindus, are deluded, and waste their precious life in recitation of mantras, in fast, pilgrimage, building up temples and in several other indirect ways. Yet we do not see them blessed by God with a pie more on that account, nor any disease cured thereby. In this way too, many a Hindu gets degenerated. But they seek consolation for their failure in that they might have faltered or gone wrong somewhere in their performance of the rituals, or they would be blessed with the fruits thereof in another life. Thus, by taking to unreasonable and unjust paths also, Hindus degenerate. They cannot but fare otherwise. If a just ruler were to appoint any one to a post, he ought to discharge his duty loyally and honestly. The king will be pleased, and he is raised to a higher post, and thus he is led to a happy life. If on the other hand, he does not discharge his duties properly, but attends on the king to secure his favour, what would be the result! Surely he becomes a victim of the king's anger and consequent punishment, and thus falls down from his erstwhile happy state. If a father were to entrust a son with a plot of land for cultivation, he ought, in due reverence to his father, cultivate the land properly in season, and thus he is enabled to lead a happy life. If on the other hand, he becomes idle and wastes his time in evil ways, or in the company of the wicked and, allowing the land to remain uncultivated, looks up to his father's favour for his wherewithal for his livelihood, he incurs but the great displeasure of his father, with the further consequence of his land being taken from his charge and entrusted to another son. Thus as he is found wanting, he comes down from his original happy position. If those who assert that the Almighty, the Fountain of justice and the Father of all, has in His divine mercy, granted us an earth of unlimited fertility and prosperity and blessed us with sufficient strength for exertion and perseverance, were but to exert according to their respective capacity and not remain idle, they can get on happily here, and be qualified for the enjoyment of the life hereafter too. On the contrary, if they remain idle without taking to any work, they will have to suffer even for their daily bread, and be forced to take up to several ways, unjust and indecent. They will have to cause harm to others. If the Almighty is one that justly metes out punishment for the guilty, they will be victims of such punishment too. Surely that is the way how they would ruin themselves. Not knowing the real meaning of the authorities quoted above, and sticking fast to Swakarma, as meaning nothing but sacrificial rituals, Hindus have set their face against physical exertion, and resorted either to the rituals of sacrifice, vow, fast, idol-worship and the like as the means to destroy their enemies, to attain sovereignty over kingdom and all prosperity, thus wasting away immense wealth in those rituals, or have remained completely indifferent to all vicissitudes of time, leaving themselves to the care of a fate. It is to this attitude that we have to trace the prevailing present degeneration of the Hindus. As a contrast, the English, holding fast to physical exertion as the one means for elevation, have been ever exerting, industrious and persevering, with the result that they are today not only our rulers, but masters in all fields of activity with laurels to their credit. It is in vain that we take to ritualistic Karma, like sacrifice, vow and the like, in the implicit faith that, if such Karma is done disinterestedly and in a spirit of dedication to God, it would conduce to God's blessing, mental purity and jnana. For we see those very orthodox of the society, who have been following the path of rituals from time immemorial, condemn and keep afar some of their own race as low or untouchable. If, by such longstanding and hereditary practice of ritualistic Karma, they have gained a little of God's blessing or mental purity or jnana, would they hate one another, without having attained any feeling of equality towards their fellow beings? A chief cause for the degeneration and downfall of the Hindus is their hatred of their own brethren as of a low caste. If some of the sons of a father be strong, and as such, they hate their weak brothers as of no concern, it is but natural that they incur their father's displeasure, and go down in the scale of his estimation for want of union and fellow-feeling. Likewise, if some of the strong sons of the same Heavenly Father, were to keep afar their weak brothers as inferior and hate them, if there is a God who metes out just reward and punishment, those orthodox who stick up from time immemorial to ritualistic karma, ought in fairness to be the victims of that God's wrath and consequent punishment, that could not but pave the way for their own degeneration and downfall.

ON SACRIFICE

- Those that are given up to rituals, are contented by mere names, and are deluded by the several kinds of sacrifices, chanting of mantras (Spells), offerings in the fire and the like.

- Is not sacrifice a highly wicked deed? Are not animals slaughtered in yaga (sacrifice)? Is there any wicked deed in the world equal to slaughter? From the justice of our own ruler even the dull can clearly understand that there is no wicked deed greater than doing harm to another. Theft, assault, deceit and the like crimes have each its appropriate punishment. A man is sentenced to death only for the crime of murder. This clearly proves that killing is the greatest of cruel deeds, and this is, as such, admitted by all religions too. Even the religions which differ in their view as to what is righteous and what is unrighteous, or virtuous and sinful, are unanimous in declaring that there is no pain greater than killing or doing harm. If a perverted fool were, for the sake of mere opposition, to say that there is no pain in killing, will he give his consent to cut off a bit of flesh from his body? No. If we do the same by force, he will cry aloud. Does he not thus cry aloud on account of the pain? Hence even the fool who speaks to the contrary has to admit that killing causes pain. Let it be. Even the beasts and the birds like fowl, goat, dog and the like which have no power of reason to discriminate between virtue and vice, do teach us that doing harm causes great pain. When we slaughter them, they shake their legs and cry out loudly. When we approach a beast and rebuke it, or speak false things to it, it feels no pain. What other deed is more wicked than slaughter, which even such dumb animals teach us as most painful and sinful? Is not such deed becoming of tigers and other cruel beasts? They have no power of reason, nor do they live upon plants and vegetables. To live, they must kill. We can find solace for their cruel action in that way. Is not the man who takes to killing, a greater tiger than the ordinary one, since God has provided him with many things in this world for his livelihood without having resort to slaughter, since he has been blessed with a faculty of reason, and since he has before him many good Sastras and wise folk to instruct him, even if he be ignorant? Is it not unreasonable too to slaughter an animal in sacrifice for the sake of dispelling one's own sin? If one's finger is affected with poison, can it be cured by cutting off another's finger? How can we blame Vasishta for condemning those sacrificers of animals like unto beasts? All religions are unanimous in the view that the Almighty is Viswambhara or the Ruler of the universe and is ever contented. Can such a God be a vile wretch to hanker eagerly after flesh? Or has He become a victim of fever and such diseases, eagerly looking up for something to gratify his voracious appetite in convalescence? Is He the victim of any disease, which has made him physically weak, or is He like a fox feeding on dead bodies?

What is the meaning of the Hindus' offering flesh to God by way of worship? It is replied that they do so not for God, but they perform such animal sacrifices to please Indra and the like Gods to obtain their grace. Such God and Gods are said by Puranas to live upon nectar. It is for this reason that gods are called Amritandhas (those whose food is nectar). Further they have in their possession the so called Kalpaka tree, capable of granting them all their desired objects. As such they can be in no need of divine food too. Hence it is neither becoming nor reasonable to include Indra and others in the category of flesh-eating animals like fox and so forth. Alas! It is a pity that our people offer such worship, unapproved by all religions and unendurable even for the very Almighty. It is becoming only for a fox or a tiger that has no power of reason, that can find a relish for blood or flesh, and not for man. As such, what wonder that the sage Vasishta has condemned those who propitiate God with the offering of flesh in implicit faith in the Lord's grace thereby as unto beasts, since they, like tiger, kill animals? Will a father, however wicked and cruel he may be, kill his own child and eat it? In that view also, is not the Almighty, the Father and Mother of all the world and the people therein? Are not all beings His issue? Will He therefore be pleased if His own child is killed, and that flesh offered to Him in worship? Even the cruel tiger does not kill its own cub and eat it. As such, does not this practice give room for other religions to laugh at Hinduism when it is explained that the God of the Hindus is worse than a tiger, addicted to the vulgar flesh, and heartless and cruel to the core? What is the meaning of worship wherein flesh is offered? We need not care for the contempt of this practice by other religions, nor for God's disapproval. The more we dive deep in the matter, the more cruel and painful appears slaughter. We shall take for granted there is some race superior to us. If we take for slaughter one of us either for food or worship of that race, how much will he feel sorry? Can we give full expression to his then situation, except to say in short, that he will beat his own breast, bitterly cry and show all indescribable pangs of agony? Why go so far for an illustration? How much does a man feel sorry even for his own natural death as a consequence of some disease? Though he knows it to be the inevitable lot of all mortal, with what great anxiety he tries to save himself from the clutches of death by all means possible, however great the expense may be to bring in doctors and be treated by them, or to offer prayers and perform rituals to please and worship God for His grace. Even then, at the point of death, wherein consolation is to be had as that is the inevitable lot of all, his sorrow and that of his kith and kin are really indescribable. Having had this very human experience at hand, knowing well that all beings have, like us, that attachment towards their offspring and fear of death, and that this horrible practice is to be put a stop to, man yet indulges in the practice of the cruel slaughter of fowls, goats and other animals, like tiger killing the cow, or the cat killing the rat or the fox killing the fowl. Is this cruel practice verily the Dharma (virtue) of man? It is the nature of the beasts for the strong to prey upon the weak. If man also resorts to that, he degrades himself unto a beast, nay, worse than beasts. My view is that it is more horrible, sinful and cruel to kill fish and the like than catching a man, cutting his neck and eating his flesh. For in human society, to cheat the implicitly faithful, or to harm the innocent helpless, is considered a very serious crime, and anyone who commits this offence is condemned by the entire society, and branded with the abusive term of 'a great sinner'. If we see in this light, fowls, goats and the like put implicit faith in us and approach us when we call them. They take us to be their masters. Should the master in whom is places such implicit and full confidence, take the life of the fowls by wringing their neck? Is the master a fox or a cat? Is not that slaughter a clear case of breach of trust? We do not see anybody to take up their cause, however much they might be harmed. Hence they are little helpless orphans too. Is it not then a great sin to kill such helpless being? Man has his own strength and power of intelligence and reason. He has also several friends, kith and kin and relatives to save him from calamity. Nay he has even the protection of the great lord, the king of the realm. In this comparative state of man and animals, who is worthier for pity? Which is the greater crime, killing a man killing an animal?

When we think about seriously, we do not see the noble virtue in man. Is not 'Not to give pain to another' the highest virtue enjoined by the compassionate great?

- There is pain only when there is a mind. God has not blessed plants with a mind. Hence in cutting them, there is no sin of doing harm, as we have no pain when we cut our hair, and no sin also in doing that. If there is sin, we cut so many hairs when we get shaved, and thus we are liable to the guilt of having committed many sins. Hair also grows with the help of oil and other things. They are also destroyed when there is a lack of such nourishment, or when they are cut. They have also growth and decay like plants. But there is the sin of doing harm in harming only beings with a mind susceptible to both pain and joy. That is the reason why no religion has enjoined sin in feeding on plants. All religions have unanimously accepted feeding on vegetables and plants. But they are not so unanimous in slaughtering and feeding of beings.

ON WEALTH

- When there is in yourself the thing to satisfy your hunger, alas! Why should you, for the sake of earning money, take to a garb, and deceive the world?

- If there is no sufficient money in your possession, you can take to manual labour and maintain your body. Should you resort to unrighteous deeds? There is one to see everything.

- Money earned by robbery or by illegal means, will never accompany you in your death. Then why should you take up to unrighteous deeds. Man should shun the ghost of desires.

- If you entertain any desire, however small, for another's wealth, that is equal to theft. That is what the great seers have declared in yoga sastras. Who knows it?

- If there is a chance to come by money, the wealthy and the learned too, will not hesitate to cut the throat of the victim with a knife. What wonder then that others resort to it!

- If you cause any pain to beings, that is verily said to be equal to the killing of beings. Even in actually killing animals, people are not afraid of that truth.

ON PENANCE

- Penance is a kind of inflicting harm. All difficult practices, like putting up with hunger, thirst, heat and cold, are included in penance. From these result loss of physical strength and several diseases. When our physical body is a boat to take us across the ocean of worldly existence, and when that body is affected by a leakage or the like, that tells upon the happiness of the self. Is not this a crime of committing suicide? If God metes out condign punishment for a crime, there is every chance for those who take up to penance and austerities to be visited with his punishment, as kings punish those who attempt to commit suicide.

ON BEGGING ALMS

- My view is that having had property originally, to have cast away that and to take up to begging, is highly sinful. Men earn money in several ways, some illegally by giving false evidence or by deceiving or robbing others. When a jnani takes to alms, he runs the risk of enjoying a share of the ill-gotten fortune too, and thus becomes liable for a share of the sins also, caused in the making of that ill-gotten fortune. Further at the mere sight of a beggar, many generally think, 'really a nuisance! How not to give anything?' and thus give him something most grudgingly. Thus jnani incurs the sin of having caused harm also to those in ease and comfort. This is a defect also for their noblest virtue of Ahimsa or harmlessness. Moreover, when one has to live upon begging, one is liable to fall sick, not getting regular food at times, and what is got at times may be quite unwholesome too. This affects not only his steadfastness in Ahimsa but he may becomes a victim of sorrow too.

ON RAJA YOGA

- Yoga has two aspects, external and internal, of which the former is not important. Vedanta is included in that external aspect. It is only to guide those, who have misunderstood the external aspect of Yoga, i.e., Vedanta, as sufficient for the attainment of Salvation, into that internal aspect viz. Raja Yoga that it is declared that the Vedanta practice and Vedantic knowledge alone are not sufficient.

ON AHIMSA

- Not to cause pain is verily the highest virtue.
- Sacrifices and the like rituals lead but to ignorance and pain.
- When we think about, in accordance with Yoga Sastra, the full significance of the word 'Ahimsa (non-injury)', all virtues are included in this one word. For, Ahmisa is verily not to cause pain to any being either by body, mind or word.

ON SENSE CONTROL

- If control of senses were to mean remaining motionless like a pillar, destroying all the senses, the great yogis of yore would have had no chance of writing treatises on yoga, and becoming the benefactors of the world. As such, we may have to call them as bereft of sense control. The meaning of sense control is the gaining of such a control over the senses that they can be directed to the right path as intended by the yogi. If that does not become possible, the result is harm to oneself and others too. The goal of eternal bliss cannot also be attained, one will have to live long in hell. If the driver of a coach has not the ability to control and drive the horses alright, they will bolt away from the straight road. The driver runs the risk of injury to himself, or of exposing himself to the offence of running over the people passing on the road, with the result he might be imprisoned, as a punishment for the offence of rash driving. If, on the other hand, he is able to control and drive the horses properly, he can drive safe to his destination, finish his business there, and return home happy, without causing injury to any one. Likewise, if there is control of the senses, he can remain in society, finish his mission there and reach the abode of Bliss Supreme. Thus in absorption of the mind is also had the control of the senses. Sense control is not to be understood to mean the entire destruction of the senses.

On Ananda (Bliss)

- Ananda (Bilss) is verily supreme above all, because, all religionists, Christians, Muhammedans, Buddhists, Hindus and all, do alike wish for bliss. They are given up-to mutual wranglings on the score of superiority of their respective gods and religions. When Christians preach that you will gain Salvation only if you believe in Christ, Hindus and other religionists do not, in the least, like it. When Muhammedans preach that Muhammedanism is the only superior religion and that only by embracing that faith you can attain salvation. Christians and others do not approve of it. Thus, whatever is spoken of as superior by the followers of one religion, all that does not meet with the accord of the followers of other different religions. Thus do all the theists, with their different ideas and notions about God, extol their own religion and their own respective duties as superior and supreme. The atheists negate the very existence of a God. Whatever is worshipped by the theists as supreme, that is not accepted even as small deities by the atheists. They do not believe in the very existence of a God. But all of them, those atheists, and theists with different conceptions about religion and God, do extremely wish for bliss. Hence, it is clear that Ananda (bliss) is supreme above everything.

- Bliss alone reigns supreme.

- Absorption of the mind in itself is verily bliss.

ON VIRTUE

- He is a fool who goes after a vote of the majority to conclude that two and two makes four. In all virtuous good things, it is the view of the party, howsoever in a minority that sticks to truth that should be accepted.

ON SALVATION

- What is known as Mukti or Salvation is but the absorption of the mind in the Supreme of the nature of Sat (Reality), Chit (Energy) and Ananda (Bliss). How is this absorption possible? It is possible when the mind is concentrated on that spot which is pointed out by the Guru as the spot wherein the Atman is located. This can be illustrated as follows, when salt is placed in a place of water, it gets dissolved in the water, and we see then but the one form of water alone. Likewise, the mind also united with the Atman, gets absorbed in the Atman, and there remains the one form verily of the Atman. There is nothing else to be styled as a second. There is neither the egotism of 'I-ness' too. Thereby results the loss of the conception of duality, and dawns the experience of non-duality. This is a Advaita or monism. This is verily Rajayoga. This is in short salvation.

- The salvation from misery is called Mukthi.

ON RELIGION

- Every religion undergoes difference in accordance with the scale of mental purity and knowledge of the Founder of that religion. All religion were not recorded in writing at one and the same time. At first it was recorded in one way. In course of time, it was found to be wanting, and had to be rewritten according to the changing needs of the time. Likewise, religious teachings had to undergo several changes with the onward march of time. Thus in course of time, several differences crept into religions. Those religious works, which were written by authors who had attained a high level of mental purity, a sense of equality towards all beings, power of knowledge and logical reasoning, are all faultless: While those which were not so inspired, were lacking in merits, and became the cause for religious differences and wranglings.

- What is required for the present times is a - Universal religion - religion of bliss, that would bring into it's fold all the followers of the several religions now given upto warring and dissentions, and all those atheists who not believe in the existence of God, to live amicably a life of harmony and peace.

ON THOUGHT

- Is it not for want of due thought that man wastes his life as a sinner and like unto a beast, in spite of his being born as a man qualified to attain Salvation? If we think deep, is there any room to be deluded in this worldly existence?

- He who has no such inclination, has no cause for any such suffering. O Disciple! Therefore think well. Then only you will come to know that this worldly existence which appears to be all pleasure, is nothing but pain, a calamity.

ON DESIRE

- There is pain only when there is desire. In the eagerness of desire for liquor, one takes to drink, becomes intoxicated thereby, falters and falls down, gets bruised on nose, face and knee, becomes an object of laughter for the public, and has thus to feel sorry within oneself.

CONCLUSION

- It is common that man accommodates man, helps him and shows kindness and sympathy towards him. But there is in all these one underlying spirit of self interest which impels him to that service either on account of a love towards his own species or of a desire for something in return, a meed of praise and the like. To style a man as selflessly devoted to the cause of others, he should be one who thinks that all beings do desire and have a right to live a life of happiness and freedom and thus extends his sphere of service to include innocent beasts and birds. Even if he is not disposed to render them any help, it would but suffice if he is not inclined to do them any harm. How ungodly it is to slaughter His own offspring and offer it in sacrifice to God, the Universal Father? How cruel to think that the Universal Father is so wicked as to accept those offerings and be pleased towards His devotees.

- What we require now is a Dharma which would infuse in all of us the luminous spirit of thoughtfulness, wisdom, manliness, boldness and bliss and which with its weapons of experience, wisdom and reason would mince to pieces all the causes of dissensions communal or otherwise. That is indeed the steadfast and real Dharma of the Self. Spread the gospel of the noble path self control whereby all fanaticism, religious or otherwise, would be crushed and the mind kept steady and steadfast, unswerving on no account. Then will dawn that harmony and happiness which are now far away from us. The whole world will then exult in ecstatic bliss.

References

1. *Anandadarsamsam* - Brahmananda Swami Sivayogi, Published by Sidhasramam, Alathur.
2. *Mokshapradeepam* - Brahmananda Swami Sivayogi, Published by Sidhasramam, Alathur.
3. *Ananda Sutram* - Brahmananda Swami Sivayogi, Published by Sidhasramam, Alathur.
4. *Ananda Matha Parasyam* - Brahmananda Swami Sivayogi, Published by Sidhasramam, Alathur.

Twelve

Literary Contributions of Brahmananda Swami Sivayogi

Sivayogi's Literature

Brahmananda Swami Sivayogi's works were meant to reform the society in which he was a part and parcel. As a man of letters he couldn't get wide recognition in his life time. It was because he moved his pen along paper and paper and paper, without interruption, against superstition and irrational things found in his society and religion. As superstition and religions had an upper hand in those days the real beauty of his literature and value of his words were veiled by opinion leaders of the time in which most of them were stood for religion and superstition.

From 1893 to 1928 he had written thirteen books and edited another one. Among those fourteen books only one is in the Sanskrit language and all the other books are in the vernacular Malayalam language.

The reason for his selection of Malayalam language as a literary medium was that he preferred to communicate in the language of common folk. He was well aware of the fact that almost all of the superstitious beliefs and irrational customs were among the common folk. If the reformations is not started from the lower strata, he thought, there will be no benefit by his work to the society.

Sivayogi's literary career can be divided into three distinct periods such as reformation period, refinement period and renovation period. As a reformation leader he wrote six books such as *Sivayoga Rahasyam* in 1893, *Sthree Vidya Poshini* in 1899, *Sidhanubhuthi* in 1903, *Mokshapradeepam* in 1905, *Ananda Kalpa Drumam* in 1905 and *Ananda Suthram* in 1910.

Sivayoga Rahasyam is a long poem in Malayalam. In it he says that one should experience the bliss eternal instead of worshipping different forms. Further he says that only by joining of mind with the 'Atmah' (Soul) one will experience the bliss eternal. His concept of yoga is also briefly described in the book. Through this book he tries to educate people to control the mind by means of Rajayoga and proclaims that religious practices are worthless in the attainment of salvation.

He lived in a society where people believed that giving education to girls is not a necessity. He proved, through his book called *Sthree Vidya Poshini* that girls have the right to get knowledge as the boys. Not only that, he proclaimed that only through giving education to girls the society will improve. As every other learnt men he was also in the belief that women are the lamps of houses. If the lamps did not supply with oil of education they cannot give enough light to the other members of the family. The book is in the form of verses.

In *Sidhanubhuthi,* a long Malayalam poem, he says that only by purification of mind one can get the eternal bliss. The book also says that caste and religion can make only external differences and all human beings are internally alike.

Mokshapradeepam, Sivayogi's popular book, is a marvellous work which depicts a collection of Sivayogi's ideals. It is really a threat to orthodox religions. It covers real yoga, refutation of caste, religions, holy baths, vows and upholds, principles of Sakti, humanism, manly effort, absorption of mind. It also gives an elaborate description on the eight fold yoga.

Ananda Kalpa Druman is a collection of hymns to Subramania, Sakti, Krishna, Rama and Siva. Actually he did not addressed the lords external to human body. Subramania, Sakti, Krishna, Rama and Siva are symbols. These are forces hidden in human body. In that way it can also be considered to be one in the group of reformation works, as it forces men to worship not external Gods but internal forces.

Ananda Sutram the last book written in the reformation period, shows that the bliss eternal is the only God universally acknowledged as Supreme; Yoga is but the union of unto that glorious bliss eternal; sacrifices, vows, pilgrimages, idol worship and the like rituals are but hindrances to salvation; and the importance of remain steady with the evenness of mind.

Before starting of the refinement period Sivayogi had edited a book called *Ananda Sopanam*. It comprises a collection of letters written by his devotees and disciples praising Sivayogi's work. It gives a picture of how Sivayogi's work influenced the society.

During the refinement period which lasted from 1914 to 1920, he wrote five books entitled *Rajayoga Parasyam* in 1914, *Vigraharadhana Gandhanam* in 1916, *Ananda Vimanam* in 1916, *Ananda Matha Parasyam* in 1919 and *Ananda Kummi* in 1920. During this period he was to free or become free from impurities. *Rajayoga Parasyam* is a book on Rajayoga as the name implies. In it Sivayogi explains what is Raja Yoga and how it can be practised.

Vigraharadhana Gandhanam is a book against idol worship. According to him, idol worship is a irrational thing. He, with the aid of logic and sacred books of Hindus, proves that nothing will get by worshipping idols.

Ananda Vimanam, a short book, asks people to discard religions which make distinctions.

Ananda Matha Parasyam is a short book which describes what is Ananda religion and how it is scientific.

Ananda Kummi is in the form of Kummi songs, a very popular verse form of Malayalam. It depicts the harmful sides of caste system, religion, and superstition. It also upholds manly effort.

During the renovation period he wrote only two books entitled *Anandadarsam* in 1927 and *Anandadarsamsam* in 1928. His aim during this period was to rebuild the religious thoughts and to give a fresh start to the society.

Anandadarsam is the collection of Sivayogi's thoughts. In it he comments on Advaita, superstitions, truth, ego, soul, bliss, thought, God, fasting, karma philosophy, Christianity, Jnana path, idol worship, Buddhism, mind, sacrifices, Vedanta, Yoga, etc.

Anandadarsamsam is a short form of Anandadarsam.

Thirteen

Notes of Credit

Many persons, from all walks of life, appreciated Sivayogi and his reformational works. The following views of some eminent persons will give a vivid picture on how acceptable Sivayogi and his ideals were to the intellectual field.

"We have been touched by the simplicity and atmosphere of purity and calmness of this Ashram".

K.R. Narayanan
(President of India)

"I am happy to have been in this hallowed spot, the radiating centre of the doctrine of supreme ecstasy, purity, equipoise, abolition of all divisive thinking and equality towards all....... Such a mental approach puts you above sorrow. I trust this lofty institution inspired by a saintly soul, will help to reform and uplift mankind."

Justice V.R. Krishna Iyer
(Former Chief Justice, Supreme Court of India)

"For long I have been looking forward to have the good opportunity of visiting the Sidhasramam. It was indeed very delightful and useful to spend some time with Swami Sri Nirmalananda Yogi. Hope, I will have many more occasions to have more intimate relations with the Ashram and its erudite Yogis."

Nitya Chaitanya Yati
(Writer, philosopher and founder of East-West University of Brahma Vidya)

"Presently under the guidance of Nityachaitanya Yati, I am preparing an M.A. thesis in psychology on the theme of source of happiness in man. I sense the benevolence of an unseen hand which brings me unexpectedly to this centre of enlightenment, peace and bliss."

Peter Oppechur
(A student from U.S.A.)

"The founder of this Ashram was one of those great sons of India, who preached about human values and high ideals of love and compassion for the mankind. Let his preachings inspire in all for a glorious and prosperous future of this land."

Chandra Shekhar
(Former Prime Minister of India)

"A famous Ashram, not only in Kerala, but outside also as the centre of origin of a revolutionary doctrine".

Panampilly Govinda Menon
(Former Union Law Minister)

"It was a great pleasure to visit this Ashram that is based on unity and peace. I hope the ideals of the founder Brahmananda Swami Sivayogi will find expression in the social life of the people."

Jayaprakash Narayan

"I have always admired that the Guru Brahmananda Swami Sivayogi sounded with such firmness in his own time when Kerala was steeped in negative forms of ritualistic attitudes. The Sivayogi's call has done much to clear the clouds of superstition and ignorance and helped many men and women to hold their heads high in self-respect and with a high sense of human dignity."

Nataraja Guru

"I have had occasions to know about the ideals and the working of this Ashram. The founder was a teacher of mine. So it is with peculiar pleasure that I visited this place again and learned more about its growth and activities at the present time. It is gratifying to find that the present Swamiji continues the work of Sri Brahmananda Swami Sivayogi and strives his utmost to spread his ideals and teachings before the growing generations."

K.P. Kesava Menon
(Former Chief Editor, Mathrubhumi)

Reference

Visitor's diary kept in Sidhashramam.

Part II

Selected Works of Brahmananda Swami Sivayogi

Fourteen

Ananda Sutra

(The String of Bliss)

आनन्द एव विजयते।।
अहिंसैव परमो धर्मः।।

Bliss alone reigns supreme.
Not to do harm is verily the greatest virtue.

Preface

Like mercury, sugarcane and coconut. Hinduism is a mixture of good and evil. If mercury is taken after due purification, with all its impurities removed, that itself turns out to be a divine elixir. We would thereby be relieved of this misery of diseases, and could live happily. Likewise, if Hinduism is duly observed, setting aside all its evil parts like traditional practices, we would be relieved of the misery of worldly existence, and could remain in the ecstasy of bliss eternal. It is only when we taste the juice of the sugarcane, throwing aside its hard joints, rind and fibre, or when we eat the kernel of the coconut, discarding its shell and fibre, that we feel them relishing. If we were to take mercury without removing its impurities and duly purifying it, under the impression that it is all created by God, that He would not create anything unnecessary and so everything has to be taken, that will lead but to several diseases, without any chance for happiness at all. If we swallow the sugarcane with its joint and rind it will stick up in the throat, and will lead to great pain and trouble, and you will never get at the juice. If we bite with our teeth the fibre and shell of the coconut, we run the risk of losing our teeth, discharging blood and suffering great misery. In the like manner if we observe Hinduism without discarding its evil side of caste distinctions and the similar traditional practices, and the false texts therein enjoining those practices, under the impression that they are all laid down by God, or declared by the great sages, or that they are existing from time immemorial, or that all of them are authoritative, there is no chance at all for that ecstasy of bliss supreme, but only misery eternal will result. This is verily and daily experience of the world too. Hence the urgent necessity to reform Hinduism; and those qualified to do it are the reigning Hindu Kings of the Country. For, when Kings impose any new taxes or introduce any new legislation, though they may not be to the welfare of the subjects, the latter do implicitly submit to them. Needless to say therefore that they would obey them when their kings work for their great religious welfare. Hinduism will then become really entitled to be known as Aryamatha. Under the present situation, to style Hinduism as Aryamatha, is like styling a veritably blind person as the most handsome. Yet since Hinduism has the one excellence of having in it the gem of yogic knowledge, it can be styled Aryamatha, just as the ocean goes by the name of Ratnakara (repository of gems), since it is the fountain source and seat of gems. Hindus can never be styled Aryans (venerable). For, they do not deal in the gems of yogajnana, but are only dealers in ignorant ritualism. It is but proper to style a man who dives in and takes pearls from out of the Ratnakara and deals in them, as a dealer in pearls. But it is never proper to call one who catches fish and deals in it as a dealer in pearls. Likewise, to style Hindus, devoted to the code of ignorant ritualism, as Aryans, is not at all becoming too. Those Hindus, who adhere to the distinctions of caste and ignorant ritualistic practices, fall a prey to the whales and crocodiles of rituals like sacrifices, idol-worship and so forth of the ocean of Hinduism, and go in vain to ruin and destruction. Just as one plucks all the herbs in the forest without knowing the particular efficacious herb that would help to cure him of his disease, so also, many without knowing the true and only path to bliss, suffer great misery by taking to the recitation of several religious works, by undergoing rigorous vows and fasts, by building temples at immense cost and worshipping idols, and by resorting to the rituals of sacrifices, pilgrimages and so forth. The reason for such great misery is to be traced to their blind implicit faith in the false texts and in the

Acharyas devoted to the cause of ritualism. If that misery born of the immemorial implicit faith is to be destroyed, we should act up to the following words of the Sage Vasishta:

युक्तियुक्तमुपादेयं वचनं बालकादपि।
अन्यत् तृणवत् त्याज्यं अप्युक्तं पद्म जन्मना।।

This means, "we must accept reason even though it be uttered by a child. That which is not reasonable, should be discarded as silly trash (dry grass), even though it be the word of Brahma, the God of Creation". If, on the strength of this authoritative text, we discard the unreasonable, we get the chance to discard all false texts and all those ritualistic practices enjoined by them, like caste distinctions, sacrifices and so forth, which do not stand the test of reason. Thereby, there will disappear from our midst that waste of money, wanton bickering, want of harmony and union, and extreme misery. When according to the above dictum, we accept the reasonable, we stand to take to the practice of yogajnana, which stands the test of reason. Thereby we get the chance to enjoy worldly pleasure and everlasting bliss. We become verily entitled to be called Aryans. I have shown in this work in the chapter on yogamahatmya (or the greatness of yoga,) on the strength of the authoritative texts, reason and experience, that yoga stands the test of reason and unites one into bliss supreme. I have further shown in this very work in the chapter on Dukkhasutrakhandana (snapping the thread of misery), on the strength likewise of authoritative texts, reasoning and experience, that the false texts, ritualistic practices and the actions of the Acharyas devoted to ritualism, are but unreasonable and conducive to misery. Hence they are not described here.

O ye seekers after truth! What has been laid down by Vasishta, that reason should be accepted even if it be uttered by a child and that which is unreasonable should be rejected even if it be the utterance of the God of Creation, is one that would be welcomed even by the seekers of truth in other religions, like Christianity and Muhammedanism. It is such an important glorious dictum. As such none can claim to be an Aryan, whosoever he may be, if he is of the view that if the speaker is powerful, he is to be accepted, even though he speaks unreasonably, and vice versa, if he is powerless he is to be shunned, even though he speaks but reason. All of them are destined to become but a prey to great misery. If it is argued that it is out of our reverential regard to the great men of the past that people act up to their words and fall a prey to misery, are not Vasishta and others of the seat of knowledge, great men of the past? If those their words are taken as authoritative, then one would gain the knowledge that great men would speak but reason, and not anything that is opposed to reason. None will have the chance of being deluded in the false texts, seeing them labeled as spoken by Brahma, or by Vishnu, or by the sages, or that they are the Vedas, Upanishads, Bhagawad Gita and the like glamorous names of reputed religious works and religious teachers. Nor will they have the chance to believe a thing as real, merely because it is generally observed by a majority and that will ensure to the greater welfare only. If some of the past heads of our family had led their lives in utter ignorance or in great self conceitedness or in rank debauchery and drunkenness, are we, out of our reverential regard to them, to take up to their ways to our utter ruin, or are we to take up to the ways of those past heads of our families who were full of knowledge, were bereft of all self-conceitedness, had an outlook of equality, were men of reason, untainted with the vice of quarrelsomeness, and contented in ever lasting bliss, and thus raise ourselves to an exalted position of esteem? No religionist ever says that there is any head of family greater than God (bliss eternal). Even in the case of what has been created by that universal head, viz, God, we accept only what is good and reject what is bad. Not even the greatest devotee of God does out of his extreme devotion to him ever takes in the joint, rind and fibre of the sugarcane because they are all created by God.

He rejects them and takes only the sweet juice. As such, if our ancestors have observed both reasonable and unreasonable, we have to take up the reasonable and reject the unreasonable. This work 'Anandasutra' has therefore, been, written by me as an epitome of only the good side of Hinduism, rejecting the evil side of it, like unto the kernel of the coconut within, rejecting the outer shell and fibre of it, and the sweet juice of the sugarcane, discarding its hard joint, rind and fibre. As such this is of greater use than the Vedas, Sastras, Ithihasas and Puranas to all aspirants after salvation, who wish to be relieved of misery and to exult in ecstasy of bliss eternal. Is it not so? Is it not better that the man, who is desirous of wearing a garland of peals, should but pearls direct? Then he can atonce accomplish his desire. Without doing so, if he, deluded by the word Ratnakara, a synonym for ocean, were to attempt to dive into the ocean in search of pearls, he would not easily come by his desire. He would have to suffer great many troubles. Perhaps he might find a watery grave without achieving his desired object. For, the ocean is vast, pearls flourish only in special places therein, and except those who are well familiar with those special spots, none else can locate them correctly. Hence the fond amateur will have to dive in several places, take in a lot of salt water, expose himself to great suffocation and to run the risk of becoming a prey to the ferocious aquatic animals, like crocodiles, whales and so on. Therefore, if one, deluded by the glamorous names of Veda, Sastra, Smrithi, Purana and so forth, and by the impression that only by going through them all that one could attain bliss, were to attempt to do so, he will have no easy chance to come by that bliss everlasting. For, the Vedas, Sastras and the like are so vast as unto an ocean. Further they are, like unto food adulterated with poison, mixed up with false texts. Like pearls in the vast ocean, truth is embedded only in certain places in the Vedas and Sastras, and that has been entirely shrouded by the false code of ritualism, which enjoins several ritualistic practices. Hence people have the only chance to go to ruin, exposed as they are to great misery, observing various ritualistic practices deluded by the false code of ritualism, without knowing the real gist of Vedas, shrouded as it is by that false code, just as men fall, becoming a prey to the misery of worldly existence without knowing the self, shrouded as it is by the gross body, and as they perish in great misery by partaking food adulterated with poison. That is verily what we see in our daily experience of the world. Is it not so? The man who desires to wear the ornament of gold, should buy gold and make the ornament. Instead of that, if he, deluded by the word Ratnagarbha (having gems within) a synonym for earth, were to begin to dig the entire earth in search of gold, his lot is but extreme misery. For all do not know where gold is beneath the earth. To illustrate, only some of the experts among Englishmen have been able to discover the gold mines in Kolar and other places, and to take gold out of them, by reducing the quartz to powder, and washing them to drive away all the crusts of stone, sand and other impurities. None of the Hindu Kings who own those domains for a long period of time, nor the Acharyas, have ever been able to do likewise. So also, none, but those steadfast in the experience of bliss eternal, will ever be able to pick up the gems of yoga from out the earth of Hinduism, removing the impurities of ritualism. None but a herbalist will be able to pick out the particular medicinal herb from out of the several plants that grow in the forest, and none but a specialist will be able to remove the impurities of mercury. So also, none but those that are steadfast in the experience of bliss eternal, can discover the real authoritative texts, rejecting the weak and false ones of Hinduism, and thus to reform that religion. That is the very reason why even at present several Acharyas, in their blind faith in the false texts, do block the door of salvation (the way to bliss) with stones, and lead people to perform sacrifices, and thus subject them to great trouble and misery. Since my Siddha works like Mokshapradeepa and others, which have been composed by me by way of reforming Hinduism to save people from their daily misery, and lead them to taste the ecstasy of bliss, have been found to be of a great use to the blessed souls of the seekers after truth, I have taken up the authorship of this work 'Anandasutra' too. But many do revile at me for bringing out Mokshapradeepa.

I shall mention here some of the reasons why people do thus indulge in vilifying me. I have in my work 'Mokshapradeepa' criticised and condemned the existence of caste distinctions and their respective duties, and the eating of fish and other animal food. Hence the reader, who has really grasped the gist of Mokshapradeepa, gets the knowledge of equality that all beings are like unto himself. Therefore, even those, who are alleged to be of low caste, begin to believe that there is none superior to them as of high caste and the like, and thus they do not show the same respect towards the superior caste as they were wont to show previously. Hence it is that the self conceited Brahmins and the high caste Sudras do denounce me as they stand to lose the respect and caste pride, in consequence. Those who are addicted to the eating of fish and flesh, do denounce me, since I have condemned their practice. Some denounce me out of mere jealousy. The ritualists blame me because I have condemned ritualism. Even though my work Mokshapradeepa is one that gives light to all alike, yet some among the low caste do praise it, since no work like Mokshapradeepa has till now seen the light of print, to relieve them of their sorrow that they are of the low caste. As such, the reason why some among those alleged low caste do denounce me, is that they have discovered of late a new reform in their religious view. They have taken up to the building of new temples, installing idols therein, and, like Brahmins, to the wearing of the sacred thread, and worshipping idols in truly ritualistic fashion. Mokshapradeepa stands in the way of such so called reforms. Hence it is that some of the Ezhuva Community denounce me. Some of the seekers after truth among those Ezhavas have, by going through my work Mokshapradeepa, come to realise that the ritualistic practices of idol-worship and the like, are but false and are in vain. Hence they have no regard for temples and the priests therein. That tells upon the respectability and priesthood of the priests and the religions teachers among Ezhuvas. That affects their income too. Hence they denounce my work 'Mokshapradeepa', thinking that only by the non-dissemination of knowledge among the Ezhuvas, they could maintain unabated for ever that respectability towards Ezhuva priests and religious teachers. They even compel some of the poor among them not to read Mokshapradeepa. All these are but the effusion of their ignorance, and not the fault of my work Mokshapradeepa, just as Brahmins interdict Sudras from going through Vedas and allied works. If I remain silent afraid of these denunciations, in the consolation that a human tongue overpowered by bile will but taste bitter even the sweet sugar, there is no chance for me to express my gratitude towards the venerable seers of the past, whose works have stood me in such good stead for my self realisation, nor any chance to contribute to the welfare of mankind. To be afraid of denunciation is not in the nature of men of our type. Is it not so? For it is said:

साधुभिः पूज्यमानोऽपि पीडयमानोऽपि दुर्जनैः।
समभावो भवेद्यस्य स जीवन्मुक्त उच्यते।।

"He is a jivanmukta, (liberated while alive) who remains equanimous both in the fulsome praise of the virtuous and the vituperation of the vicious".

निन्दन्तु नीतिनिपुणा यदि वा स्तुवन्तु
लक्ष्मीस्समाविशतु गच्छतु वा यथेष्टम्।
अद्यैव वा मरणमस्तु युगान्तरे वा
न्यायात् पथः प्रविचलन्ति पदं न धीराः।।

"Let the moralists condemn or praise. Let Fortune embrace or forsake. Let Death overtake this very day or in another yuga. The bold never falters from the path of righteousness". The gist of this verse is that the bold would never swerve from the path of righteousness, whatever calamity they might be exposed to. 'Even if the burning firewood is kept downwards, will its flame go anywhere except upwards? If a lighted torch is shown near the waters of the ocean, will that water ever get heated?' Even if the sweet smelling champak flower is denounced as foul-smelling, it will only smell fragrant. Even if the moon be condemned, she will only bring refreshment to all. Likewise, are the great minds too. Even our yogis and jnanis of yore have not refrained from criticising ritualism and illuminating yoga jnana, out of any fear of denunciation of the ritualists. Hence it is that I have been able to taste the ecstasy of bliss eternal, and it is my duty too to follow in their wake to bring the ecstasy of bliss to others, to denounce ritualism and illumine the path of yoga. That is the very reason why I have composed this work 'Anandasutra'. The denunciation arising out of this is. I consider, but an honour to me. Since even the extremely handsome Hinduism is affected by the foul disease of the leprosy of caste distinctions, Hinduism has become untouchable to the virtuous, to their own kith and kin among the Hindus, and to other regionalists. In such a situation, what chance is there to live happily in amity and harmony? What chance is there for progress among the Hindus? Who will side with the leper? The leper, be he though handsome, is sure to meet his end as a deformed being. Even his own wife and children become disgusted with him. It is such a leprosy of the distinctions of caste that I have denounced in my work Mokshapradeepa. In addition to this great disease, Hinduism is affected by a great demon too — the demon of Ritualism. Owing to the scourge of this demon,

Hindus suffer untold miseries. I have but offered in sacrifice this horrible demon of Ritualism, in the fire of yoga, mincing him to pieces with the weapon of jnana. Since I have treated that foul leprosy of the distinctions of castes, and offered in sacrifice the dreadful demon of Ritualism, Hinduism shines in my Siddha works in that transcendental form of exquisite bliss, deprived of all its deformity of form and mad guise. This is the excellence of my Siddha works. On account of this, the seekers after truth among the Hindus and those among other religions who denounce Hinduism, have written to me in terms of great appreciation and hearty congratulation. Further, many of them have approached me in my holy hermitage, and received spiritual instruction too from me. They still hold correspondence with me in the wonder of their experience of yogic bliss. There is no necessity to mention this fact here. But since I have already mentioned that some denounce my work Mokshapradeepa, I have mentioned this fact here but to show as a palliative that there are others who welcome and praise it. There is no remedy to put a stop to the vilification indulged in by the ritualists blindly, without any thought over the matter, even though they are shown authoritative texts, unimpeachable reasoning and patent experience. They have understood Veda to mean that code of ritualism which enjoins the observance of caste distinctions, the performance of sacrifices and other rituals. But jnanis understand this ritualism to be a false code, which fosters an outlook of inequality, encourages mutual wrangling and leads to eternal misery. Hence when such a code of ritualism is denounced by jnanis, they are taken to be and looked down upon as missionaries that denounce Hinduism. What remedy can there be for stopping such denunciation, and discard of the reasonable words of the jnanis! Be that as it may. If it is asked then what the Veda is according to the jnanis, I shall answer.

"परात्मा वेद्यते येन स वेदो वेद उच्यते।"

So says Sivaswarodayam. This means 'That is Veda' through which "Bliss supreme" is attained. The root 'Vid' means 'to know'. Thus, when we look into the etymological meaning of the word Veda, we understand it as meaning knowledge, and not ritualism. As such, to understand Veda to mean ritualism, and, in that light to be indulging in its performance, are both unreasonable and miserable, just as coconut is taken to mean the outer fibre and making use of it in the daily food preparations, or devouring it tearing it with the teeth. As sprout in the seed, the words of the great contain within themselves their real meaning or significance. If that meaning is grasped on careful consideration, that is itself an excellent weapon to refute the meaningless silly arguments of the opponent. To illustrate, if an ugly person is brought before one who knows what really beauty is, and if it is argued that the ugly man before him is a handsome person, and if, in proof of it, certificates of several persons are produced too, the man with eyes will only throw them aside. Likewise, the entire world of yogis who indulge in bliss eternal, in their knowledge of the true meaning of Veda, will throw aside all authorities produced before them to prove that caste distinctions and caste duties are the initial steps to attain the state of bliss supreme and that they are enjoined by the Vedas too. To illustrate, I quote the following from Amanaskakhanda. (अमनस्कखण्ड)।।

"आत्मनस्तत्वमज्ञात्वा मूढश्शास्त्रेषु मुह्यति।"

"Without knowing the truth about Atman, i.e., the nature of bliss supreme, the ignorant gets deluded in Sastras". Will he, who has really known that truth, ever be deluded in the Sastras? Will he ever go in for misery by taking to the workship of idols, to the performance of sacrifices and other ritualistic practices, and that at the expense of immense sum? Will he lead others also to the same path eventually to their great misery ? Will anybody who has tasted the kernel of the coconut, be ever deluded in its shell and fibre and tear them off with the teeth? Will he ever advise others to do the same to the loss of their teeth too ? None should be deluded by the mere names of Acharyas, Yogi, Jnani, Vedas and Sastras. For it is said in Amanaskakhanda:

कुलाचाररतास्सन्ति गुरवो बहवो मुने।
कुलाचारविहीनस्तु गुरुरेको हि दुर्लभः।।

"Innumerable are the Gurus who stick up to their castes and caste practices, i.e., who take pride in their caste superiority and respective duties pertaining to it. But rare indeed is the Guru bereft of such caste and caste practices".

"न वेदं वेद इत्याहुर्वेदे वेदो न विद्यते।"

So says Sivaswarodaya. This means 'Veda' cannot be said to be real Veda. There is no Veda in Veda.

3. Further we see the following in Mundakopanished:

अपरो ऋग्वेदो यजुर्वेदः सामवेदोऽथर्ववेदः।
शिक्षा कल्पो व्याकरणं निरुक्तं छन्दो ज्योतिषमिति।।

Neither the Rig Veda, nor Yajur Veda, neither Sama Veda nor Atharva Veda, neither Siksha (the science of intonation) nor Kalpa (the code of rituals and ritualistic rules), neither grammar, nor Nirukta (Vedic etymology), neither chhandas (Metrical science) nor astronomy, is of primary authority, but they are all only secondary.

According to the above texts, we come to understand that those Acharyas, who stick up to caste practices, and those Vedas and Vedangas, are not primary authorities. To explain how it is that Veda is denounced as no Veda, people deluded in the distinctions of castes and caste practices, enjoined by the false texts interspersed in the Vedas and Sastras, as poison mixed in milk, suffer great misery, and eventually go to ruin, and those Gurus, intent on caste practices, do but increase and intensify the distinctions of castes and caste practices, which are instrumental for their misery and ruin. Hence it is that it has been denounced, pointing out the right path for people to exult in the ecstasy of bliss, lest they should fall a prey to those false texts that go by the name of Vedas and Sastras, and to those religious teachers.

"भेदबुद्धिरविद्येयं सर्वथा तां परित्यज।।"

So says Vasishta. This means that the outlook of inequality and distinctions, is what is called Avidya or ignorance and that it is to be shunned always.

When such are the authoritative texts, and when we are all born of the same race of bliss, it is indeed most unjust to lead the world to misery, laying down several kinds of unrighteous and evil practices, causing people to wrangle mutually in the superiority and inferiority complex of castes, and in the touchability and untouchability among them. Hence it is verily right to denounce as of secondary importance those Acharyas who hold fast to castes and caste practices, and those Vedas and Sastras which advocate the same. Then what are those portions of Vedas and others that are of primary importance?

"अथ परा यया तदक्षरमधिगम्यते।।"

So says Mundakopanishad. This means, That is primary (of

supreme importance), whereby the indestructible (everlasting) bliss is attained. It is by yogic knowledge that such an eternal bliss is had. Hence that is the only primary one. To cite authority:

"अयं तु परमो धर्मो यद्योगेनात्मदर्शनम्।।"

So says Yajnavalkyasamhita.

That indeed is the most primary of all where through Yoga, the Atman or bliss eternal is seen.

तैलधारामिवाच्छिन्नं दीर्घघण्टा निनादवत्।
अवाच्यं प्रणवस्याग्रं यस्तं वेद स वेदवित्।।

This is what has been advised by Krishna to Arjuna in Uttaragita. "When a bell is rung, there is a chiming sound which continues long unbroken like the flow of oil. Likewise, it is he who knows the indescribable continuing sound of Pranava, that really knows the Veda." This knowledge too is only had through yoga. Hence those alone who have yogic knowledge, are the real knowers of Veda. Those who study and receite the four Vedas, who intonate duly the Pranava `om' and those who are given up to ritualism, do not know the real Veda. It is said in Sivajnanadeepika.

"वेदो गर्जति गोकर्णे तं वेदं वेत्ति को भुवि।"

"Veda resounds in Gokarna, i.e., the Sushumna. Who in the world knows that Veda."

I have shown in this work in the chapter on the greatness of yoga that the primary Veda of yogic knowledge unites one unto bliss eternal. I have further shown in the chapter on Dukkhasutra Khandana (or snapping of the thread of misery) herein, that ritualism leads men astray from that bliss into misery. Hence this Anandasutra is verily the most important of all Sutras (aphorisms) in Hinduism, to unite men unto bliss, i.e., to salvation. The code of ritualism was drawn up at a period when mental purity and knowledge had not attained their maturity. It spread everywhere and began to take root in the soil, flower and bear fruit. The code of knowledge came into existence at a later period when mental purity, knowledge and the virtues of the outlook of equality and the like had ripened in full. In the midst of the exuberant growth of ritualism, that divine creeper of knowledge cannot grow and consequently withers away. If only the entire jungle is reclaimed and good seeds are thrown therein, those seeds can grow. Then how to reclaim? As said in Sivajnanadeepika.

"ज्ञानिनो दुर्लभा लोके कर्मिणः कोटिकोटयः।"

"Rare are the jnanis, while innumerable are the ritualists". The entire world is overspread with ritualists. On account of their power and influence, it has become difficult to reclaim the jungle of ritualism. Hence these rare jnanis of the several periods have been able to reclaim the same but in their works. Only thus much I have been also able to do. What can the junior member of a family do, even if he be wise, if the head of the family reduces all the lands of the family to his own possession, wins over all the members to his side and takes to unrighteous ways and actions? The junior will not be able to exercise his authority. Without the bare means even for his livelihood, his only lot is to pass his days, seated in a corner of the house, complaining in vain as follows:- "The conduct of the head of the family is not at all right; what can I do? Indeed a great sinner he is! The cruel man puts me to starvation and leads me to misery. What is the use of being born in an affluent family?," and so forth. The power of the head of the family has grown to be highly extraordinary. I have shown in the chapter on Dukkhasutrakhandana herein, on the strength of authoritative texts, unimpeachable reasoning and common experience, the various cruel deeds of the head of the family of ritualism, whereby the members are put to starvation, made to roam about here and there, kept under vigil, exposed to wind, rain and heat and led to take up to several horrible practices, thus leading them to misery and their eventual ruin. In a way it is better to maintain silence and make no reply to those who side with that family head and denounce me, just unto crows that caw in muster when a stone is dropped into their midst. For, the head of ritualism is very rash and audacious, lacking in prudence. He has on his side many an adherent too. Who is there to come to our help if he instigates his followers to attack and assault us? That ignorant head of ritualism has driven out even the great sage Buddha, the ocean of all good virtues like knowledge, compassion, and so forth. It is verily that ignorant head of ritualism that has taken and is taking the Hindus to degradation and destruction, and it is the duty of kings to remove him from his management. It is only at that time that Hindus will have any progress or welfare. Then only will Hindus be really worthy to be styled Aryans. O! The family head of ritualism! We are subjected to great misery from a very long time past by the management of your powerful agents, and Acharyas, exposing us to starvation and several hardships and ritualistic practices. Even after having had the freedom to live comfortably owing to the excellence of the British administration, and even after the introduction of several reforms in our midst, we pass our days in great misery on account of the intolerable atrocities of your agents. Therefore, we request you to entrust the management to a junior member of mature yogic knowledge and retire yourself with your agents to rest. If you are reluctant to do so, it is but enough if you refrain from inflicting harm on those children who act up to the dictates of your junior members of yogic knowledge, and from demolishing the communion halls of yoga built by them. Then we will be saved of filing suits in the courts of law on those scores. O you, The family head of Ritualism! O you, his agents, may you not discard this request of this Sivayogi. Let prosperity and progress be on the increase.

As milk is beneficial both to the weak and the strong, so is Rajayoga capable of bringing salvation to all alike, irrespective of sex as man and woman, of being literate or illiterate, rich or poor and of being the low caste Pana or his wife or the Paraya. Alas! even the wise, not knowing the truth about Rajayoga, are sunk in deep ritualism.

2. If under the impression that Gita advocates the performance of duty in a spirit of disinterestedness, you become deluded therein and give up the easy path of Rajayoga, you are sure not to attain that exquisite bliss supreme, but will, like Arjuna, only perish on the way. Therefore by all means, give up the delusion of ritualism.

3. Some ritualists do, without any sense of shame, rush to journals and periodicals to gain prestige thereby with false things about me, that Sivayogi has been vanquished. But those who know of my teachings, will only take it as worth the news that a swarm of moths has put out the blazing fire.

—Brahmananda Swami Sivayogi.

A

आनन्द एव विजयते।।
अहिंसैव परमो धर्मः।।
Bliss alone reigns supreme.
Not to do harm is the greatest virtue.

आनन्दसूत्रे आनन्दमाहात्म्यप्रकरणम्।।

The chapter on the greatness of Ananda in the work Anandasutra

Ananda or Bliss is verily supreme above all, because, all religionists, Christians, Muhammedans, Buddhists, Hindus and all, do alike wish for bliss. They are given up-to mutual wranglings on the score of superiority of their respective gods and religions. When Christians preach that you will gain salvation only if you believe in Christ. Hindus and other religionists do not, in the least, like it. When Muhammedans preach that Muhammedanism is the only superior religion and that only by embracing that faith you can attain salvation. Christians and others do not approve of it. Thus, whatever is spoken of as superior by the followers of one religion, all that does not meet with the accord of the followers of other different religions. Even among the Hindus who are the followers of the one religion of Hinduism, when Saivates proclaim that God Siva is supreme, the Vaishnavas do not like it. When Vaishnavas proclaim that Vishnu is supreme, Saivates do not approve of it. When Yoga is extolled as supreme, the Vedantins strike a discordant note. When Vedanta is acclaimed as superior, the yogin dissents from that. Thus do all the theists, with their different ideas and notions about God, extol their own religion and their own respective duties as superior and supreme. The atheists negate the very existence of a God. Whatever is worshipped by the theists as supreme, that is not accepted even as small deities by the atheists. They do not believe in the very existence of a God. But all of them, those atheists, and theists with different conceptions about religion and God, do extremely wish for bliss. Hence it is clear that Ananda or bliss is supreme above everything.

2. Even the lower orders of beings, like beasts and birds, do desire for happiness. When it rains the birds take to their nests, or

find shelter in places not exposed to rain water. Even the bitch that generally sleeps on the floor or on the ashy heaps - does, when she gets a chance, get into the seats of her master on the verandah or into his bed or chair. When we pass our hand over the cows, patting them and scratching them with our little fingers, they remain calm without budging an inch or eating their fodder, overcome by the happiness due to the patting and scratchings. It is on account of their desire for happiness that they all behave thus. Hence the very behaviour of cow, bird, bitch, dog and all animals goes to show that Ananda or bliss is verily supreme above all.

3. Human beings stand foremost among all created beings. Look at their activities. Some take to the raising of crops, exposed to all wind, heat and rain. Some resort to high mountain ranges and dense forests inhabited by wild ferocious beasts like tigers and so forth, and grow tea and coffee there. Some take to the wide ocean inhabited by crocodiles and whales. Some catch fish therein, while some dive in search of pearls. Some take to the practice of acrobatic feats on very thin wires where a slip means death, or on poles, and some join circus troupe. Some go to distant lands and far off shores, crossing the deep and vast ocean, in pursuit of trade and commerce. Some are given up to study from their very childhood, keep long vigils, spend immense money, go to foreign countries like England for the prosecution of their further studies, and after a long stay and years of study there, pass high examinations, become barristers, judges, collectors and hold other high offices. Thus several people are engaged in several pursuits of life. Needless to describe them in detail as it is within the common knowledge of all. Thus, people by their respective pursuits of life make great fortunes, with which they maintain their body, ward off all untoward calamities, accomplish their desired objects and live in happiness. It is clear therefore that the activities of all worldly people are but for the acquisition of happiness or bliss. If misery were to be the result of agriculture, trade, learning and holding offices of administration, few would ever dream of taking to those pursuits of life. From these facts also, it is clear that bliss is supreme above all.

4. Now take the case of ritualists. They worship God,

observing vows like Ekadasi and so forth, keeping fasts and long vigils, spending large sums of money in the construction of temples and in the worship of idols, and roaming about by way of pilgrimages to distant places like Kasi, Rameswaram and so forth. Some worship God, becoming great devotees, yogis or jnanis, giving up as trash all worldly objects and possessions, not so easily possible of renunciation. All these their activities are not in their desire for misery, but for happiness alone. If worship of God is eventually to turn out as misery, few will dream of taking to such a worship, or even if they have the knowledge that worship of God will not conduce to happiness, none will ever worship God. This clearly shows that Ananda or bliss is supreme above all.

5. Some, when they find what are supposed to be the agents of bliss, such as wife, children, husband, venerable parents, affectionate brothers and sisters warm friends and close relations and the like, work against their happiness, do forsake them, may cause them hurt and even put them to death. This also proves that Ananda is supreme above all.

6. Some who look upon their body as supremely dear, which they would like to protect at all costs, even at the sacrifice of their entire fortune, wife, children and all, by seeking the aid of doctors, even though they are close to their centenary and by worshipping God, are seen to destroy it suddenly when it stands in the way of their happiness. To explain when one sees no chance for any happiness owing to incurable disease or similar calamity, one is seen to commit suicide by taking poison or by hanging oneself or by shooting oneself dead. This also shows that Ananda is supreme above all.

7. When a man of pride in caste superiority who wards off the lower castes from approach and orders them to go far apart, lest he should be polluted by their approach, is attacked by any serious disease, and if one, that was warded off earlier, happens to be a physician, he is invited, taken inside the house, seated near the sick bed, and gets himself examined, treated by him for restoration of normal health. The doctor is respected and given money too by way of fees and presents. This is a practice that obtains among all religionists, who pride as the followers of different religions. From this also it is clear that Ananda is supreme

above all. Thus, as we think over the several facts in turn, it becomes clear that men and all beings are actuated by the one desire for happiness in some way or other. Hence it is universally acknowledged that Ananda is supreme above all. It is within the experience of all followers of religions that the moon is cool, that water is a cold liquid that quenches thirst, and that food is an object that satisfies hunger. Likewise, the greatness of Ananda too is within the experience of every religionist. Hence to prove it, I need not explain in detail and enlarge this volume. Then if it is asked why it is that Ananda is supreme above all, the answer is that we are all the children of Ananda, being born of it. It is the common experience of the world that children do desire to see their father, do feel great joy when they see him, and think of him as great. It is because that bliss is the one father of all the world, that all followers of religion desire after it like, and Ananda appears supreme above all. When our natural father does anything to hinder our happiness, we forsake him. Therefore it is clear that our real father is not our natural father, but is Ananda. Likewise, when our mother or relations stand in the way of our happiness, we forsake them all too. Hence it is also clear that our real mother and relations are but Ananda. That is the reason why Ananda ranks supreme above all. We love all and everything, deluded in the fact that they are all conducive to our bliss. When we see them to be a hindrance to our bliss, we forsake them all. Hence it is clear that Ananda is verily the real father, mother, friend and relations, fortune, everything and God supreme too. If we are the children of misery, we ought to long for misery. Even kid, calf and puppy do not desire after misery. Therefore, all of us are the children of bliss. The authoritative texts also proclaim to that effect:

"आनन्दाद्ध्येव खल्विमानि भूतानि जायन्ते।
आनन्देन जातानि जीवन्ति। आनन्दं प्रयन्त्यभिसंविशन्ति।।"

So says the Yajurvediya Taithareeyopanishad. "All these beings are born of bliss. All these born live through bliss. Finally all set out in search of bliss and attain that bliss, i.e., salvation". O ye seekers after truth! All religionists can, from the nature of worldly existence itself, believe this text as correct and true. It is enough if we think over it a little. Man and woman get united on account of bliss in that union. From that union are born children.

Thus, it is clear that Ananda is the cause for origin. It is a common saying with the people, "I have no happiness. Why should I live? It is better to die". Further, we see people committing suicide when affected by intolerable pain, or attacked by any incurable disease. The happy do not resort to any such end. They desire to live for ever. Thus, it is also clear that it is through Ananda that all people live. Finally all set out in search of their desired salvation, that bliss eternal wherein there is no misery whatsoever, and after great trials and hardships, attain it. Thus, we find that the above text which declares that Ananda is verily the cause and prop of all origin, sustainment and dissolution, is in fact correct and true. Hence it is clear on the strength of authoritative texts reasoning and experience that, the entire living world is held up strung as it were in the string of Ananda. That is the very reason why Ananda or bliss reigns supreme above all among the followers of all religions.

Thus ends of chapter on the greatness of Ananda in the work 'Anandasutra' composed by Brahmananda Swami Sivayogi.

B

आनन्द एव विजयते।।

अहिंसैव परमो धर्मः।।

आनन्दसूत्रे योगमाहात्म्यप्रकरणम्।।

Greatness of Yoga in the Work Anandasutra.

I have already explained that Ananda is supreme above all, and all beings are after it. Now we have to consider the way to come by that bliss. Union with Ananda is verily the means to attain it. The means to taste sweetness, is verily the union of the tongue with sweet objects. We have only to eat sweet things to taste sweetness. The way to enjoy sweet fragrance is verily the union of the organ of smell with fragrant objects. We have to smell fragrant objects to enjoy fragrance. The means to enjoy music is but the union of the organ of hearing with good music, i.e., we must hear the very music. To enjoy coldness, we must be united with cold objects, and likewise, to enjoy heat, we must come in contact with hot objects. Thus, to enjoy respective objects, we must get ourselves united unto those very objects. So also for the attainment of bliss, we must get ourselves unto Bliss, and Bliss alone. The scriptures also proclaim to that very effect. It is said in Yajurvediya Taittreeyopanishad:

रसो वै सः रसं ह्येवायं लब्ध्वाऽनन्दी भवति।।

"He the Paramatman or the supreme soul (God) is verily Ananda. It is only by attaining Ananda one can be blissful".

Since it has also been thus declared, the chief means to attain Ananda, is verily to get the mind united unto bliss and be absorbed in it. This is verily Yoga. To cite textual authority:—

1. योगश्चित्तवृत्तिनिरोधः।। (Padanjalayogasutra)

"By Yoga is meant the restraint of the activities of the mind". When the mind is concentrated in Anandasthan (आनन्दस्थाने) the spot where from Ananda emanates, and the activity of the mind is restrained, i.e., the course of the mind towards the external objects of the senses is checked, the mind gets united unto bliss, just as the water, which flows out from a tank through the sluice, flows into the tank itself, if obstructed.

2. ऐक्यं जीवात्मनोराहुर्योगं योगविशारदाः।। (Devi Bhagavatha)

"Yoga is but the union of the individual soul with the Supreme Soul".

3. सं योगो योग इत्युक्तो जीवात्मपरमात्मनोः।। (Yajnavalkyasamhita)

"It is the union of the individual soul with the supreme soul that is known as yoga".

It becomes clear from the above texts that the supreme soul is Ananda, and it is only by getting united unto that Ananda or bliss, that the individual soul attains bliss. That union unto Ananda is verily yoga, is also shown by the above three quotations. It is but reasonable too that when united unto bliss one attains bliss. To illustrate when we suffer from heat, if we come into contact with water, we are relieved of that heat and enjoy coldness. Likewise, when the mind that is affected by the miseries of worldly existence gets absorbed unto bliss, we are relieved of these miseries and attain bliss. It is declared in Mandala Brahmanopanishad:

"एवं सह जानन्दे यदा मनो लीयते तदा शांभवी भवति"

When the mind gets absorbed in its own inherent bliss, then we attain yogamudra known as Sambhavi. Thus, it is clear that the chief means to come by Ananda is verily yoga. Since all religionists and atheists who deny the existence of God, are in search of happiness, and since it has also become clear that it is yoga that unites one unto bliss, it is to be concluded that all those religionists who quarrel on the difference of religion, all theists and everybody should take to yoga, if they desire to attain bliss. Be it so. No follower of any religion ever says that water can be had without coming into contact with water, or sexual happiness can be enjoyed without coming into contact with woman. Likewise, none is ever seen to say that without union unto God, that happiness from that God can be had. If it is asked why then so much importance is attached to Yoga, I shall explain. When we practice Yoga, we enjoy within overselves the sight of several objects such as moon, sun, fire, lightning, of lamp winkling. Bindu or brilliant dot of light, star, the lustre of nine gems, the sacred triangle indicating the point of concentration, clear sky, variegated sky, infinite lustre, lotus, the sky of variegated colours, endless light, the lotus, colours, blue, yellow and red and other grand signs; We begin to hear some sounds like those of bell, blowing conch, of the musical instruments like Veena, flute, the drums like tabor, kettle-drum, and of thunder and so on. Sometimes we enjoy bliss and the pleasure of agreeable touch and several odours. At times we see within us realised sages and gods. When any of these is experienced, it is only that man that so experiences them, knows the awe, wonder and bliss of the mind. It is indescribable in words even for him. On account of these marvellous signs, the mind of the aspirant is captivated sometimes by the divine odour or taste, at times by the luminaries like Sun and so forth, sometimes by the pealing note of bells, and so on, and thus, struck with awe, becomes overpowered by them, and gets gradually absorbed into the great bliss supreme. Is not this state of the mind one to be wondered at and devoutly wished for? The ship, that is tossed about in the stormy sea without any idea as to the directions of quarters, on account of the dense gloom of clouds and thick darkness, reaches the harbour, either with the aid of the light of the lighthouse, or by the sudden dispersal of the clouds and the appearance of the moon, or with the aid of the rising sun at dawn. Likewise, the mind that is tossed about in the ocean of worldly existence, owing to the thick darkness of ignorance, touches the shore of bliss, with the aid of the light of the luminaries and the like symptoms that dawn in the mind through yoga. Just as the bees in the forest locate with the aid of fragrance the spot where the lotus grows, reaches it and sucks the sweet honey from it, the mind that roams about in the forest of sensual sphere, finds out with the aid of the divine odour of yoga, the unseen bliss supreme, and exults in its experience, just as the baby that is crying without any sleep is lulled to sleep, hearing the lullaby of its mother, the mind that is afflicted with the misery of worldly existence, hears the divine sound of ringing bells and so forth, that are experienced in yoga, and goes into the yogic sleep of bliss. Are there in the path of devotion or in the path of jnana any of the divine signs that lead the mind to get absorbed into bliss supreme? No. Without the experience of such marvellous signs, how can the mind get absorbed into that supreme bliss eternal? Unlike the phenomena of this visible world, this eternal bliss absolute is not visible to the senses. If it were likewise visible, the senses will run after it, as they run after worldly objects of pleasure. The mind of the worldly man rushes towards worldly objects, only because it thinks there is happiness in them. Even in this visible world, if we want to reach a destination not known to us, we seek the aid of a guide to lead us. As such, how will the mind get absorbed in the invisible bliss absolute, without the aid of any attractive sign leading to the same, or of any stimulation of happiness in it? It is indeed difficult for the mind to get united unto bliss otherwise. Hence it has been said in Yogasikhopanishad:

ज्ञाननिष्ठो विरक्तोऽपि धर्मज्ञो विजितेन्द्रियः।
विना योगेन देवोऽपि न मोक्षं लभते विद्ये।।

"Though a man be steadfast in jnana, or be entirely averse to and bereft of all desires in sensual objects, though righteous and self controlled, though he be even a god, without yoga (union unto bliss), he will never attain salvation". When such is the case even as regards gods, needless to say anything about man. The gist is, that, without yoga, no salvation is possible. We shall think over a little in this context.

The word Moksha means release from misery. The word Bhakti means devotion or attachment to god (of the nature of bliss). The expression jnana means the knowledge about the nature of that bliss absolute. Without getting ourselves united unto that bliss absolute, how will we be released from misery? Will we, when afflicted by heat, get any relief in that affliction and feel cold by our devotion to water, or by our knowledge that water is cold and tones down all heat? We have to get ourselves into actual physical contact with water to be relieved of the affliction of heat, and to enjoy the refreshing coldness therefrom. Likewise, the mere devotion to and knowledge of the object of bliss, can never ensure to us the release from misery and the attainment of bliss. It is only by the actual union with bliss, we will be relieved of our misery and gain bliss. In the course of the practice of yoga, there arise, within the mind of the aspirant, the above mentioned marvellous signs of ringing bell, divine lustres, and extraordinarily sweet tastes, odours, touches and so forth. Hearing and seeing them, exulting and wonder struck, the mind is overpowered and captivated, and gradually gets absorbed in bliss eternal. Hence it is quite appropriate that yoga means union. The highly authoritative text of **युक्तियुक्तमुपादेयं** also advocates what is reasonable is to be accepted. Bhakti and jnana, being but the constituent elements of yoga, are included in yoga. Hence it is that the word yoga is seen affixed to Bhakti and Jnana as Bhakti yoga and jnanayoga. It is not because that those two paths are as important as yoga that they are thus used. To cite authority, it is said in Yogasarasamgraha:

"योगाङ्गेषु ज्ञानभक्तिकर्मादिषु च योगशब्दो
योगसाधनत्वान् मोक्षोपायत्वाच्च गौण इति"

"The affix `yoga' added to Bhakti, jnana, karma, and so forth, the constituent elements of yoga proper, is because they are the means for yoga and for salvation. As such, that is only of 'secondary importance'. It is not because those paths are primary yoga that they are named as Bhaktiyoga and so on. Some extol Bhakti and jnana, as Bhakti alone or jnana alone will lead to salvation. Such kind of fulmination ends in the praise of yoga proper. To explain. If we describe the merits of a man, that turns out to be a description of the man himself. Likewise the description of Bhakti and Jnana, which are the constituent elements of yoga, turns out but to be a description of yoga proper. Just as the small measures like the Malabar measure, Ollack, Uri, Nazhi, Edangali and so forth, are included in the bigger measure of `Para', just as streams, rivers and the like get themselves absorbed in the ocean, so also Bhakti, Jnana and the like, are included in yoga proper. Hence the best means to attain bliss eternal is verily yoga. As the bigger measure `para' is not contained in the smaller ones like ollok and others, as the ocean is not contained in the smaller repositories of water like streams and rivers, as man is not included in his merits so also, yoga is not included in Bhakti and Jnana, but transcends them all. Thus also it is clear that yoga is the best means to attain bliss. Nor can the opponent argue that yoga is contained in Bhakti, Jnana or in any other cult or creed. For, if it were so contained, those texts which give prominence to Bhakti, Jnana and so forth, would have reasonably mentioned therein the marvellous signs of bliss of yoga, such as the sounds of bell, drum, veena, flute, and so on, of the lustres of lamps, sun, moon and the like, and of the divine odours, tastes, touches and so forth. They have not done so. Theretore it is clear that yoga is not contained in them. Further, it also becomes clear that there are not in Bhakti. Jnana and the like, as there are in yoga, those marvellous signs of bliss, as sound, lustre and so forth, which stand out as real guides to point out the unseen bliss and as attractive objects to captivate the mind. This also goes to show that yoga is the best means to attain bliss. Authoritative texts also declare to the same effect, to cite:—

1. पुमान् जन्मान्तरशतैर्योगेनैव प्रमुच्यते

"Even though a man may take several births, he is relieved of misery and attains bliss through Yoga alone".

2. The following text appears in Yogabeeja:

तथा योगेनं रहितं ज्ञानं मोक्षाय नो भवेत्

"Jnana bereft of Yoga is never conducive to Moksha or release from misery, and to salvation or bliss".

3. It is said in Yajnavalkyasmriti:-

अयं तु परमो धर्मो यद्योगेनात्मसाधनम्।।

"That is indeed to supreme duty or virtue where, through Yoga, the self or bliss is discovered and realised".

4. Further it is said by the sage Matanga

शान्तये कर्मणामन्यद्योगान्नास्ति विमुक्तये।।

"To destroy Karma or action and to attain eternal bliss, there is no means other than Yoga".

5. We see the following in Garuda Purana:-

तथा यतेत मतिमान् यथास्यान्निर्वृतिः परा।
योगेन लभ्यते सा तु नचान्येन तु केनचित्।।

"The man of intellect should so exert as thereby to come by bliss supreme. That is had through Yoga, and not by anything else".

6. Further the Srutis declare:-

अथ तद्दर्शनाभ्युपायो योगः।।

"Yoga is the means to discover that bliss supreme"

7. The following occurs in Yogasikhopanishad:

ज्ञाननिष्ठो विरक्तोऽपि धर्मज्ञो विजितेन्द्रियः।
विना योगेन देवोऽपि न मोक्षं लभते विधे।।

"Even though a man be steadfast in jnana, or averse to worldly objects of pleasure or well versed in Dharma or righteousness, or self controlled, or even if he be a god, without the aid of Yoga, he will not be relieved of his misery, and attain bliss". When it is thus established that even gods should seek the aid of Yoga to attain bliss, needless to say of the state of man. The gist is that without Yoga man can never attain bliss eternal and supreme.

8. We find the following texts in Bhagawad Gita.

तपस्विभ्योऽधिको योगी ज्ञानिभ्योऽपि मतोधिकः।
कर्मिभ्यश्चाधिको योगी तस्माद्योगी भर्वाजुन।।

"The Yogi is greater than the man of penance. He is greater than the man of jnana and the man of Karma. O Arjuna ! be thou therefore a Yogi" Krishna has rendered all help to Arjuna even while his own sister Subhadra was seduced away by the latter. Like unto a servant, he has driven the chariot for Arjuna. These show what unbounded affection had Krishna towards Arjuna. To such a hearty friend, what Krishna advised for the attainment of bliss, was nothing but Yoga, as the best means for it. Thus on the strength of authorities it is clear that Yoga is the best and most important means. I do not intend to cite further quotations for fear of enlarging this treatise. Yet to prove that there are marvellous indicative signs of bliss in Yoga, I shall dilate a little by further authorities. We see in Mandalabrahmanopanishad:

"आदो तारकवद्दृश्यते ततो वज्रदर्पणं तत उपरि पूर्णचन्द्रमण्डलं, ततो नवरत्नप्रभामण्डलं, ततो मध्याह्नार्कमण्डलं, ततो वह्निशिखामण्डलम्"

"First is seen by the initiate in Yogic practice what looks like a star, then what looks like a well cut sparkling diamond and a bright mirror; Thereafter what looks like the disc of the full moon. Hence what looks like the circular radiance of nine gems. Then what looks like the splendour of the noon day sun. Then is seen a right of flaming fire as the next in order".

"स्फटिकधूम्रबिन्दुनादकलानक्षत्रखद्योतदीपनेत्रसुवर्णनवरत्नादिप्रभा दृश्यन्ते"

"To initiate experiences `the brightness of crystal, the colour of smoke, the Bindu or dot (of the mind), the Nada, the Kala, the radiance of the star, the firefly, the lamp, the eye, gold, the nine precious gems and the like'".

"आकाशं पराकाशं महाकाशं सूर्याकाशं परमाकाशं इति पञ्च भवन्ति। बाह्याभ्यन्तरमन्धकारमयमाकाशं, बाह्याभ्यन्तरे कालानलासदृशं पराकाशं, बाह्याभ्यन्तरे परिमितद्युतिनिभं तत्वं महाकाशं, बाह्याभ्यन्तरे सूर्यनिभं सूर्याकाशं, अनिर्वचनीय ज्योतिस्सर्वे व्यापकं निरतिशयानन्दलक्षणं परमाकाशम्"

"There are five kinds of ether, known as Akasa Parakasa, Mahakasa, Suryakasa and Paramakasa. Akasa is both externally and internally full of darkness (productive of stupor). Parakasa is both in the exterior and the interior like the fire of the deluge. That existence which both in the exterior and the interior resembles radiance beyond measure is Mahakasa. That which both inwardly and outwardly resembles the sun is Suryakasa. That radiance which transcends description, which pervades every where and is of the nature of bliss par excellence is Paramakasa". These are the characteristics of the five kinds of ether mentioned above. Further it is said as follows in Hamsopanishad:

"चिणिति प्रथमः, चिञ्चिणीति द्वितीयः, घण्टानादस्तृतीयः, शंखनादश्चतुर्थः, पञ्चमस्तन्त्रीनादः, षष्ठस्ताळनादः, सप्तमो वेणुनादः, अष्टमो मृदङ्गनादः, नवमो भेरोनादः, दशमो मेघनादः"

"The first is of the character of the 'chain' sound. The second is of the character of the 'chini' sound. The third is like the sound of a bell. The fourth is distinctly like the blast of a conch. The fifth is like the note produced by the wire of a harp. The sixth is like the sound of cymbals (made of bell-metal). The seventh is like the sweet note of the flute. The eighth is like the sound of a kettledrum. The ninth is like the sound of tabor. The tenth is like the thunder of a cloud".

Thus, the practitioner of yoga experiences ten kinds of nada or sound. Here the nadas are mentioned in the general serial order in which they are gradually experienced. But at times they may be experienced otherwise than in the order given above. Some may experience only some of the above nadas or sounds. Likewise too the experience of lustre may be seen deviated from their order described. Some many experience only some of the lustres. Some may experience merely bliss alone. Some may have the experience of nada (sound) earlier, and some the experience of lustre too likewise. Some may experience several indicative signs simultaneously. These can be known at length on going through the siddha work 'Mokshapradeepa'.

It is said in Patanjalayogasutra:

"विषयवती वा प्रवृत्तिरुत्पन्ना मनसः स्थितिनिबन्धिनी"

"When there arises the experience of the sensual object, the state of the mind becomes conditioned by it".

To explain. Vishayavathi means having vishayas or pertaining to objects of senses. The vishayas or objects of senses are sound, taste, touch, form and smell. The sound herein means those sounds of bells and so forth. The touch refers to that feeling pleasure of touch in the nirvana plexus. Form has reference to the aforesaid sun, moon and other signs. Taste refers to that sweet juice oozing through the uvula, and smell refers to the divine odour enjoyed at the tip of the nose. Pravrithi means visibility or actual experience. Utpanna means born. If among these five objects of sense, any one is experienced, the mind exults in it, being captivated by it and gets absorbed therein. It is within the experience of us all too, that, when the mind begins to enjoy pleasure, it remains rivetted to it in ecstasy. Is it not on account of being attracted by the external objects of pleasure, like the sweet melody of music, the pleasant feeling of touch or contact or the beauty of form or the agreeable taste of an object or by the sweetness of odour that the mind rushes after them, exults in them, and remains immersed in the ocean of worldly existence? Likewise, it is, that the mind becomes captivated by the divine sound of bell and so forth, exults in them, and, struck with awe, gets absorbed into that bliss supreme, i.e., attains salvation. This is within my own personal experience. Hence even the veritable illiterate man and woman can through Yoga get absorbed in bliss. Should one study Sastras to taste sugar? Should one be a master of astrology to know whether one's body is black or white? Should one go through Vayu Purana to feel whether a touch is pleasant or not? Should one master the full significance of the logical maxim 'Gandhavati Prithivi' (earth is characterised by smell) to enjoy sweet smell? Likewise, one need not take to the study of the Sastras to hear the nada or sound of bliss, or to enjoy the ecstasy of bliss, or to see the lustre of Ananda, or to experience the sweet touch and odour born of bliss, and to get absorbed in bliss eternal. He need not even know a single letter of the alphabet. Some of my disciples are verily non-lettered. I am a witness to their exulting in the ecstatic bliss of Yoga. I am also a witness to the fact that many learned in the Vedas and Sastras observe the code of ritualism, discriminate according to the Vedantic method about what is Atman and what is non-Atman, yet not having a particle of the taste of bliss, wander forth in long pilgrimages to several temples and sacred places to their lasting misery. Some among these Vedantins and ritualists have sought refuge in me, received spiritual advice from me, and remain contented. Of this also I am a witness. Extraordinary indeed is the greatness of Yoga. This meets with the approval of jnanis too. To cite.

नादानुसन्धान नमोऽस्तु तुभ्यं त्वां मन्महे मान्यतमे लयानाम।
भवत् प्रसादात् पवनेन साकं विलीयते विष्णुपदे मनो मे।।

"Salutation unto thee Nada, that is heard within incessantly. I respect thee as the supreme means for the absorption of the mind. For with thy aid, my mind gets absorbed along with my vital breath in the region of Vishnu, i.e., bliss complete and absolute". This quotation is from `Yoga taravali" of Sankaracharya, not the Acharya of the present day, but the original founder Sri Sankara himself. He is a great man who took up the cause of Vedanta, advocated and disseminated it everywhere. From the above words of this great personage, it becomes clear that Yoga is superior to Vedanta and that it was through Yoga he was able to attain bliss supreme. Further, to cite from another Vedantic treatise, the Panchadasa Prakarana of Vidyaranyaswami.

"बहुव्याकुलचित्तानां विचारात्तत्वधीर्नहि।
योगो युक्तस्ततस्तेषां धीदर्पस्तेन शाम्यति।।"

"Those that are disturbed in mind by several affairs, will not be able to know the truth by the vedantic process of discrimination about Atman non-Atman. It is verily yoga that is suited to them. With the aid of yoga, the pride or exultation in worldly existence is destroyed".

Vidyaranyaswami was a very great vedantin. From the words of this great one too, it becomes clear that vedanta is not powerful, like yoga, to destroy the pride of worldly existence, and to grant bliss absolute. Be it so. The great sage Vedavyasa is the author of Vedanta Sastras. It is he who has written the commentary on Patanjali's 'Yogasutra'. It is because that he has known that yoga is more powerful to unite one unto that bliss infinite, that he has advocated that Vedanta suits only those having the necessary qualifications prescribed in Vedanta, and not for those not so qualified, and for them yoga alone is suitable. This is proved by the following text of Vedanta, viz. Vivekachudamani.

"मेधावी पुरुषो विद्वान् ऊहापोहविचक्षणः।
अधिकार्यान्मविद्यायां उक्तलक्षणलक्षितः।।"

"He alone is qualified for the knowledge of self, who is endowed with a high intellect, deep learning, who is proficient in the complete discussion of a subject both positively and negatively, who has given up all desires in worldly objects and is possessed of the other three means prescribed in Vedanta". Since it is laid down thus, it becomes clear that Vedantins themselves do admit that Vedanta will not conduce to the salvation of those men and women who have not the necessary prescribed qualifications set forth above. While on the other hand we see in the world many a man and woman, without those qualifications, yet is longing for salvation. What is their go? Is it not unjust and most pitiable that only the qualified should enjoy happiness, and not others, that only the learned should taste sugar and not the illiterate, and that only the learned should be treated and cured of their diseases and not others? Is such a state desirable? No. Both parties should be benefited and for it, the only go is to seek refuge in yoga. For, like unto a specific that cures all of their diseases, and blesses them with health and happiness yoga brings relief to all men and women in their misery, irrespective of their qualifications whether they are of high intellect and deep learning, or have the proficiency for complete discussion, and grants them all bliss supreme.

To cite further, the sage Matanga says:

ब्राह्मणक्षत्रियविशां स्त्रीशूद्राणां च पावनम्।
शान्तये कर्मणामन्यद्योगान्नास्ति विमुक्तये।।

"For the Brahmin, Kshatriya, Vaisya, Sudra and for women, there is nothing else other than yoga that would destroy their Karma, relieve them of their misery and lead them to bliss.

Further, it is said in Vishnu Dharma:

यच्छ्रेयः सर्वभूतानां स्त्रीणामप्युपकारकम्।
अपि कीटपतङ्गनां तन्नः श्रेयः परं वद।।
इत्युक्तः कपिलः पूर्वं देवैर्देवर्षिभिस्तथा।
योगएव परं श्रेयस्तषा मित्युक्तवान् पुरा।।

"May you be gracious enough to instruct us as to what is most beneficial for the welfare of all human beings, even woman, worms and birds. Thus was Kapila addressed in the past by the gods and the divine sages, and he replied them that it was verily the path of Yoga". During the time of festivals, many rush to the temple, hearing the insignificant sound of drums and the noise of the bursting *Kadana*, and seeing the lights, the fire-works and the illuminations therein. Needless to describe the state of these people if they chance to hear the divine and exquisite melody of bells and the like, and to see the lustres within themselves of the marvellous experiences, that are had in the practice of Yoga! Should any one point out the way to be united unto bliss eternal? Should any one recommend that the insignificant worldly objects of pleasure should be given up! Should any one advise the man who has tasted milk to give up his rotten gruel? Are Bhakti, jnana and the power of full reasoning necessary to stimulate one to rush to the temple on hearing the din and tumult of the festival therein? No. Likewise, neither Bhakti, jnana, nor other full power of reasoning is necessary to see the yogic marvels in the temple of the body, and be united unto bliss. That is the very reason why Kapila also has observed that yoga alone is for all the chief and surest way to bliss everlasting. And this great Kapila is the author of the Jnana Sastra, known as Samkhya. Since he also has thus observed, it is clear that Samkhya lacks the efficiency of yoga to lead one to bliss. Now let us take the view of the Tarkikas or logicians. These take their stand on logic, and denounce both Vedanta and Samkhya. Their school too pays great regard to yoga. For it is said in Karikavali, a treatise on the sastra of logic:

"योगजो द्विविधः प्रोक्तो युक्तयुञ्जानभेदतः।
युक्तस्य सर्वदाभानं चिन्तासहकृतो परः।।"

"Yogis are of two sorts, namely, Yuktas and Yunjanas. Their contact with yoga to know the invisible is also of two kinds. The Yukta yogi always sees the invisible, but the Yunjana yogi requires the aid of contemplation, i.e., he has to meditate to see the invisible. The Tarkikas are armed with the weapons of the power of expression and reasoning to denounce all. Such Tarkikas and the great seers of Samkhya and Vedanta, have paid great regard to yoga. Since, unlike in Yoga, there are not in Vedanta, Samkhya or any other system, those marvellous signs of the sound of bell and the like, that would lift up even the illiterate man and woman from the well of worldly misery, since the gists of Vedanta and Samkhya are not easy of comprehension even for the learned great, and since even some among them, having, through the power of discrimination of what is Atman and what is non-Atman, received the spiritual advice of the great maxim `I am Brahma', set apart the mind as non-Atman, giving it full scope to do anything it likes with the view what the mind does is not binding on the Atman, and are thus see indulging in unrighteous deeds, without trying to absorb the mind, it is clear that even for the jnanis, the easy way to find out that bliss infinite, is verily the path of yoga. It is said in Tejobindupanishad:

"महावाक्यार्थतो दूरे ब्रह्मास्मीत्यतिदूरतः।
तच्छब्दवर्ज्यस्त्वं शब्दहीनो वाक्यार्थवर्जितः।।
क्षराक्षरविहीनो यो नादान्तज्योतिरेव सः।।"

"What is far remote from the import of the great maxims, what is beyond the conception of the maxim `I am Brahma', what cannot be implied by the word `That', or connoted by the word `Thou', what cannot be externalised by the import of the maxim `Thou art that', what is without any decay and non-decay, that is verily the internal radiance of Nada" To explain. The radiance of bliss cannot be experienced by the mediation of the maxim `I am Brahma', after receiving the spiritual advice of the great Vedantic maxims, having mastered the Vedantic discrimination of what is Atman and what is non-Atman. But when one is raptly intent on the sound or Nada, experienced in the practice of Yoga, that radiance dawns within oneself in the midst of that Nada. Further it is laid down in Prabodha Sudhakara:

"नादाभ्यन्तरवर्ति ज्योतिर्यद्वर्ततेहि चिरम्।
तत्र मनो लीनं चेत् न पुनः संसारबन्धाय।।"

"When the mind is absorbed in the radiance that dawns when one is attentively listening to the marvellous Nada or sound heard within, then there is no further bondage of worldly existence.

We see the following in Skanda Purana,

"आत्मज्ञानेन मुक्तिस्स्यात् तच्च योगादृते नहि"

"Through the knowledge of the Atman, one is relieved of misery, and attains bliss and verily that knowledge of the Atman is not had without Yoga".

Only by the contact with a cold object, one can experience coldness. So also, it is only by the union with bliss that one can have the knowledge born of the experience of bliss. It is this same knowledge born of experience that is known as Aparokshajnana or direct cognition, and Sakshatkarajnana or realised knowledge. This same experience of the absorption of the mind in bliss is known as Mukti or salvation, as Nirvikalpa Samadhi (non-differentiated concentration), as Raja Yoga and so forth I have explained all these in my work 'Mokshapradeepa'. Even though I have conclusively established, on the strength of authoritative texts, illustrations and reasoning, that to be united unto bliss through yoga there is no necessity for the study of the Sastras and so forth, I shall once more prove it by texts:

न मीमांसातर्कग्रहणगणितसिद्धान्त पठनै-
र्न वेदर्ग्वेदान्तैसस्मृतिभिरभिधानैरपि च न।
तथैव च्छन्दो व्याकरणकवितालंकृतिमयै-
र्मुने तत्वावाप्तिर्निजगुरुमुखादेव विदिता।।

So says Amanskakhanda.

"Neither the study of Mimamsa (Sastras of Vedic interpretation) nor of logic, neither of Astronomy nor of the four Vedas, neither of Vedanta sastras, nor of smrithis, neither of lexicons nor of metrical science, nor grammar, neither of poetry nor of rhetoric, will ever lead one to bliss supreme. That bliss can be had only through the path revealed by the preceptor". Then arises the scope for the questions, "If it is really so, how is it that the incomprehensible Vedanta is taken as part of Yoga and with such an incomprehensible part in it. Yoga too becomes incomprehensible.

The defect of Vedanta pointed out earlier that it cannot suit men and women who have not the power of full reasoning and the like, affects Yoga too". I have answered this question in my work Mokshapradeepa I am but propounding Rajayoga, the essential and real part of Yoga, refuting that part of it which tends to physical fatigue and which is non-essential. That essential part of Yoga is easy of both comprehension and practice for all. Listen:

1. सुमनः पल्लवामर्दे कश्चिद्व्यतिकरो भवेत्।
परमार्थपदप्राप्तौ न तु व्यतिकरोऽल्पकः।।

2. गच्छत्यवयवस्पन्दं सुमनः पत्रमर्दने।
इह धीमात्ररोधस्तु नचावयवचालनम।।

This is what is seen in Vasishta as spoken by the sage Vasishta to Sri Rama. The meaning is 1. "A little exertion is needed to crush the petal of a flower, but no exertion at all is necessary to attain bliss eternal" 2. "To crush the petal of a flower, the physical limb has to be moved (in exertion). To attain bliss eternal, not even the limb need be moved! It is enough if the activity of the mind is checked". What is here said by Vasishta viz. इह धीमात्ररोधस्तु (here it is enough if the mind is checked), is verily what has been explained by me earlier by the aphorism योगश्चित्तवृत्तिनिरोधः (Yoga is the restraint of the activity of the mind).

Further it is said by Swatmarama Yogindra:

"उन्मन्यवाप्तये शीघ्रं भ्रूध्यानं मम संमतम्।
राजयोगपदं प्राप्तुं सुखोपायोऽल्पचेतसाम्।।"

"I am of opinion that the meditation concentrated at the eye brow is the easiest means to get the mind absorbed in bliss. This is the easiest way to attain Rajayoga even for those of small intellect". When the path is thus easy for even men of small intellect needless to say how much easier it would be for the intelligent wise! Indeed it must be very easy. The following appears in Sivasamhita:

"आलोक्य सर्वशास्त्राणि विचार्य च पुनः पुनः।
इदमेकं सुनिष्पन्नं योगशास्त्रमतं तथा।।"

"After deep consideration on examining all Sastras, the fact that has become most evident is that Yogasastra is the one and only worthy Sastra". The following is taken from Brahmajnana Tantra.

"मथित्वा चतुरो वेदान् शास्त्राणि विविधानि च।
सारं तु योगिना पीतम्"

"The Yogi tastes the gist that is churned out of the four Vedas and the diverse Sastras". If we think over what has been spoken by me hitherto, there can be no chance to say why so much stress has been laid on Yoga. It will be seen that verily Yoga, and nothing but Yoga, is the only suitable and best means to get united unto bliss, both for the literate and the illiterate, men and women, young and old. I have proved at length the superiority of Yoga in my work Mokshapradeepa. Hence I stop from further dilation of the topic in the doubt that some may accuse me of repetition.

Thus ends the chapter on the greatness of Yoga in the work Anandasutra composed by Brahmananda Swami Sivayogi.

C

आनन्द एव विजयते।।

अहिंसैव परमो धर्मः।।

Dukkhasutra Khandanam

The snapping of the thread of misery

I have already explained the greatness of Ananda and that of Yoga which unites one unto that Ananda or bliss supreme. What is required further is to find out the cause why such a Yoga is little practised and little known to the world, and to root out that cause. The cause for that lack of practice and publicity of Yoga, has to be traced to the delusion of the world in ritualism (the thread of misery) advocated by the false Sastras. Some may at once say, "What a wonder this! We have heard of Sastras. But are there texts to be branded as false Sastras?". This I shall explain.

1. नानाकपटशास्त्राणि प्रपञ्चकथितानि वै।
दृष्ट्वा विश्वासपूर्वं तु विद्वानपि चलत्यहो।।

2. प्रपञ्चं कर्मसंछिन्नं तत्सङ्गत् कर्मठा जनाः।
तस्माद्यः पुरुषो लोके कर्मत्यागी स ईश्वरः।।

3. इदं पापमिदं पुण्यमिति बिभ्यति कर्मठाः।
दृष्ट्वा कैतवशास्त्राणि वाग्दंभघटितानि च।।

4. तेषां गत्यन्तरं सिद्धं जन्ममृत्युजरास्पदम्।।

5. चित्तक्षोभकरैरुग्रैस्तपोभिश्च व्रतैस्सदा।
मुह्यन्ति प्राणिनो देवि वागुरेष्वण्डजा इव।।

These are from the work of Sivajnana Deepika: They mean:

1. Various sorts of false texts are proclaimed in the world. Seeing them, the wise also implicitly believe in them and go astray.

2. The world is over-powered by Karma or rituals, and on account of the association with those ritualists, all have turned out to be ritualists. Therefore, he who gives up ritualism is verily Iswara or God.

3. Seeing the false Sastras composed by the pedantic scholars, the ritualists are driven to the fear of 'This is meritorious and this is sinful'.

4. Their daily lot is nothing but birth, infirmity of old age and death.

5. O Goddess! as birds caught in the nets, beings are always deluded by rigorous vows and austerities which tend to the unsteadiness of the mind, i.e., to misery. From these texts, the following six facts are conclusively established:

1. That there are false texts.
2. That even the wise are led astray by their implicit faith in them.
3. That all people are attached to ritualism.
4. That the man who has given up all ritualism is like unto God.
5. That the lot of those who believe in ritualism is nothing but birth, decay and destruction.
6. That the Sastras, that enjoin ritualism, are called false Sastras, since ritualistic practices lead to unsteadiness of mind, and consequent misery.

Now we shall consider, in the light of reasoning and experience, whether these facts are true. It is the desire of all people to be relieved of misery and to live in happiness. Just in opposition to this natural desire of all, rituals lead men astray from Ananda into misery. To illustrate. When we observe the fasts of Ekadasi and the like, we feel the misery of starvation. Greater still is the misery when we take to penance. Diverse indeed are the kinds of misery when we go on long pilgrimages to Kasi, Haridwar, Rameshwaram and other places, exposed to heat and wind, not having food at the usual proper time to which we are accustomed, exposed to starvation, to the fatigue of the journey, to the lack of sound sleep and so on. What all sorts of miseries are we confronted with on account of the building of temples, worship of idols, performance of sacrifices and so forth? They are indeed hard and impossible to describe. We can but briefly conclude that all ritualistic practices partake of the nature of misery. Neither reason nor authority is required in the face of one's own actual experience. Yet Hindus have an unbounded faith in textual authority. There are some among them who, even if they are told that sugar is sweet, and even if they are made to taste that sugar and know it to be sweet, yet would fondly insist that some textual authority is required to prove that sugar is sweet. Therefore, I shall quote a few authoritative texts to show that rituals lead only to misery, but never to happiness.

कर्तव्यतैव परमं दुःखानां दुःखमुच्यते।
तत् सत्वे तु कथं तेस्तो दुःखाभावः सुखञ्च तत्।।

"The conception of a necessity to have to perform particular fixed duties, is indeed the greatest of all miseries. When that prevails there is no relief of misery, nor will one have happiness". When one cannot remain at ease and in steadiness on account of ritualistic practices, it is nothing but misery. There is no happiness. Can there be any happiness of sleep when one takes the part of an actor during night and plays on the stage? Can there be coldness but heat when fire is handled?

यावत् कर्तव्यवेताळात् न बिभेति दृढं नरः।
न तावत् सुखमाप्नोति वेताळाविष्टवत् सदा।।

"As long as man is not afraid of the ghost of rituals, till then he has no happiness, as unto one under the influence of a ghost." The man under the influence of the ghost suffers great misery, shaking, running, quivering, trembling, biting teeth, jumping into water, climbing up trees and not taking food and sleep properly. Likewise do those deluded by ritualism suffer great misery, getting up before day break even in the coldest season, rushing up to the tank for a dip and throwing themselves into the water, with shivering body and biting teeth unable to bear the cold, climbing up trees to gather flowers for worship or entering, in search of them, lotus ponds and forests, and not having proper food and sleep owing to their vows and fasts. Therefore, one should be afraid of ritualism like unto a very ghost, and give it up entirely. Without giving up Karma, there is no chances for happiness at all. My view is that it is not enough if we are afraid of ritualism like unto a ghost only. The man under the influence of ghost roams about only in a limited space. That does not appear to affect him too seriously, since he is out of wits, and that too affects him only and none else, and is not deliberately embraced. While those under the influence of the ghost of ritualism, wander out to several distant places and temples like Kasi, Haridwar, Rameshwaram, Gokarnam and so forth. Some even take to a circumambulation of the entire world. They spend large sums of money for the performance of several rituals, and expose themselves to great loss and tribulation. Observing rituals in ardent faith and delivering lectures on them, they transform many into ritualists. Thus they lead not only themselves but others too to great misery.

The ritualists vilify those Jnanis who denounce these practices as unnecessary and of no purpose. They cause hurt to them, and even the jnanis who have no fear of death, are afraid of them. There is no chance to throw the seed of yoga on earth that would bestow bliss eternal. Since ritualists have strewn all places with thorns and stones, there is no chance for the jnani to tread a step. That is the reason why the immemorial yogic knowledge has become extinct among Hindus. That is the reason why the religion of Buddha too, even though he is acknowledged to be an Incarnation of Vishnu, does not bear fruit, and that is the very reason why I have also to pass my days in this remote corner. It is in undoubted fact that in future also the lot of Hindus is nothing but misery, having no chance to reach the abode of bliss through the path of yogic knowledge. For the ritualists are blocking with stones the door to bliss, that cannot be removed by any, whether yogi or jnani. The gist of this is that works that intensify ignorant ritualism are daily on the increase in the world. The man under the influence of the ghost will not be able to bring such a lasting menace to the world. Hence, it is that I have observed that rituals are not to be afraid of only as much as unto ghosts. The above two texts are quoted from the work 'Tripura Rahasya Jnana Khanda'. By these authoritative texts, by reasoning and by experience, it is well established that ritualism is the thread of misery, that takes one away from bliss and leads to great suffering and misery. It is not enough if it is said but once that it is a false Sastra, not even if repeated thus a thousand times. Therefore, what has been said in Sivajnanadeepika (many are the false Sastras) and so forth, are to be highly esteemed and respected. Be it so. I am quoting below what was advised by Vasishta to Sri Rama.

कालं यज्ञतपोदान तीर्थदेवार्चनभ्रमैः।
चिरमाधिश्तोपेताः क्षपयन्ति मृगा इव।।

"People pass long days like unto beasts in great distress, deluded in the observance of sacrifices, penance, giving alms, pilgrimages and propitiation of gods." The world praise those who have performed sacrifices with the honorific title of Dikshitar. Likewise, they praise as blessed those persons who had taken to pilgrimages. If it is asked whether it is justifiable on the part of Vasishta to have branded them as unto beasts, the facts set forth by me earlier, on the strength of scripture, reasoning and experience to prove that rituals partake of the nature of misery, are but enough to clear any such doubt and satisfy the questioner. Yet I shall explain a little more. It is said in Devi Bhagwata. '**पापं हिंसा समं नहि**'।।

"There is no sin equal unto doing harm," whereas in sacrifices animals are slaughtered. Is not slaughter a great sin? Is this the virtue of men? No. This is but the nature of beasts. The big fish preys upon the smaller ones, the snake feeds upon frogs, the fox on fowls, the cat on rats and the leopard on cows and cattle. Likewise, to get hold of the goat forcibly, to shut up its mouth and nose to suffocate it, crush its testicles and thus kill it, and feed upon it - how can such an act be the virtue of man? Is the man who performs the sacrifices a tiger or man, leopard or fox? Might is right is a law of the jungle. Hence it is verily justifiable and befitting to have denounced those who perform sacrifices. If the followers of other religions were to ask us: 'Why is it that in sacrifices you kill animals and offer worship with their flesh? Are your Gods and Goddesses addicted to flesh eating or are they like unto foxes that are after meat. That that is so is verily proved by your actions and rituals, what reply can we give them? It is indeed justifiable to have denounced those performers of sacrifices who resort to such unrighteous actions which cannot be explained in any reasonable way.

I quote the following from Bhagawat Gita.

1. ईश्वरः सर्वभूतानां हृद्देशेऽर्जुन तिष्ठति।।

"O Arjuna! God abides in the heart of all beings."

2. It is said in Sivajnanadeepika **देहो देवालयः प्रोक्तः** 'The body is called the temple of God'.

The meaning of the above texts is verily the experience of men of our type too. As we think over this, it becomes clear that those who kill beings do but destroy the temples of God. It is a pity that those ritualists who spend large sums of money in building temples, installing idols of stone and worshipping them in the fond hope that they stand to gain thereby great merit, paradise and salvation, have not the knowledge that by slaughtering animals, they are incurring the great sin of destroying the highly sacred temple of body. Who in the world can say that it was not justifiable on the part of Vasishta to have denounced those performers of sacrifices as unto beasts? '**ज्ञानेन हीनाः पशुभिः समानाः**' (Those bereft of knowledge are like unto beasts), so says the authoritative text too. Since flesh is contemptible and since one has to incur the sin of doing harm to come by it, many among men do not take to meat-eating. As such, those who worship God in the hope that flesh is an article of worship dear to God and Gods, do denounce thereby those very gods as possessed of intellect lower than that of men. Hence it is highly justifiable to have condemned those who slaughter animals in sacrifices. When God is the universal father, when all beings are His children, what a perversion or lack of intellect it is, to offer His child in sacrifice to Him in the hope that He will feed up on the flesh of his dead body, be pleased and bestow all blessings? Those who think thus, and slaughter animals in sacrifices, are verily the denouncers of God. Even dogs and tigers do not kill and feed upon their young ones. Thus they denounce God by their sacrifices that God (bliss) is more cruel than dogs and tigers, and is a despicable being that feeds upon the flesh of the dead body of His own children. Hence, it is heartily to be congratulated that the performers of sacrifices are rightly condemned. When we are pierced by a thorn in our foot, or when we get a wound, how much do we suffer from the pain caused thereby? Having this human experience, who else but a heartless sinner would dare say that Vasishta was not justified in condemning those men as unto beasts who, like tigers, kill animals without any pity in their sacrifices, in spite of witnessing their last agonies, crying, and shaking their limbs when they are slaughtered? It is an ardent belief of the ritualists that God will grant all desired objects to those who do meritorious deeds. The meaning of the Devibhagavat text '**दया समं नास्ति पुण्यं**' is, that there is no merit like unto pity. Hence these people ought to take to pity. As such, who else but the heartless sinner in the world, would dare say that

Vasishta was not justified in condemning as unto beasts, those men who, in opposition to the above text, commit the sin of injury?

To quote from Devibhagawata.

1. आत्मवत् सर्वभूतेषु चिन्तनीयम्।।
2. आत्मदेहस्य रक्षांर्थ परदेहनिकृन्तनं न कर्तव्यम्।।
3. जीवतव्यं प्रियं नूनं सर्वेषाम्।।
4. कर्मणा मनसा वाचा सर्वभूतेषु सर्वदा।
अक्लेशजननं प्रोक्तं अहिंसात्वेन योगिभिः।।

This last is from Yajnavalkyasamhita. The meanings of these texts are respectively:-

1. All beings are to be looked upon as unto oneself.

2. To protect one's body, one should not destroy anothers' body.

3. All beings verily desire to live.

4. What yogis mean by non-injury is that none should cause any misery to any being by deed, mind or word. Further, it is said that 'not to do harm is the greatest virtue' (अहिंसा परमो धर्मः).

Are these authorities and highly superior texts, enjoined for beasts or for men? One should not even in mind think of doing harm to another. Then that itself, according to the texts, is tantamount to doing harm. As such, who else in the world but a Rakshasa or demon would dare say that Vasishta was not justified in condemning those men as unto beasts, who do harm deliberately by mind, word and body, in their performance of sacrifice? The followers of all religions who hold different views on what is Dharma (virtue) and what is Adharma (non-virtue), do all in one voice approve that there is no misery greater than doing harm. If, on the view that something should be said to the contrary, a fool is to argue that injury is not painful, will he admit any one to cut off some flesh from his body? No. If we try to do so by force, he will cry aloud. Is not that cry due to pain? Therefore, even the rogue, who argues to the contrary, admits that injury is painful. Be it so. Even beings like goats and fowls, which have not the power of reason, nor the discrimination about merit and demerit, instruct us that injury is a great pain. When we slaughter them, they cry out shaking their legs. But if we approach animals and vilify them and speak false things about them, they do not suffer any pain thereby. As such, what else other than doing harm is an unrighteous deed, which even animals teach us to be highly painful? It is indeed very necessary to denounce those men who do unrighteous action in their performance of sacrifices. Some religionists argue that the texts which insist on the necessity of pity and prohibit killing, are in reference to pity towards men and to the killing of human beings. Those who thus argue, are thereby indirectly denouncing the great authors of those texts as mere insignificant beings without any outlook of equality, and are giving expression to words without any sense. To explain. Since man has an attachment or love towards his own race, since there is no practice generally of man preying upon man, since there is a kingly authority to punish the offender, if by chance one were out of anger, hatred or greed of wealth or any such cause, to kill one's fellowman, since man is able of himself and with the aid of his friends to protect himself, generally man is not able to kill his fellowman. Nor has man ordinarily any innate desire to kill another man. Thus it is clear that those great men of pity who have laid down the texts, 'Be merciful, do not do harm', have done so more in reference to helpless beings. That becomes clear from the facts set down below. Since men, being accustomed to feed on the flesh of goats and others, find a great relish for it, since those beings are not of the race of men, since they have neither the intelligence nor the power to save themselves from harm at the hands of men and since no kingly authority punishes men for doing them harm, many a helpless being is killed at ease without any scruple in a short time. Hence in the maxim laid down by the great, 'Be merciful, do not do harm', there is that powerful injunction intended to put a stop to all kinds of harm to helpless beings. If it were not so, their maxim does not really serve any great purpose, and is of no great use. Will ever the great seers who are highly imbued with a sense of equality of all beings and who are the seats of mercy, enjoin any dictum which is of no great benefit, which savours of inequality, which limits mercy only towards human beings and prohibits only the killing of men? No. If they do so, they are to be styled as narrow-minded fools, imbued with a spirit of inequality, and that partiality with a leaning towards their own kin. I am not prepared to think of them in that light. Let those addicted to flesh-eating and the heartless say that those great men have approved that no mercy need be shown to helpless beings like goats and so forth, and that they could be killed with impunity, and thereby, cast slur on those great ones. Water brings coolness to both men and animals. It is not of a nature to cool only men and not animals. Likewise, the pity of the great is never limited so as to approve of the killing of animals, and of protecting men alone. Theirs is of a nature to protect both men and animals, without causing them any distress whatsoever. Hence their pity and the virtue of harmlessness know no bounds, but are universal. To argue on the contrary, that their pity and harmlessness are limited only to the narrow circle of mankind, and thus to kill and feed upon the flesh of animals and others, are due to the relish in flesh eating. There is no doubt about it. I am of opinion that doing harm to fish and others of the type, is a greater sin than getting hold of a man and butchering him. For, in the very midst of men, if one were to commit a breach of trust, or to do harm to a helpless fellowman, the whole world looks down upon him as a great sinner who has committed the heinous sin of breach of trust, or of inflicting harm on a helpless brother. When we think over this fact, goats and the like thrive by putting their trust in us. When we call them, they come near us. They take us to be their masters. Is the master in whom is placed full implicit trust, to behead and kill that one so trusting him? Is the master a wolf, tiger or a fox? Is he not thereby committing the sin of breach of trust? However much these helpless beings are subjected to harm, none is seen to taken up their cause. Thus it becomes clear that they are helpless. Is not harming such beings the great sin? Man has his own physical strength and intelligence. To save himself from untoward calamity, he has for his aid his own brothers, sons, friends, relations and others. Further, there is also the king, the great lord and protector of all. As such, who is worthy to be an object of pity? Which is the greater crime? Hence who in the world would dare say that Vasishta was not justified in condemning those men as unto beasts, who slaughter animals in sacrifices? Is not inflicting harm, the characteristic of a tiger? It has no power of reason, nor does it live upon plants and vegetables. To live, it has but to resort to doing harm. In spite of men having several things in the world to live upon without resorting to harm, in spite of their being endowed with the power of reason, and in spite of their having several, wise men and good Sastras to instruct them, if they lack knowledge the man who takes to do harm ought to have been condemned by Vasishta as a greater tiger, worse than the ordinary one.

Some argue that sin is only for those who kill, and not for those who buy fish and flesh from those who kill. This is also unreasonable and untenable. Even though one murders another, the abettor also is punished under the law by the king. Likewise, even though it may be another that actually kills goats, fowls and the like, those who buy their flesh and feed upon it, do rightly deserve to be punished. For if there is none to eat, there will be none to kill too. Therefore, it is really those that eat the flesh, that induce the killing of those beings. When a trade lacks demand for its wares, the trader in those wares incurs loss, and closes his business. Likewise, if there is no customer to buy fish and flesh, the man who resorts to killing will retrace from that business of harm, and stop it.

Some argue that since fish and the like are seen relishing to men, they are ordained by god to be fed upon. Otherwise there cannot be any relish for men in those articles of food. If this argument were right, then we ought to console ourselves that men, who have a desire for another's wealth or wife, are justly ordained by God to commit theft and adultery. In this light, none is to be punished for the crimes of theft and so forth. For, the thief takes to theft since he finds a pleasure in stealing, and that pleasure is due to the dictate from God. If one resorts to an action due to a pleasure in it, as impelled by God, the king who punishes such a one, becomes guilty before God, and none should transgress the command of God. Further, we are calmly to surrender ourselves to tigers when they attack us or our cattle. They should not be shot at or killed. Is it not due to the dictates of God that they find a relish in our flesh and the like? We are thus to console ourselves. All those who argue in this line, do so simply out of their own relish for flesh. It is such a section of arguers that have mixed up in Hinduism the ritualism of sacrifices, accompanied with slaughter of animals, and this has been corroborated by Vedavyasa, who arranged the Vedas, as seen from the following quotation from his work Devibhagawata:

द्विजैर्भोगरतैर्वेदे दर्शितं हिसनं पशोः।
जिह्वास्वादपरैः कामं अहिंसैव परा मता।।

"Those twice born who are addicted to sensual enjoyment, and who are slaves of the tastes of their tongue, have incorporated into the Vedas, the ritualism of slaughter in sacrifice. Not to do harm is indeed the greatest virtue." Those who resort to animal sacrifices contrary to the above maxim have been condemned by Sri Krishna too, in his discourse with Uddhava, as we see from Bhagawata.

ते मे मतमविज्ञाय परोक्षं विषयात्मकाः।
वृथा पशून् विहिंसन्ति हिंस्यन्ते प्रेत्यतैसतु ते।

"Those addicted to sensual pleasures, not knowing the underlying truth of my teachings, do in vain resort to the slaughter of animals, and they are, in turn, slaughtered by those animals after they are dead". Krishna has thus condemned them, because they slaughter innocent animals without knowing the real animal that is to be slaughtered. What is that real animal that is to be slaughtered according to that underlying truth of his teachings? To cite from Sivapurana Deepika.

रागाद्यवयवोपेतं अज्ञानपशुपातकम्।
अवशं तु कुमार्गस्थं हत्वा होतव्यमादरात्।।

"It is that wicked beast of the mind with its limbs of love, hatred, anger, lust and the like, which strays into the evil path, which is not under control and which is overpowered by ignorance, that is to be killed and duly offered in sacrifice." From this, it is clear that the animal slaughter mentioned here, means the control of the mind, and not the killing of goat by holding fast its legs, closing its mouth and nose and suffocating it to death. Even if all the animals of the world are thus offered in sacrifice, it results in the increase of sin and misery, and the animal of the mind will not be won over. Only when that is won, there will be an end to misery. To illustrate, when the mind remains in the state of Sushupthi or deep sleep, none feels any misery. Likewise, if the mind is absorbed in bliss, misery ceases and bliss dawns. This is verily yoga. This is verily the slaughter of the animal in sacrifice. Not knowing this real truth, the ritualists are deluded. The fact of their delusion and the cause of it have been mentioned by God Vishnu in Garuda Purana too, Listen:

नाममात्रेण सन्तुष्टाः कर्मकाण्डरता नराः।
मन्त्रोच्चारणहोमाद्यैर्भ्रामिताः क्रतुविस्तरैः।।

"Men becoming satisfied with mere names, and intent on ritualism, have become confounded by the several kinds of sacrifices, embracing the recitation of mantras, performance of homa (offering to the fire) and the like". The first two feet of the above verse **नाममात्रेण सन्तुष्टाः कर्मकाण्डरता नराः** (becoming satisfied with mere names, and intent on ritualism) and the last foot **भ्रामिताः क्रतुविस्तरैः** (are confounded by the several sacrifices) clearly bring out the fact that people have become intent on ritualism, merely by hearing the renowned glamorous names of authors and works which exclaim `as revealed by Vedas, Smritis, Upanishads, Bhagawad Gita, by Lord Krishna, by God by the seers and sages' and so forth, and not on account of their intrinsic love for it, engendered on due consideration whether those works are composed really by those authors, and whether the sacrifices referred to therein are reasonable and justifiable, and so they take to those rituals in a delusion. Likewise to people take to penance, pilgrimage and idol-worship, similarly getting deluded in texts. They are all of the nature of misery I have clearly shown, on the strength of texts, reasoning and experience explained hitherto that bliss can be had, if only they are given up. Still, since it is more useful to prove it still further, I shall explain a little more.

Penance is also a kind of inflicting harm. All difficult practices, like putting up with hunger, thirst, heat and cold, are included in penance. From these result loss of physical strength and several diseases. When our physical body is a boat to take us across the ocean of worldly existence, and when that boat is affected by a leakage or the like, that tells upon the happiness of the self. Is not this a crime of committing suicide? If God metes out condign punishment for a crime, there is every chance for those who take up to penance and austerities to be visited with His punishment, as kings punish those who attempt to commit suicide. Since there is the injunction that no being is to be harmed, is it reasonable to do harm to one's own Atman or self? No. Let it be. Their action is of the nature of destroying their own temple of body, the temple of God. It partakes also of the nature of denouncing God. Since they explain by their actions that God takes pleasure in seeking persons in distress, who are unable to put up with their hunger, thirst and so forth, they are verily the denouncers of God. Even a man of pity never takes delight in seeing another man in distress. As such, can it be pleasing to our Father, God (bliss) to see His children in distress? Is it not verily one's enemy that exults in joy in one's distress? Is God our enemy? Nor does anybody acquire Yogic knowledge too by resorting to fast and suffering thereby. Hence it is that Vasishta has condemned those who take to penance. God Vishnu also has condemned them in Garuda Purana.

"एकभुक्तोपवासाद्यैः नियमैः कायशोषणैः।
मूढाः परोक्षमिच्छन्ति मम मायाविमोहिताः"।।

"Deluded by (illusion or ignorance), those fools wish to see my form of bliss invisible, by resorting to such vows, as taking food once a day, and fasting and the like, which are all tending to weaken the body."

Sri Krishna has condemned those who resort to penance in the Bhagawad Gita.

"कर्शयन्तः शरीरस्थं भूतग्राममशेषतः।
मां चैवान्तः शरीरस्थं तान् विद्धयासुरनिश्चयान्।।
अशास्त्रविहितं घोरं तप्यन्ते ये तपो जनाः।।"

"Know you those of Asuric nature who cause fatigue to me seated in the heart, and to the body constituted of the five elements and perform penance, not approved by Jnana Sastras" To explain:-

Is it not doing harm to give no food to the members of the family and expose them to the pangs of starvation? Will not such a head of the family who inflicts that harm, be denounced by the public? Is it not like unto that to give not food to the family members of the Prana and the organs of sense in the house of the body, and thus put them to distress? Surely those who act thus, are verily Asuras or demons. That is the very reason why God Krishna has also denounced them. Hear then what that fasting and that penance are, which are not thus denounced by the great, which do not lead people to distress causing fatigue and weakness to their physical body. I quote from Varahopanishad.

1. उपसमीपे यो वासो जीवात्मपरमात्मनोः।
उपवासः स विज्ञेयो न तु कायस्य शोषणम्।।
2. कायशोषणमात्रेण का मुक्तिरविवेकिनाम्।।

These texts mean respectively:

1. The preposition 'upa' means 'near', and so Upavasa means 'to be seated near'. That is Upavasa where the individual and the Supreme souls dwell in close proximity, and not the weakening of the body by undergoing fasts.

2. What salvation can be had for those lacking in prudence by the mere wasting of the body? There is no chance for any salvation at all.

It is said:—

"मनसश्चेन्द्रियाणां च निग्रहः परमं तपः।।"

"The best penance consists in controlling the senses and the mind". The above texts clearly prove that controlling the mind is real penance and real fasting. As described in the chapter on the `greatness of Yoga', control of the senses and the mind is had when the mind is got united unto the Supreme soul (bliss). Thereby too there is had that Upavasa of the proximate dwelling of the individual and the Supreme souls. As we think over the real meaning of authoritative texts, both penance and upavasa eventually turn out to be Yoga. Will the great seers lead men to miserable rituals resulting in the destruction of the self through fasting and so forth, without leading them to Yoga which unites all unto bliss everlasting? Since pilgrimages entail great physical fatigue owing to the long and distant journey involved therein, with the risk of having no chance for proper food in time and of great physical fatigue, pilgrimage also is beset with the defects and evils of penance set forth above. Holy baths during pilgrimages may help to remove the dirt of the body, but not the impurity of the mind. Many take to pilgrimages, yet they are seen, in spite of such holy baths, possessed of those very impurities of mind like love, hatred and so forth which they had before they set out on their pilgrimage. There is not even the slightest change in their state or bent of the mind. Nor do we see any dawn of knowledge either after pilgrimages. When we take any medicine to be cured of a malady, that malady has to be cured, or at least it must result in some other benefit to us. If these two things are not possible, why should we undergo great physical trouble and fatigue on the score of that medicine and subject ourselves to great trouble and loss? Even those who always have their abode in those sacred places of pilgrimage, and have sacred baths daily, are also seen largely beset with those impurities of love, hatred and the like of the mind. Nor do we see in them any superior knowledge or excellence too. From the facts set forth above, it is clear that there is only evil and no good from pilgrimages and holy baths. Hence it is that those who indulge in them and waste their time in vain, are condemned like unto beasts by Vasishta. God Vishnu also has likewise condemned them in Garuda Purana.

आजन्ममरणान्तं च गङ्गादितटिनीस्थिताः।
मण्डूकमत्स्यप्रमुखाः योगिनस्ते भवन्ति किम्।।

"We see frogs and fishes living in the sacred rivers like the Ganges from their birth to death. Do they turn out to be Yogis?". Hence how will man, by a dip in them by once, become pure? The gist is that man is, like frogs and fish, a sect that gets deluded in water. Listen to what the great sage Veda Vyasa says in his Devi-Bhagawata:

क्षलयन्तीह तीर्थानि सर्वथा देहजं मलम्।
मानसं क्षलितुं तानि न समर्थानि वै नृप।।
शक्तानि यदि चेत्तानि गङ्गातीरनिवासिनः।
मनुजाद्रोहसंयुक्ताः कथं स्युः पाविताशयाः।।

"O King! baths in the holy waters may remove the dirt of the body, but they are not capable of removing the dirt of the mind. If they are, on the other hand, capable of doing so, and if it is argued that those that live on the banks of the Ganges are of pure mind, will they ever indulge in doing harm to men?" The gist is that since even those who live on the banks of the Ganges are seen to do harm, it is clear that holy baths have not the power to purify the mind. But listen to what that holy place is, that is referred to by the great seers. It is said in Yogasikhopanishad:

1. इह नाडीनदीप्रोक्ता शरीरे वर्तते सदा।
   पवनस्य गतिस्तत्र सर्वतः स्नानमुच्यते।।
2. सुषुम्नैव परं तीर्थम्।।

To translate these texts:

1. "There is in this body a river of the name of Sushumna nerve. The entrance of the vital breath into that nerve is verily the bath in all ways".

2. The chief holy place is verily the nerve Sushumna. When the mind is concentrated in the Sushumna, the spot of bliss in the body, the vital breath also enters it along with the mind. This is within the personal experience of men of our type. Thus it is established that what it meant by bath in the holy water, is verily Yoga that unites the mind unto bliss eternal. Worship of God is likewise the Yoga that keeps the mind united unto bliss. To cite authority, hear what Vasishta says in Vasishta.

शमबोधादिभिः पुष्पैर्देव आत्मा यदर्च्यते।
तत्तु देवार्चनं विद्धि नाकारार्चनमर्चनम्।।

"Know that as the worship of God, wherein the God of Bliss in the temple of body is worshipped with the flowers of the calmness of mind, knowledge and so forth. Real worship of God is verily the absorption of the mind in bliss. On the other hand, worshipping idols made of stone, wood or metal and so forth, is no worship of Iswara". It is to such idols that people offer their worship. That is why Vasishta has condemned them also as unto beasts, who worship God in that way. Those people are condemned by Sankaracharya and others too. It is in Sivanandalahari:

गभीरे कासारे विशति विजने घोरविपिने
विशाले शैले च भ्रमति कुसुमांर्थ जडमतिः।
समर्प्यैकं चेतः सरसिजमुमानाथ भवते
सुखेनावस्थातुं जन इह न जानाति किमहो।।

"The man of weak intellect wanders about in search of flowers of worship, getting into the deep waters of the lotus lake, or entering dense forests, or climbing up high mountains. O God! Man knows not how to remain happy united unto bliss, offering the chief flower of mind unto you. Alas! What a great wonder!" Hear what another realised soul has given expression in Tamil.

"Ettinaittan Kallukalai Poozithalum
Heenarkalae Unkalukku Mokshamundo"

"O ye stupid fellow! Whatever or how many so ever stones you worship, you will not be released from misery, and attain bliss".

"Natta Kallu Daivamentu nalupushpam charthurir
chuttivantu munu munentu chollum mantramethado
Natta Kallu pesumo, nathanullirukayil
Chuttta chatti chattukam karichhuvai ariyumo".

This means: "People offer a few flowers under the impression that the installed idol of stone is God. What is that mantra which you repeat "munu munu" after going round that idol? Will the installed idol speak, if the God is within it? Will the hot ladle in the vessel know the taste of the preparation made therein?". This is the word of Siva. I do not add here the texts condemning idol-worship, for fear of enlarging the size of this work. I shall mention but a few of the evils of idol-worship which have been the cause for condemning it.

1. Like sacrifices, penance, pilgrimages and similar ritualistic practices, worship of God also leads men to misery. Therefore all those evils that are shown to arise from sacrifices and the like, on the strength of scriptural texts, reason and experience, are seen in the ritual of the worship of God too. As the fervour for worship increases, the delusion in the different entities of God also increases. When we see the text that Siva is Supreme, we take to the worship of Siva. When we see the text that Vishnu is Supreme, the mind goes after Vishnu, and the man takes to the worship of both Vishnu and Siva. When later he hears that God Ganapati is the deity that wards off all obstacles, the mind becomes inclined to that, and he takes to the worship of Vigneswara. When he hears that Sakti is Supreme above all for, without Sakti or Power everything is helpless, and without the aid of that Sakti, nothing is possible even for gods like Siva and others, his mind runs after that Sakti, and he takes to the worship of that Sakti or Power. Thus deluded in the existence of several deities, people take to the worship of the idols of those deities, and run the risk of great misery without the chance even to take food in time. Some are confounded with the doubt whether, in taking to the worship of Vishnu also, they would not incur the wrath of Siva, who might think that He is looked down upon as an inferior deity, incapable of granting the desired objects of His devotees. Some argue that Siva is superior, and people thus wrangle mutually. The knowledge that the one blissful object that is Omnipresent and pervades all, is

that object of bliss, and the consequent bliss arising out of such knowledge, do not seem to dawn in those worshippers, but what is seen to dawn in them daily is nothing but ignorance. In acting up to the scriptural injunction that one should enter the temple and worship God only after taking bath, the ignorance, that by bathing only, one would attain purity, and that bath is thus a chief agent for purity takes a strong hold on the people. The danger in this is, that they would never approve of that superior knowledge, that the bath mentioned above, refers to the removal of the impurity of the mind, which alone can make one pure, and not the mere dip in water. This is a developed stage of ignorance.

2. Accustomed to worship God with the articles of water, fragrant flower, frankincense, light and offerings of food, there becomes firm in men the ignorance that those are really the articles of worship. The danger from such a hold of ignorance is, that they do not pay any regard at all to the superior knowledge contained in Sankara's teachings.

"समर्प्यैकं चेतःसरसिजमुमानाथ भवते
सुखेनावस्थातुं जन इह न जानाति किमहो"

That only when the one lotus of mind is dedicated (got absorbed in) unto God (bliss), there is the chance for the attainment of that bliss everlasting. On the other hand, they will take up arms if advised thus. Nor will they retrace from that misery that results from their wandering forth in search of flowers of worship, such as basil leaves, Vilwa leaves, lotus and so forth, wherever they exist. This is also a developed stage of ignorance arising from the practice of idol-worship.

3. Accustomed long to worship idols installed in temples, people become steeped in the deep faith that they are varily the real temple and the real God. The danger that arises out of this superstitious yet strong faith, is that they would care but a trash for your advice that they are treading the wrong path, that their present mode of worship is wrong, that they would be relieved of misery and attain bliss, only if they get their mind absorbed in the God that is within themselves, pointing out authoritative texts in support of that advice, such as quoted below from Sivajnana Deepika and Bhagavad Gita respectively:

1. देहो देवालयः प्रोक्तः

2. ईश्वरः सर्वभूतानां हृद्देशेऽर्जुन तिष्ठति।।

These texts mean: "(1) The body is the temple of God (2) O Arjuna ! God abides in all beings within their hearts." They may even take you to task for imparting such advice. This is but another developed stage of ignorance resulting from idol-worship.

4. Many take to fasting in temples, observing the vows of Pradosha, Ekadasi and so forth. If you speak to them: 'This is not correct. Upavasa does not mean fasting. Upa means 'near' and 'Vasa' means dwelling. Hence upavasa means the abiding of the individual soul close by the Supreme Soul; if you thus quote the texts of Upanishad and expound their meaning they would not listen to you. On the other hand they may accuse you as being a Christian, a Missionary or a Buddhist and of denouncing Hinduism. "From time immemorial temples are built, and idols therein are worshipped at great expense by the Brahmins, the rich and others. Are they all ignorant? We shall show you are long what we can do against you. We are going to publish a work shortly criticising your Mokshapradeepa wherein you have condemned ritualism". Thus and so forth the ritualists argue and threaten, and come to quarrel against me. This is another highly advanced stage of ignorance, the result of idol-worship. People may have reason to blame me if I found a new religion and advocate the same. Let them accuse their Vasishta, their Vishnu, their Siva, their Krishna, their Vedavyasa, their Sankaracharya, their Gods and sages, as Christians missionaries, Buddhists and so on. Let them publish a book criticising the works of the great men mentioned above, like Vasishta and others, and the Vedic texts. The ritualists have every right to do so even long long ago. Why have not they really attempted at that till now? Nor do they attempt now. What is the meaning of wreaking their vengeance and audacious threats and hatred against me alone? Is it because they think I am not so powerful as they? Wonderful indeed ! Wonderful ! If some of the weak descendants of the powerful ancestors of the past were to distribute by way of charity the great fortunes hoarded up by them, Namburis, Patters, Nayars, Ezhuvas and all, would receive it in joy. Even though he be a Chandala, an unapproachable, who offers money, those who regard themselves as superior, do welcome

it, and receive it gladly. Even if he be a non-follower of Hinduism, say a Christian, a Muhammedan or a Buddhist, that offers money, that is readily and gladly welcomed by the Aryans (Hindus). The followers of all religions do the same. If money could be received from any hand, what objection could there be to receive the wealth of knowledge from all, whoever they might be. The wealth of knowledge has even the power to purify the mind, but wealth or money proper has no such power. As such, under the impression that knowledge is not worthy of acceptance from all, and that a jnani is not powerful, to speak rashly of him in disrespect, is nothing but the effect of hatred and jealousy, the ignorance of the gist of Hinduism and the long acquaintance with and observance of ritualism. If in the beginning some have taken to some faith, and in due observance of it, have become accustomed to it for a long time, they would never like to be criticised as to their mode of life. They will, if you do so, only come to quarrel with you. To illustrate. If you address those who are accustomed to eat fish or meat, criticising their partaking of them, they would never agree to your view. They would discard it overboard saying that those objects of meat and fish have been created by God for human consumption. Is it not, because they are accustomed to such a despicable diet from the very beginning of their life, that they find it difficult to give it up? If children are not from their very childhood given such a diet, they would find no relish at all in it. There is no doubt as to it. Since Brahmins are, from their very childhood not accustomed to eat fish or flesh, they appear to them foul-smelling and non relishing. They need no advice that flesh should not be eaten. Nor do they find it hard to put up with any lecture that condemns fish and flesh eating. Likewise, if people had not taken to idol-worship and the like ignorant practices from their very beginning, the ritualists among them also, will not find it hard to put up with the lectures of jnanis, criticising that, by such practices, there is no chance to attain bliss. Even Christians and Muhammedans who denounce Hinduism, take delight in hearing from us yogic knowledge, that is the gist of Hinduism. Since such lectures on the pure knowledge of such greatness, are unendurable to the ritualists among Hindus, since they are found to exult in the superiority complex as high and low, without any outlook of equality of vision, rituals foster but ignorance. They do not work out purity of mind. They lead only to bondage. The ignorant deceivers attach undue importance to ritualism, and deceive the world. Rituals block the door to bliss. God has not laid down any injunction that only particular persons are to perform particular rituals, and that if they do that, they would be granted the fruits of those respective rituals. People take up to several rituals as befitting their nature. The world is deluded like the blind following the blind, and suffers great misery. In spite of my restraining from giving expression to authoritative texts, which proclaim in corroboration of the above statements and which rush up to my mind in emulation. I am not able to control them, and they rush forth from out of my mind. Listen, O ye men ! to the authorities that proclaim that rituals lead to increase ignorance.

यथामावास्यान्धकारं मेघावरणं वर्द्धयति तथा कर्म अज्ञानं वर्द्धयति।।

"Just as dark clouds intensify the darkness of the new moon night, so also do rituals increase ignorance". Thus is laid down in the Vedantic treatise "Vasudevamanana".

To prove that neither Gods nor the rituals like sacrifices and the like, will ever conduce to purity of mind, I quote the following from Devibhagavata.

न देवा न च शास्त्राणि न व्रतानि तपांसि न।
न मखा न च दानानि चित्तशुद्धेस्तु कारणम्।।

"Neither the gods nor the learning of many Sastras, neither vows nor penances, neither sacrifices, nor giving alms or gifts, would work up for the purity of mind". This reminds me of the discourse between Krishna and Arjuna in the Gita. Hence I quote the advice of Krishna to Arjuna found therein.

यतो यतो निश्चरति मनश्चञ्चलमस्थिरम्।
ततस्ततो नियम्यैतदात्मन्येव वशं नयेत्।।

"The mind that is unsteady and ever wavering, has to be controlled from its running after all sensual objects, and has to be concentrated to the spot of Ananda". To this advice Arjuna asks Krishna:

चञ्चलं हि मनः कृष्ण प्रमाथि बलवद्दृढम्।
तस्याहं निग्रहं मन्ये वायोरिव सुदुष्करम्।।

"O Krishna! The mind is indeed wavering and highly affecting the body and the senses. It is indeed very powerful too. To think of controlling such as mind, is like that of attempting to tie down the wind".

To such a statement of Arjuna, could not Sri Krishna have replied, 'O Arjuna! I shall bless you and get your mind purified and under your control'? Where then was that extraordinary power of Krishna who encouraged Arjuna to take up arms with the high hope of killing the heroes in the war, and of getting the kingdom of Pandavas? Could he not have granted Arjuna the purity of mind by a mere blessing? If he had been able to do that, would he have replied him as follows?:

"असंशयं महाबाहो मनो दुर्निग्रहं चलम्।
अभ्यासेन तु कौन्तेय वैराग्येण च गृह्यते।।"

"O Arjuna! There is no doubt that the mind is given up to wavering and is difficult of control. But it can be brought under control through practice and non-attachment or averseness to worldly objects." It is in this way that Krishna, the visible Incarnation of God, has advised his intimate friend Arjuna. This means that the mind is to be purified and brought under control, that its absorption into bliss is our responsibility, and that it is to be accomplished by giving up the worldly objects, knowing the evils thereof, and practising the mind in concentration and that it is incapable of being accomplished with the aid of the God, and the performance of sacrifices, and other rituals. As such, what a lack of thoughtfulness it is to hold the view that, by the daily recitation of Bhagawad Gita, God will be pleased and will bestow mental purity and salvation, and likewise the same, by the performance of sacrifices and other rituals, and thus to be deluded in the various ritualistic practices. It is the view of our people that mental purity and bliss are things to be bought of another, as we do about grain, money and other wares. Be it so. I shall quote here from Vyasasmriti to prove that rituals lead to bondage, and that they are not to be performed.

कर्मणा बध्यते जन्तुर्विद्यया च विमुच्यते।
तस्मात् कर्म न कुर्वन्ति यतयः पारदर्शिनः।।

"Man is bound down by ritualism, and is released from it by

knowledge. Hence those aspirants after bliss eternal, do not take to ritualism."

Is it not due to the knowledge that rituals lead to misery, that jnanis of real knowledge have given up all rituals? Hence the text that, through knowledge, one is released from bondage, is one based on experience. Is it not on account of being long accustomed to ritualism, that ritualists do not pay heed to the several Sastras of jnana, that are dinned into their ears, and still insist on the performance of such rituals? Therefore the text that man is bound by ritualism, is also one born of and based on experience. Further it is a tenet of Hinduism that as one continues in the performance of rituals, one has to take births again to enjoy the resulting fruits of those ritualistic practices. The ritualists hold fast to that view too. As such, karmins or ritualists have no chance at all for salvation at any time. For, it is our experience that to whatever practice we are accustomed, therein our attachment goes on increasing. Some take in the beginning to small quantities of meat, wine, ganjam opium and the like, and in due course, they begin to indulge in them beyond limits. People take to adultery, perjury and other crimes scarcely, and in great fear at the start. Becoming gradually accustomed to that, they indulge in them extremely without any scruple of conscience at all. When thus we find that peoples tendency goes on increasing as they continue to resort even to activities that are despicable and shameful, it is needless to say how much more their fond and fast attachment for ritualistic practices, such as sacrifices, vows, pilgrimages, worship and the like should go on increasing, when they see that the same are praised and practised by the venerable Acharyas and the learned scholars, and are proclaimed by the code of ritualism, which enjoins, with high hopes though false, that the performance of rituals like sacrifice and so forth, would gain them all prosperity and heaven, that action performed in a spirit of disinterestedness would work out for one's purity of mind and so forth. As men continue to engaged in the performance of rituals, so much their attachment for them goes on also increasing. Can that lead otherwise, to an inclination of the mind towards jnana? As we sow seeds of paddy, it is verily paddy that grows up ten fold. Likewise, the inclination for ritualism goes on increasing from one birth to another birth, and from that to the next future birth and so on. Consistently with this increase their hatred towards jnana and jnanis also, goes on proportionately increasing. As firewood added to fire increases the flame, so also attachment to ritualism and aversion to jnana go on increasing, as a consequence of which, attachment is persisted in and jnana is discarded. Such a state leads only to misery, is what is really confirmed by textual authorities, reason and experience, and that leads nowhere to salvation. The text 'Karmana badhyate' (man is bound down by Karma or rituals) is always to be remembered. O ye of the caste of bliss ! Listen to the authorities that declare that those intent on the distinctions of castes and caste practices, are ignorant men and deceivers of the world. The following are the words of Vishnu as we see them in Garuda Purana:

1. स्वस्ववर्णाश्रमाचारनिरताः सर्वमानवाः।
न जानन्ति परं धर्मं वृथा नश्यन्ति डाम्भिकाः।।
2. क्रियाऽयासपराः के चित् व्रतवर्यादिसंयुताः।
अज्ञानसंवृतात्मानः सञ्चरन्ति प्रतारकाः।।

These mean! "All those men, who cling fast to the practices of their respective castes and stages of life, do not know of the supreme virtue of salvation. In vain they rush to ruin, self-conceited".

O ye who exult in the pride of caste duties! If there is any benefit in taking pride in the distinctions of castes and in the observance of respective caste duties, will God Vishnu condemn them as self conceited, who rush to ruin, as we see from the text 'Vritha Nasyanthe' quoted above? No. As long as we hold fast to the distinctions of castes and caste practices, so long our chance is only for ruin. To illustrate "I am a Brahmin and superior by caste. You are of low caste and are to stand apart". Thus and so forth do men of respective castes, pride in their caste superiority. As they go on doing thus, their outlook of inequality also widens. As that outlook of inequality increases, the chances for the outlook of equality and union among men become far remote, and dissensions ensue. Thus it is that the Hindus have fallen to ruin, and are falling so at present. This I have detailed at length in my work 'Moksha Pradeepa'

2. "Some are keen about actions like building temples, performing sacrifices and so forth. Some take to fasts and pilgrimages. Thus, not knowing the Atman, out of their ignorance they wander about as deceivers". The real significance implied by the word `Prataraka' in the above second sloka, is that those who hold fast to caste and caste practices, become themselves, out of their ignorance, a prey to ruin, and they deceive others by leading hem astray from the path of bliss, deluding them by their teachings.

It is heartily to be welcomed that God Vishnu has rightly condemned them, as unto deceivers, who lead people astray from the real right path into the wrong one, Be it so.

O ye aspirants after bliss ! The Yogasastras also proclaim that rituals are a hindrance to bliss. To quote from Sivasamhita.

"यज्ञश्चान्द्रायणं कृच्छ्रं तीर्थानि विषयानि च।
दृश्यन्ते च इमे विघ्ना धर्मरूपेण संस्थिताः।।"

"Sacrifice, the vow of Krichtra Chandrayana, holy place, and sensual objects, which appear in the form of Dharma or merit, are really hindrances". People perform sacrifices and so forth in the belief that it is Dharma, or ordained merit. They are, on the other hand, really hindrances to the attainment of bliss. Further,

प्रातः स्नानोपवासादि कायक्लेशविधिं त्यजेत्।।

"Hatayogapradeepika"

"One should give up all those practices, like early bath, fast and the like, which tend but to physical fatigue". O ye ritualists, who believe in Bhagawad Gita! Krishna himself has said in the Bhagawad gita that God has not enjoined particular duties for particular men. Each one takes to that action that befits his natural disposition.

"न कर्तृत्वं कर्माणि लोकस्य सृजति प्रभुः।
न कर्मफलसंयोगं स्वभावस्तु प्रवर्तते।"

So says Bhagawad gita in verse 14, chapter V "God creates neither agency of action, nor action for men, nor does He work out the fruit of their action. It is but the natural disposition of beings that works out". To explain: You are a Brahmin. The duty prescribed for you is the performance of sacrifice and the like. You are the agent qualified for that work. If you duly perform that, your duty, you will enjoy such and such fruits. You are a Sudra. Your duty is to serve the Brahmins; you are the agent qualified to take up that work. If you do it rightly, you will reap such and such fruits. You are a Kshatriya. You are a Vaisya. Your respective duties are government of the country and carrying of commerce. God has not laid down in this way, any rule enjoining particular duries for particular class of people, particular agents for particular actions, nor particular fruits for particular actions. But each man acts up as stimulated by his natural disposition or inclination. The man of evil propensity takes to evil deeds, while he of good natural disposition takes to good and virtuous deeds. Thus the activities of all Hindus, and the followers of other religions, like Christians and others, are in accordance with their natural disposition. Is not this verily within our own experience? As such is there any reason to quarrel and hate, now is in the past, on the score of facts like. 'I am a Brahmin. The duty enjoined by God for the Brahmin is the study of Vedas and scriptures. That is prohibited to the Sudra. He is not allowed even to hear the scriptures'. If God has enjoined particular duties for particular men, will they be able to transgress it and take to another duty? No. This world itself is an illustration to testify to it. O ye disputants! Can you alter the bitter taste of the neem tree? Can you whiten the black crows? Can you make the sweet sugarcane to taste bitter? Can you do away with the heat of the fire? Can you put out the light of the sun? Can you prevent your death, and live immortal. Neither man nor any object in this world can alter even one of the dictates of God. As such if Vedas, the respective distinctions of castes and caste practices, are really enjoined by God, no one can go against them, no Brahmin will be able to take up to the duty of Sudra, nor any Sudra to that of the Brahmin, and none among the Brahmins and the Sudras, will ever be able to become Christians. No Brahmin will be able to give up the study of the Vedas, the performance of sacrifices and the like, which are prided upon as the exclusive privilege enjoined by God on Brahmins, or to take up to the study of English, and to pronounce the English language. The elephant can never turn itself out into a goat and bleat like the latter, and vice versa. As we think over thus, it becomes clear that those respective caste distinctions, and that ritualism that enjoins respective rituals are all enjoined by those men who are self-conceited, who have not the outlook of equality, who are heartless, and are not possessed of due thoughtfulness and knowledge. It is by resorting to the performance of sacrifice and the like rituals, in all implicit faith in them, that even Brahmins have now to maintain their livelihood by taking to agriculture, trade and service to others, by holding several administrative positions, studying the English language and by resorting to several other pursuits of life. If the caste distinctions and the respective caste practices are ordained by God, it is some ritualist among the Hindus that is to rule over the country today in all glory and prosperity. Such is the efficacy of ritualism as laid down in Dattatreya Tantra quoted below:

अङ्कोलवृक्षमारूढो जपेदेकाग्रमानसः
राजाधिराजो भवति नान्यथा शिवभाषितम्।।

"If one climbs up the ankola tree, and be meditating with a concentrated mind, one is sure to become the overlord of kings. This word of Siva cannot work out to the contrary".

Thus taking to such a meditation could not a Hindu reign as the Emperor? Why should you take up arms against the just and impartial British Government, clamouring for Home Rule? Hinduism contains within itself the device to come by sovereignty even without a war. Listen to another quotation from the above Dattatreya Tantra:

"कुङ्कुमं चन्दनं चैव कर्पूरं तुळसीदळम्।
गवां क्षीरेण तिलकं राजवश्यकरं परम्।।"

"Vermilion, sandal paste, camphor, basil leaves, crush these all together in cow's milk, and apply a mark of it on the forehead. The king is sure to be won over to you thereby !" Cannot a mark of this be applied, and thus the English Emperor be won over, and thereby gain self-government? Why the necessity of a revolt or war against the just British King? To quote from Bhagawad Gita:-

"इष्टान् भोगान् हि वो देवा दास्यन्ते यज्ञभाविताः"।।

"The Gods, propitiated through the performance of sacrifices, will bestow upon you all your desired objects". This shows that you can come by all your desired objects, including self-government, by performing sacrifices. Then why the necessity to take up arms against the just British King? O Friends! Let go sovereignty. Can you not propitiat God by your sacrifices, and get, through their favour, at least as much wealth as is necessary to maintain your body? Then, will you have to give up your caste duty of Vedic study, performance of sacrifice and the like, and take to trade and so forth, and thus suffer? Is it not to be condemned that one should give up one's natural caste duty? O ye Sudras! Some of you also condemn me who am devoted to jnana, and my works. The reasons for this is to be traced to that implicit faith of yours that the castes and the caste practices, observed by you from time immemorial, are enjoined by God. Why should those of you who cling to that faith, give up your caste duty of serving Brahmins? Your duty, as laid down in Manusmriti is verily to serve the Brahmins '**शुश्रूषैव हि शूद्रस्य**' (Verily service of the Brahmin is the duty of Sudra). Therefore, you are to understand that your duty is but to serve Nambudries and Patters, and obey what they dictate unto you. Is it right on your part to pose as masters, instead of seeking your livelihood by doing manual work unto them, as they dictate, in their compounds, gardens or fields, or by tending their cattle? Indeed wonderful! You and the Brahmins hold fast to the code of ritualism, only to raise revolt against jnanis, while you throw overboard that very code, which you consider as divinely enjoined, as a trash, when it concerns matters where you are self-interested. If it is really ordained by God, you will not be able to discard it as you like. That you are thus able to do so, is itself proof positive that it is not so ordained. If we think over duly on the matter, it will be clear that neither God has any necessity to promulgate such a code too. If God has a desire to found a religion, prescribing particular castes and caste duties for particular men, and thus make them observe the same. He as All-powerful, could make all observe the same duty for ever. God, being omniscient, can as well foresee what we are in need of. As such, He has no necessity, like unto kings who are not omniscient and who frame new laws at intervals and amend the existing ones, of introducing any changes in the Vedas and Sastras at intervals through Pandits, in the impression that the injunctions laid down by Him earlier, are not right. Does He make any change at intervals in the grains, like paddy and so forth, and in water, air, fire and so on, seeing that they were not rightly created in the beginning? No. Therefore to think, on account of the mere mention of the names of the authors of texts, that God has not that omniscience in matters religious alone, and He has thus to make several changes in them, turn out but to be a denunciation of God. It is by believing the false texts the people thus fall victims to misery, by observing several rituals, and become averse to the path of jnana. Verily therefore it has been correctly observed in Tripurarahasya Jnanakanda as follows:

"अहो यथान्धानुगतो ह्यन्धश्चेष्टति तादृशः।
लोकस्य व्यवहारो वै सर्वस्याप्यभिलक्षितः।।"

"Alas! The ways of the world are seen to be as those of the blind led by the blind." To explain. Without knowing that the blind man has no eyes, and as such, another blind man is incapable of leading him aright, the blind follows the blind, and becoming incapable of reaching the destination, goes astray and falls into misery. Likewise, people without the knowledge to decide that the teacher of ritualism lacks in Yogic Jnana and is incapable of pointing out the right path to bliss, obey that teacher, and unable to attain bliss eternal, become prey to the misery of worldly existence.

O Ye aspirants after truth! If sacrifices, fasts, vows, pilgrimages, idol-worship and the like rituals, are conducive to purity of mind, or are the initial steps or aids to reach salvation, could there be any mention in Tripurarahasya Jnanakanda, that those who act up to the code of ritualism and the advocates of it, are like unto the blind following the blind, to their eventual lasting misery? Would it be said that ritualism, if not warded off in fear that it is like unto a ghost, would lead not to bliss but only to misery? Would it be mentioned in the work 'Vasudevamanana' that ritualism would tend to increase ignorance. Would it be proclaimed in Devibhagawata that no purity of mind could be had through ritualism? Would it be condemned in Vyasasmriti that ritualism would lead to bondage, and was therefore not resorted to by the aspirants after bliss! Would it be described in Sivasamhita that ritualism would be a hindrance to Yoga Jnana? Would it be denounced in Garuda Purana, without any hesitation whatsoever, that those who lead people to ritualism, and those who resort to it, were ignorant, self-conceited men and deceivers? Would it be condemned in Sivajnanadeepika that the Sastras, enjoining ritualism, were false Sastras, brought into existence by self-styled Pandits, and the lot of the ritualists who believed in them, was verily birth decay and death? Would it be said in the same work that even Pandits were misled by these false Sastras, and had gone astray? Would that same work mention that through ritualism the world has fallen to ruin, and praise the man, who gave it up, as unto Iswara? Would Vasishta denounce in his work Vasishta those who took up to ritualism as unto beasts? As flowers to fruits, if rituals, like sacrifices and so forth, are conducive to mental purity, and thereby to Yoga Jnana and salvation, those who resort to that path would only be praised. Why should the flower be denounced that is the cause of the fruit? Likewise, if sacrifices and the like rituals are the cause or instruments for Jnana, why should they denounced? If, as in the beginning the learning of the alphabet is the cause for the later scholarship, the performance of sacrifices and so forth, is the initial step for salvation, that would only be praised. The scholars will not denounce the infant readers and the infants. They know that, only through the learning of the alphabet, later scholarship can be had, and that it is essentially to be resorted to in the beginning. Likewise, if it is through sacrifices and other rituals that the path of Yoga Jnana is reached, the Jnanis would know that it is to be practised in the initial stages, and as such, they would not denounce it. Some argue that a Jnani is not in need of sacrifices, idol-worship and the like, illustrating the instance of the non-necessity of a boat for a man who had crossed the river, but they are necessary for one who has not attained Jnana, as a boat is necessary for a man this side the river to cross it, and reach the other side. This is not correct. It is not the practice of people who have crossed to the other side of a river, to condemn those who get into the boat to cross the river. They know they have crossed the river with the aid of the boat. If, likewise, it is through idol worship and similar rituals, that people have attained and are to attain Jnana, the Jnani would be aware of it. Therefore they will never denounce ritualists. Since, on the other hand, they are seen to denounce ritualists and condemn ritualism it is clear that it is not through ritualism that they have reached the shore of bliss, that those who take to that boat will reach only the ocean of misery, and that it is only to ward off people from taking to such a wrong path, that they have thus denounced them and that is just and highly necessary too. For, all beings are the children of bliss, and all long for bliss alone. As such, are they not to work through the path of Yoga Jnana, which unites them unto bliss. Without doing so, they resort to the rituals of misery, like sacrifices and so forth, and suffer a great deal, like unto infants handling the burning charcoal, and unto moths falling into the burning fire, out of great delusion. When a man is denounced, he will begin to think over the cause for such denunciation. As he thinks over, he will come to understand the absurdity of his actions and the ensuing misery from the existence of caste distinctions and caste practices. As he begins to understand, he will give them up, and will begin to enter the path of bliss. It is, with the object of thus uniting all unto bliss, that Jnanis have criticised and condemned ritualism. In spite of such denunciation, alas! no one cares to think for a moment the cause why it is, that they of the superior caste have come to be condemned as unto beasts, and those practices of idol-worship and the like, observed by them as Aryan practices, have come to be criticised. Alas! If no one takes to such a consideration of the matter, is it not the dire need of the time to establish Jnana Yogasalas (Communion Halls of knowledge and Yoga) in several places, initiate people into that path of Yoga, and to deliver lectures on its in all places? Then all will come to understand the heart of Hinduism. Knowledge, harmlessness, truth, pity, pleasure, contentment, peace, outlook of equality and the like virtues, will flourish in our midst, and we will not take up to mutual quarrelling, like unto the natural enemies of animals like dogs and so forth. The harmony and union that have now disappeared from our midst, will begin to approach us, and we will be able to attain worldly happiness and bliss everlastings.

O ye seekers after truth! Since we are all after bliss, and since the great Sankaracharya was one exulting in the bliss of yogic knowledge, if it were a great Ananda Yogapranabhyasa Sala (Hall for the practice of blissful yogic knowledge) open to all, that was established at Kaladi, the place of his birth, it would have encouraged many to open yogajnanasalas in several places, and the society would derive all the benefits of yogajnana described above. It is said in Bhagawad Gita:

"यद्यदाचरति श्रेष्ठस्तत्तदेवेतरो जनः।।"

"What is observed by the illustrious, that is verily imitated and taken up by others". This fact is within the experience of all too. As such, if a college of yogic knowledge were set up at Kaladi, should we say anything of the unrivalled benefit to the world therefrom? It is verily the all powerful Acharyas, the rich and the learned, that are to take up at first such a noble cause. Then all Hindus will follow them. Who is there to obey my followers? I am not possessed of great affluence, nor of the title of Acharya. Neither am I a lord, nor do I hold any high and influential office. I have no titles of honour, nor any retinue of bodyguard and other paraphernalia. It is only the words of those that have such assets, that the majority would follow. Then, why is it that the powerful rich do not stop their zeal for building temples and attempt to encourage the dissemination of the supreme yogic knowledge? It is only through that yogic knowledge that Hindus would become entitled to be called Aryans (the venerable). How is it that they give up such an exalted state and advocate the unbecoming practice of ritualism? The installation ceremony at Kaladi has in reality turned out to be a renewal, lest the immemorial ignorance be barred by limitation. As many a person, with extreme devotion, and with coins of silver and gold and other offerings of presents, has worshipped the Swami, the officiating head of the ceremony of the installation of the idol therein, much money has been drained out of Kerala. As such, it was a great pity that, out of the vast sum collected from Kerala, not even a fraction of it has been devoted to the cause of Malayalees, in lifting up those struggling in misery, devoted to the performance of evil ritualistic practices. Neither the sanctified holy water, nor the offering of a few flowers, can ever dispel ignorance. Nor do we see those, that offer them, and those, offered the same, deprived of ignorance. The practice of sipping the holy sanctified water, resorted to by the Hindus from time immemorial, has turned to be one of the poisons of ignorance, and the installation of idols to be that of ignorance. O God! None are seen to instal the deity of jnana, and to distribute the holy water of the ambrosia of jnana! Another swami set out towards the north. He began investing the sacred thread to some section of the people, who were not accustomed to it previously. Under the delusion that Brahmins, on account of the habit of wearing the sacred thread, and of their practice of idol-worship, have a certain superiority, and that, if their ways are accepted and imitated, there is a chance for ascendancy in the social scale, many have taken up to the wearing of the sacred thread and idol-worship. This is nothing but the wearing of the thread of ignorance. Listen to what is described in Brahmopanishad as the real sacred thread of knowledge:

1. यदक्षरं परं ब्रह्म तत् सूत्रमिति धारयेत्।।
2. यस्मिन् सर्वमिदं प्रोतं सूत्रे मणिगणा इव।।
3. तत् सूत्रं विदितं येन स विप्रो वेदपारगः।।
4. शिखा यज्ञोपवीताभ्यां ब्राह्मणो नैव नैव च।।

This fourth quotation is from Sivajnana deepika.

5. बहिः सूत्रं त्यजेत् बुधः।

These mean:

1. 'The eternal Brahma that is indestructible and has not decay (i.e., bliss), has to be understood as the thread'. Then the reason why that Brahma is to be known as the sacred thread, is explained in the subsequent texts.

2. 'It is because all the worlds are kept strung in this thread of Brahma, as pearls in a string'.

3. 'He who has known that thread is verily the Brahmin possessed of the qualifications of the recitation and the study of the Vedas.'

4. 'It is quite certain that one can never become a Brahmin by wearing the sacred thread, or by keeping the tuft of hair.'

5. 'The man of jnana should give up the sacred thread' When such is the real fact, Pandarams (professional religious beggars), Chakkans (oil mongers), Asaris (carpenters), Ezhuvas and others, take to the fashion of wearing the sacred thread, and worshipping idols, under the delusion that they will thereby rise in the social scale by a lift of caste or by a special superiority; or become possessed of a purity of mind and excellence of jnana. But we do

not see any special purity of mind or excellence of jnana in those who, from time immemorial, have taken up to the worship of idols and the wearing of the sacred thread. If they have attained any such purity, will they argue and quarrel mutually, even now, in the pride of superiority complex, as 'you are a Sudra and low'. As such, how can those who have taken to that fashion but of late, ascend in the social scale ? It is nothing but a wonder, an effusion of ignorance.

"ज्ञानिनो दुर्लभा लोके कर्मिणः कोटिकोटयः।।"

'Jnanis are but rare in the world, while ritualists can be counted in crores'. We have no go to forget the above text from Sivajnana deepika. What can we do? In the next, number four, quoted above, even the tuft of hair that is generally kept, is discarded as a sign of Brahminhood. Listen to what is said in Brahmopanishad as to what the real tuft is:

"अग्नेरिव शिखा नान्या यस्य ज्ञानमयी शिखा।
स शिखीत्युच्यते विद्वान् नेतरे केशधारिणः।।"

'The flame is verily the tuft of Agni or Fire. Likewise, he who has the tuft of knowledge is really the man of tuft. He is the learned. The wearers of the simple tuft of hair are not men of real tufts". As such, it is nothing but a manifest effusion of ignorance that heads of families do find fault with the junior members of the family, as going against the old practice, when they take to the new fashion of having their hair cropped, and that people are deluded in the ceremony of tuft and in the question of tuft. Some delude people by saying that Rajayoga is not possible of acquisition without the aid of Hatayoga. I shall briefly refute that view in this context. It is said in Sivajnana deepika:

"देहक्षोभकरैर्दुःखैरासनैः कुक्कुटादिभिः।
कर्शयन्तो वृथाऽत्मानमीश्वरं कर्मयोगिनः।।"

'The Karmayogins weaken their own self, a part of Iswara, by taking to postures, like that of the fowl, peacock and so forth, which cause but fatigue to the body, and are miserable'.

O ye seekers after truth! No difficult posture need be assumed to see the sun with our naked eye. Likewise, no aid of Hatayoga is necessary to come by Rajayoga, which exults in the sight of the sun of Atman with the aid of the mind. When a man sits for sometime in the posture of the cock, he begins to feel pain in his legs and in other limbs. Then the man becomes conscious of the pain, and thus falters in the steadiness of his concentration. Listen to what is said in Tejobindupanishad, as to what the real posture is that is to be practised:

"सुखेनैव भवेद्यस्मिन् अजस्रं ब्रह्मचिन्तनम्।
आसनं तद्विजानीयात् अन्यत् सुखविनाशनम्।।"

'Wherein the incessant contemplation of Brahma is possible at ease, know that to be the posture. (The gist is you can contemplate in any posture as you like, but you should not tire out the body). All other postures tend to destroy happiness.'

Since Hatayoga has been criticised by me along with the rituals of sacrifices and the like, you should not conclude that Hatayoga is either to be condemned, or is of no use at all. I have criticised it but to show that it is not necessary for Rajayoga. Those who argue that, without the aid of Hatayoga, Rajayoga is not possible of success are, without doubt, verily those who have not tasted the experience of Rajayoga. This I can boldly assert on the strength of my own personal experience, at the top of my voice even from the top of a mountain. Further, it can also be thus asserted in the light of reason and the support of textual authorities. I do not add all of them here for fear of enlarging this treatise. Let it be. I shall conclude the subject briefly.

O ye seekers after truth!

"चित्ते चलति संसारो निश्शलं मोक्ष उच्यते"

So says Yogasikhopanishad.

"When the mind wanders or becomes unsteady, that results in worldly existence or bondage. When it remains motionless, that is verily salvation." It is said, चलनात्मकं कर्म, i.e., Karma is of the nature of motion. Therefore karma or action causes motion to the mind. That is within our own experience too. Therefore, just as a push to a fast moving boat, the observance of rituals, like sacrifices and so forth, ensures but motion to the mind, which is by nature in worldly bondage, and intensifies and increases that bondage. If a monkey that is naturally wayward, comes under the influence of a ghost too, needless to describe its freaks and pranks. Another authoritative text lays down.

"कर्म किञ्चिदपि दुःखं भवति"

"Even a little of karma tends to bring on misery". That is verily corroborated by our experience also. All are after release from misery and for happiness. The performance of sacrifices and other rituals is, on the other hand, productive of only increased misery. As such, it is quite absurd to lay down that, before the dawn of knowledge one should resort to the observance of rituals, like sacrifices, vows, pilgrimage, idol-worship, and to believe that such observance is necessary and to observe the same. Should one eat the rind and joint of the sugarcane, before one tastes its sweet juice? Should one eat the fibre and shell of the cocoanut, before one tastes its sweet water and the kernel inside? Should one take poison first before one takes food? Should a man practise at first the art of lying that he might come by the necessary courage to speak truth? Should we pass our days long in darkness that we might become able to see the light? If, under the impression that they are created by God, and that they are verily outside too, and therefore we are to eat them first, we attempt to eat the fibre and shell of the cocoanut, or the rind and joint of the sugarcane, it will result in the loss of our teeth, discharge of blood, and perhaps in death too, since any piece of it may fatally stick up to the throat. Then there is no chance at all to taste the delicious essence within. Likewise, if ignorant rituals are resorted to till the dawn of knowledge, it will result only in ignorance and ever lasting misery. Hence Vasishta and other seers of jnana have denounced the code of ritualism, so that all may become possessed of yogic knowledge, and thus be united unto bliss eternal. Men of our type and experience will only conclude that those who on the contrary, advocate ritualism as the first step - be they world respected scholars or even Gods - are but blind men without the eye to detect the false Sastras, and without the least experience of yogic bliss. What rises forth from within the hearts of men of the experience of bliss, can only rightly be but what is conducive to the dissemination of the blissful yoga-jnana, and can never be to that of miserable ritualism. To illustrate. When a man who has heavily loaded his belly with the sweet milk porridge vomits, no trace is seen in it of any bit of fish or flesh, nor is there the odour of any liquor. When on the contrary, we see those bits, we cannot but conclude that he has taken but fish and so forth, and not the sweet milk porridge at all. Likewise, we have to conclude that the advocates and adherents of ignorant ritualistic practices are verily the seats of ignorance, and that they are never jnanis at all. We have to conclude that he who speaks falsehood is but a liar, and he who steals is but a thief. A lecturer on Buddhism is to be decidedly viewed as a Buddhist and likewise, one on Christianity, as a Christian. It is the deliberate activity of every man that is the prime test for deciding anything about him. God has not furnished any special characteristic feature to be distinguished as a liar, thief, Buddhist, Christian and so on. Likewise, God has not created any special physical feature, as tusk to the elephant, to conclude that one is a jnani. That he is a jnani, can be conclusively established only by looking at his deliberate activity. As much, those that give up the practice of jnana and advocate ritualism, can never be decided to be a jnani or a yogi. If, on the contrary, we do thus conclude, we have also to conclude that a liar is a truthful man, that an adultress is a chaste woman, that the founder of Christianity is a Buddhist, and that of Buddhism is a Christian. There is nothing more absurd, more unjust, more smacking of want of intelligence than such a conclusion. As such, and in the light of the experience of men of our type, and on the strength of authoritative texts, and unimpeachable reasoning, it is but quite becoming, and to the benefit of the world at large, that Vasishta has denounced ritualists as unto beasts, and criticised ritualism.

D

आनन्द एव विजयते।।
अहिंसैव परमो धर्मः।।

आनन्दसूत्रे शङ्काक्वादपरिहारः।।
Sankavada Parihara

Explanation and answers of doubts and arguments

1. Here in this treatise Anandasutra, are cited several texts as laid down by Siva, as enjoyed by Vishnu and so on. But it is not to be doubted thereby that I have approved of the existence of a plurality of gods, and that religion is ordained by God. I have shown herein but those texts that stand the test of reason, and are useful to the context. That is all. Let those be, by whomsoever they be spoken.

2. Sakti has been given all prominence in Mokshapradeepa. It is Ananda or bliss that is described as Supreme in this treatise Anandasutra. It is not to be doubted on that score that the two treatments are opposed to each other and are inconsistent. It is verily what is described as Ananda here, is the very Sakti referred to in the former work. I have shown in Mokshapradeepa, on the strength of scriptural texts, reasoning and experience, that it is verily that Sakti that is spoken of by diverse terms or names, like Siva, Vishnu, God, Paramatma (Supreme Soul), Brahma, Ananda and so on, and that Sakti is verily the God of all religionists. Those who have carefully gone through that work, will never have any cause to doubt or argue that Sakti is a separate entity different from Ananda or Brahma. Yet some who have gone through that work but have failed to grasp the gist, are deluded in the expression Brahma, and argue as follows:

Some among the Vedantins raise objections to the supremacy of Sakti on the strength of the usages like, "Sakti or power is lost, Sakti is reduced, Sakti has increased. There is no Sakti at all," and so forth, and then argue that Sakti is neither eternal nor full, and that it is finite, liable to changes, unlike Brahma which alone is eternal, full, infinite and immutable, and so on. By raising such objections and arguments, they raise the petard to strike their own head. To explain. The Vedantins declare.

1. ब्रह्मैव जीवः सकलं जगश्च

2. एकमेवाद्वितीयम्

Which mean (1) Brahma is verily the individual soul, and all the universe.

2. There is but one without a second.

As such, they have to admit that Sakti is verily Brahma, for there is no second. Therefore their criticism that Sakti is neither eternal nor full, but only finite, liable to undergo modifications, is tantamount to a criticism of Brahma too, as non-eternal, incomplete, finite and mutable. The expression 'Sakti or power is lost' and the like, have reference only to the power limited by the body, and that also, is an expression based on the upadhi or adjunct, namely, body. If that is objected to, Vedantins could not even raise their voice. One of their maxims is 'I am Brahma' (Aham Brahmasmi). They also declare 'Brahma is verily myself' (Brahmaivahom). Since they declare that Brahma is very myself, they cannot but admit that Brahma also is finite and liable to undergo modifications. It is only the finite object, liable to modification that could raise the voice. In the expression 'I stole', they have to admit that Brahma stole. Enough of these wrong criticisms and arguments. If it is asked which God is that, that is omnipresent, all pervading and approved by the followers of all religions, we cannot but answer that it is only that Sakti or power. This I shall prove briefly in the form of a discourse:

Question: O ye followers of several religions! Where is Brahma seated? Where Siva, Vishnu, Allah? Where is God?

Answer: He is within, without, and everywhere.

Question: How do you believe that He exists?

Answer: It is said in Vedas that God pervades all (Sarvavyapi Sah-Bhagawan).

Question: Vedas contain false texts too. Vedas speak also in diverse ways. It is also said that Vishnu has His abode in Vaikuntah, and Siva in Kailas. The Vedas of the Christians, i.e., the Holy Bible, declares that God is seated in heaven. The atheists argue that there is no God at all. 'Mrityurevapavarghah, Nasthi Paralokah' which means that death is verily salvation, and that there is no other world like heaven. The followers of several religions speak about God in several ways too. Which shall I believe? Can you prove in the light of reason, that the God, advocated by you, is pervading all and everywhere?

Answer: No we cannot. You assert that there is a Sakti. Where is that Sakti seated? Does it pervade all? If so, prove. Let us see your skill.

Question: O Friends ! It is verily on account of Sakti that you have put me this question, 'Prove, let us see your skill'. If there were no Sakti, can you move your tongue, hands, legs or any other limb. Will you be able to walk? Can any of your bodily organs do anything? Therefore it is clear that Sakti pervades all your body, tongue, hands, legs and all the several limbs. In which or whom is there not Sakti? To illustrate. All religionists speak of a Sakti, as could be seen from the following general usages in the world. "This medicine has good power. It can cure all diseases. This ox has good power. It can draw the cart even though heavily loaded. Brahma has the power to create, Vishnu has the power to protect, Rudra has the power to destroy, God has the power to do everything. This man has the power of intelligence. All my organs have power" and so forth. It is because that power is in all and everywhere, that we find such usages in the world, and that people are capable of speaking thus too. It is verily on account of power that particular movable and immovable objects are possessed of special importance or quality. Is it not on account of their power of knowledge that Vasishta, Buddha, Christ and others have become objects of praise even today? Is it not on account of the power of Sakti that Yogis also shine forth? Is it not due to power that Kings attain the status of Emperors? In which or whom is not seen the Sakti? Is it not on account of that very power that atheists argue that there is no God? But for that power, will an atheist be able to move his tongue to utter even a syllable? No religionist ever says, 'this medicine has Brahma or Siva or Vishnu or Allah, and as such, this can cure the disease'. All speak only that this medicine has power. No religionist ever says that his legs have Brahma, and so can walk, but only that his legs have power and can walk. Thus thought over, it becomes clear without the aid of any textual authority of Vedas and so forth, that it is only power that is the God, that pervades all deities, like Brahma, Vishnu, Maheswara, all founders of religions like Buddha and others, the God that is described by them, and all objects movable and immovable. Some argue that in the expression 'my power', that power is contained in me, in the expression 'power of the medicine', that power is included in the medicine, in that of 'the power of God' that power is included in God, and thus Sakti becomes included in those several objects, and is not an object separate, and as such, importance is given to those objects, and not to Sakti. To argue thus is just like arguing that in the expression 'the water or juice of the sugar cane', the water or juice is included in the sugar cane. Water is not contained in the sugar cane. Water pervades everywhere, in the ocean and in the earth. It is water that has externally become a cause or agent to water the sugar cane, helping it to grow. It is that very water that has entered the sugarcane too. Likewise, it is verily power that pervades externally to be the cause or agent to protect all objects, movable and immovable. It is verily that power that has pervaded all objects in proportion to their limiting adjuncts, that goes in the world by the name of the power of those objects, and that is contained in those several objects. It is to be understood that Sakti is not limited by the respective objects that contain it, but is infinite, that sustains the world as the primeval cause of all objects, movable and immovable, both within and without. It cannot be said that water is of several tastes, because we taste it sweet when it gets into the sugar cane, bitter when it enters the nux vomica fruit; and sour when it finds its way into lemons or limes. But water is of only one taste. It is on account of the difference in the limiting adjuncts like sugar cane, lemon and so forth, that several tastes are imposed on it. Likewise, since Sakti pervades all objects, it is on account of the difference in the limiting adjuncts that contain it, that diversity is imposed on it. Sakti supreme is but one power, full and infinite. It is said in Devibhagawata:

"एकैव च पराशक्तिः निर्गुणः परमः पुमान्"

"It is the one Supreme Power that is the Supreme Brahma, devoid of attributes".

We use the following Bahvrichopanishad:

"सैव जगदण्डमसृजत् तस्या एव ब्रह्मा अजीजनत् विष्णुरजीजनत् रुद्रोऽजीजनत् संर्व शाक्तमजीजनत् सैषा पराशक्तिः सैवात्मा यदस्ति सन्मात्रं यद्विभाति चिन्मात्रं यत् प्रियमानन्दं तदेतत् सर्वाकारा"

"It is verily that Sakti that has created the world. From that very Sakti were born Brahma, Vishnu and Rudra. All that is possessed of power are born from that Sakti alone. That which shines as Sat (existence), chit (energy) and dear Ananda (bliss) verily that Parasakti or Supreme Power that pervades all and is verily the Atman too.

It is said in Yajurveda Taithreeyopanishad:-

"को ह्येवान्यात् कः प्राण्यात्
यदेष आकाश आनन्दो न स्यात्"

"If this Ananda or bliss were not in the ether, who can stir, who can live? Verily Ananda is Atman". Since only a brief explanation of Sakti is given in this treatise, if any doubt arises about the topic, the reader is referred to Mokshapradeepa, to clear all such doubts. I have explained at length therein, on the strength of texts, reasoning and experience, the principle and the greatness of Sakti.

E

आनन्द एव विजयते।।
अहिंसैव परमो धर्मः।।

आनन्दसूत्रे शिष्योपदेशः।

Advice To The Disciple

O Disciple! Whatever calamity may befall you, do not give way to the despair that such things fall to your lot, in spite of your propitiation of bliss (God), and thus give you your devotion and practice. Because, adversity is really one's best friend and illustrious Guru. To explain. However much those rolling in luxury and affluence, without any thought about God, are addressed and advised with the support of Sastras, that they should think of God, they would pay no heed at all. But when such persons are exposed to any calamity, they would cry out, 'O Lord! O my God!', and then begin to worship God too. As such, is not that calamity their friend and illustrious Guru that reminded them of God? Did not they remain at first indifferent to and heedless of the advice of the illustrious Guru, even on pointing out the text of Sastras that they should remember Him? It is indeed adversity that has led even such persons to the worship of God. If, in this worldly existence, a man were to be accomplishing all his desired objects, according to his likes, he would never retrace from that worldliness. It is only when adversity befalls men that they would try to turn away from their worldly attachments. Therefore, adversity is a great friend to turn you away, from worldliness, and lead you to bliss. Fools laugh at the man saying, "what is the use of his worship of God ! Was he able to prevent the calamity that has befallen him? He is said to be a yogi. If he has the grace of God, will he have to suffer thus? He is indeed a false yogi" and so on. You should not be sorry on that score. Who is there that does not meet with any adversity at all? Did not the Pandavas, Nala, Rama, Gods and others, suffer from adversity? Pandavas and others were kings. They were all very very powerful, good and illustrious men, great devotees of God, and they were said to be objects of grace of God too. Where is that enviable state of theirs !

Where is their other pitiable state, when they had to pass their days in the forest like the tribes therein, and when they had to go a begging for alms, keeping their mother in the potter's hut ! We see from the Puranas that even those high souls had to suffer from extreme adversities, that might not have been the lot of even those who indulged in the performance of despicable deeds. We see even today many an adversity befalling the high-souled Mahatmas. It is only the man of little intelligence that would condemn them as not Mahatmas or high souls on that account. If it is asked, if adversity befalls also the great Mahatmas, how they are superior to the laymen of the world, it is answered as follows:-

They will never do harm to others. If at all, they do anything that will be only for the benefit of others. When adversity befalls them, they will think as follows: "Why feel sorry about this? Who can stop the course of Time? Will the adversity disappear, if felt sorry over it? Is it not the nature of the worldly layman to feel sorry? Is it not the virtue of the great to remain calm and unperturbed, without any change extremely aggrieved. On the other hand, the high souled great ones would think in another way as follows: "What is the use of entertaining hopes and desires in worldly objects? This earth was ruled over by many a mighty king, exulting in pride as `my kingdom', with great army, all paraphernalia of royalty, and the glory of all prosperity, where are all of them today? Did this earth accompany them in their death? How many do die even now? We do not see anything of theirs accompanying them. Should they not go with them, if they were really theirs. Let it be that they do not accompany them in their death. When a man suffers from any great disease, can his sons and relations share his affliction even for a short time, and give him relief? That is also not possible. Let that also be. If he desires to live in all happiness and prosperity at least till his death, in the company of his wife, children, friends and relations, is he sure of accomplishing that desire too? No. In the general course of time, everything courts destruction, and then result sorrow and misery". Thus thinking, the great ones will not entertain any high hopes or desires on worldly objects like the worldly laymen, and expose themselves to self-wrought calamities, and then suffer extreme misery, or feel aggrieved on any score. They will never be elated when they are favoured by fortune. They will never do harm to others. If at all, they do anything that will be only for the benefit of others. When adversity befalls them, they will think as follows: "Why feel sorry about this? Who can stop the course of Time? Will the adversity disappear, if felt sorry over it? Is it not the nature of the worldly layman to feel sorry? Is it not the virtue of the great to remain calm and unperturbed, without any change of mind or emotion even when exposed to grief, anger or any such passion that would naturally produce a flutter of the mind? If both the mountain and the tree equally shake when the storm blows, what is the superiority of the mountain over the tree?" Thus thinking, they will remain undaunted and firm, like unto a mountain. They will not feel aggrieved like the worldly. When they have to accomplish anything they will not, like the worldly, be moved by lust, desire, anger and the like passions. When an actor plays the part of a character, he displays in his acting the various sentiments of love, grief, the terrific and so on, that would excite like emotion in the mind of the audience too. Yet at that time, he is not really possessed of any such sentiment regarding himself. Likewise the great who, in the stage of this worldly existence, act with a show of the sentiments of love and so forth only to carry out their desired objects, do not in fact undergo any real modification of the mind. Further, as the mind of a lover is ever after the object of his love, even though he be engaged in his duties, so also the mind of the great is ever drawn to the bliss experienced within, even in the midst of their daily routine just as some clever persons deliver lectures, and function in other ways, with all, zeal and delight, under the influence of a moderate dose of liquor or any other intoxicant, the great ones carry out their objects, indulging in the dose of bliss supreme. And the marvellous bliss that is had in Samadhi or super conscious state of the mind is indeed indescribable. Thus thought over, the state of those great who are emancipated in this life itself while alive, is verily extraordinary. O Disciple ! Do remain in that firm state itself. Therefore even though beset with calamities one after another, even though the whole world may laugh at you and denounce you, your mind should remain steady and unperturbed, like the steady flame of a lamp kept in place where no wind flows. It should remain motionless, like the ocean without the wave. The mind should not be disturbed and sullied. In the disturbed water, the disc of the sun will not be seen reflected. Likewise, in the disturbed mind, the luminary of bliss will not shine out too. The mind should always be cheerful. Then, as sun in the clear water, bliss will always, shine in the mind. Know that your mind has become pure when you are not in the habit of feeling any ill-will towards those who do you any harm. If you seem to feel to entertain any such ill-will towards them, know that your mind has not become pure, and try to purify it. You are not to grow reverse to those who are not well disposed towards you. When the palate or tongue is overpowered by tastelessness, even the sumptuous meal, with savoury dishes, will but be distasteful. That disease of distastefulness has to be cured by treatment, and it is not becoming to get angry with the cooks for it. If you remain in the state of bliss, what can belittle you even if the world were to condemn you? If you are pleased and contented with a hearty meal, will hunger pinch you even if the whole world were to say that you are suffering from starvation without any means for maintenance? No. On the contrary, when you suffer extreme misery on account of dire starvation without any means for even a single meal in reality, will your hunger be satisfied if the world were to say that you are happy with a full and sumptuous meal? Therefore there is no defeat or harm to you at the censure of others, nor any gain at their praise about you. As such to be moved by the censure or praise of another is to be concluded to be but a defect of your mind and that mind alone has to be purified always. On the score of cleanliness or handsomeness, some take to daily shave and do not allow any hair to sprout. To attain beauty or purity of the mind, you should take to a daily shave of the mind. To explain. Whenever the poisonous creepers of love, hatred and the like passions sprout in your mind, they should be pruned then and there with the weapon of jnana Sastra. Even though the evils are being thus cleared, they will never be completely eradicated. To get them completely annihilated the mind should get absorbed. To be thus absorbed, the mind has to be incessantly united unto bliss. Only when the mind is thus able to be united unto bliss, it will be able to remain steady and motionless, like the steady flame of a lamp kept in a place where no wind blows, or like the calm ocean with all the waves therein fully subsided. Then only, it will be possible to live the routine life, exulting in bliss too. Does not water taste sweet if taken after eating the myrobalan fruit? Does not the hard earth strewn with pebbles and stones appear to be a downy bed to a man under intoxication? The bubble that rises up from the water, has its dissolution in the water itself. Likewise, the mind, born of bliss, has its dissolution in bliss alone. That dissolution or absorption of the mind in bliss, is verily salvation. That is real monism. That is Rajayoga. That is the attainment of bliss everlasting.

It is said as follows in Brahmajnana Tantra:

"मनः करोति कर्माणि मनो लिम्पति पातकैः।
मनश्च उन्मनीभूत्वा मुच्यते सर्वपातकैः।।

"It is the mind that does actions. It is the mind that is contaminated by the sinful deeds. When that mind is dissolved, one becomes released from all sins, and attains bliss".

We see the following in Brahmabindupanishad:

1. निरस्तविषयासङ्गं संनिरुद्धं मनो हृदि।
यदा यात्युन्मनीभावं तदा तत्परमं पदम्।।

2. तावदेव निरोद्धव्यं यावत् हृदि गतं क्षयम्।
एतत् ज्ञानं च मोक्षश्च अतोऽन्यो ग्रन्थविस्तरः।।

These mean respectively:

1. "When the mind, concentrated in the heart is restrained from running after worldly objects of pleasure, and gets absorbed, then is had that supreme state of bliss".

2. The mind has got to be restrained in the heart, so long as it gets absorbed in bliss. This absorption of the mind is verily jnana and moksha (salvation). To dwell at length on that path which gives up the absorption of the mind through restraint, is but useful to enlarge the treatise. It is indeed a waste of time. I have already mentioned herein, in the chapter on the 'the greatness of Yoga', that Yoga is verily the restraint of the mind. The above texts establish that jnana and moksha are had through that yoga alone.

Disciple: O Swamin ! Some ask as follows: "We take the photo of our father or our Guru, and keep it, and after they are dead, we look at them, are pleased, and we pay our respectful homage to them. Likewise it is, that the image of God is installed in temples and worshipped. If not, how can those poor in intelligence, and children, understand that there is a God?

Guru: O Disciple? Is it by installing idols of stone that

Christians, Muhammedans and others, instil the idea of God in those of poor intelligence and in the children among them? Can we say, because they do not instal idols that they have no idea or thought of God, or there are no devotees or jnanis in their midst?

Disciple: They have churches and mosques.

Guru: Well. If, necessary, let us also have buildings for congregational worship. Let those be called temples too. Let lectures on the truth about God be delivered therein and explained to the audience. Let spiritual instruction be imparted therein to foster the virtues of equality, calmness, pity, truthfulness and so forth, and to give up the evils of love, hatred and the like. Let there be therein spiritual discourses on God head. We are to create and disseminate knowledge through these ways. But, on the other hand, what are now taught in temples, are such ignorant lessons, as would mislead even the man of poor intelligence and children, that there are many Gods as instanced by the several idols installed therein, that they, like unto gluttons, would be pleased with the offerings of porridge and so forth, and, like unto those of poor intelligence and children, they would find pleasure in the beating of drums and in the display of fireworks, that, God would bless His devotees by their carrying out those idols in procession with all the paraphernalia of umbrella, cowries, a big retinue and so forth, like those priding in rank, title and status, that He would, like a corrupt judge, do them good by their vows and the like, that He would be pleased by His devotees wearing wet clothes, taking to fasting wearing the sacred thread and dressing in the ceremonial way. Such observances tend but to the ruin of men and loss of wealth. What a great pity is this ! It is no wonder that the descendants of those ritualists, who in former days exultingly indulged in those condemnable practices, like *Sutti* (burning alive of the widow along with her deceased husband) and human sacrifices, should put out the eye of knowledge. Yet it is a great pity that in these days when men are becoming more civilised and cultured under the benign administration of the British Government, people are led to ignorant practices to the loss of their wealth of knowledge and money. It is indeed but the misfortune of the Hindus that none has raised the revolt to put a stop to the management of the family head of ritualism and his agents, as they have done against the old evil practices of *Sutti* and the like, and have put a stop to them. O Disciple! What else did you say? Like the photos of the father and the Guru, that are preserved and worshipped in house in great joy, the photo of God is worshipped in the idols in the temple. What a wonder ! The photos of the father and the Guru are taken as they were actually seen in flesh and blood in their living state. Those photos have their shape and form. But God has no form. Then how was His photo taken? Who was the photographer? Is that the photo of God what we see engraved or carved on stones and the like, by those architects of idols and others?

Disciple: Yes. That is verily the belief of Acharyas and others. Is it not on account of that belief that they are installed and consecrated with the religious ceremonies of Prana Prathishta and Jiva Prathista?

Guru: O Disciple ! The two ceremonies mentioned above refer to the giving of Prana and Jiva, i.e., the vital breath and soul respectively.

Disciple: O Swamin ! Then how is it that the idol does neither walk, nor speak, nor eat the porridge and the like offered in worship?

Guru: If one is able to give Prana and Jiva, a dead body can as well be brought back to life by giving them to that also. Then the installers of idols, who give such Prana and Jiva, can readily make a lot of money by the revitalisation of the dead body. Should one seek after money and respectability by taking to the installation of idols? Not only thus much. Those installers of idols can themselves ever remain immortal too, by instilling Prana and Jiva into themselves.

Disciple: Swamin ! O realised Guru ! O Destroyer of the demon of ritualism. I bow down to you. Salutation unto you, the destroyer of the disease of the leprosy of caste distinctions. I prostrate unto you, the sun that dispels the darkness of ignorance. I bow down to you who have grasped the gist of Aryan religion. Salutation unto you, the reformer of Aryan religion. All respect and homage to you, the illuminator of the state of bliss Salutation.

Guru: O Disciple ! Be steadfast in bliss. Be steadfast in bliss. Be steadfast in bliss.

F

आनन्द एव विजयते।।
अहिंसैव परमो धर्मः।।

आनन्दगीता।।
The Song of Bliss
(A prose version)

1. Of what avail are Sastras and jnana to him who is united unto the power of bliss - Of what avail are Sastras and jnana?

2. What for is the desire for gold to him who has seen the resplendent power of sparkling Kundalini - What for is the desire for gold?

3. The three worlds are but a trash to him who remains in the thought of that Sakti supreme - The three worlds are but a trash.

4. Why the necessity of Vedas to see the Atman (bliss) by the incessant hearing of Nada or sound - Why the necessity of Vedas?

5. Should the eye take to the study of the Vedas and Sastras that it might see the sun - To see the sun?

6. Should the tongue be well versed in the Sastra of logic that it might taste the sweetness of sugar - should be well versed in the Sastra of logic?

7. Is there the necessity of astronomy to see the luminary within and remain in ecstasy of joy - Is there the necessity of astronomy?

8. Is there the necessity of Rig Veda to be united unto bliss within oneself - Is there the necessity of Rig Veda?

9. Should one study Sama Veda to be united unto an object of pleasure - Should one study Sama Veda?

10. Are the Vedas of Yajus and Atharva necessary to see the Atman - to see the Atman?

11. Should even the dull be equipped with the knowledge of Sastra to enjoy the pleasure of sexual union - Should even the dull be equipped with the knowledge of Sastra?

12. Likewise, to enjoy the bliss of communion with Atman, are Agamas (the sacred scriptures) and the like necessary - Are Agamas and the like, necessary?

13. The Veda dins in Gokarna. Who in the world knows that Veda - Who in the world knows it?

14. Of what use are sacrifices and the like rituals to exult in the ecstasy of Yogic path - Of what use are sacrifices and the like rituals?

15. Why the desire for earth for him whose eyes are cast towards the heaven alone - Why the desire for earth?

16. Why the Vedic rituals to exult in the immaculate Atman - why the rituals?

17. Should one go to Kasi to live peacefully in the true Kasi - Should one go to Kasi?

18. The real Kasi shines or flourishes between the nerves Ida and Pingala - there it flourishes.

19. Of what use is the fair sex for him who sees and exults in the bliss within - of what use is the fair sex?

20. Of what use are ganja and liquor for him who drinks the liquor of bliss within - of what use are ganja and liquor?

21. What for is the life of Sanyasa or renunciation to see the light within oneself - what for is the life of Sanyasa?

22. Why the necessity of Vedanta to exult in the union with the radiance, during the experience of Yogic nada - why the necessity of Vedanta?

23. What for are the impenetrable jungle and the mountain cave, to be united unto the grave - what for the impenetrable jungle?

24. Will the deer feeding upon the grass and plants in the jungle, ever have the absorption of the mind - will ever have the absorption of the mind?

25. What for is the meditation of a Personal form to exult in bliss supreme - what for is the meditation?

26. Why the necessity of contemplation at all when the mind always looks at Atman - why the necessity of contemplation?

27. What for is listening, to hear with the ear the initial sound of the mystic Pranava (Aum) - what for is listening?

28. Of what avail is the import of maxims to exult in bliss, looking at the tip of the nose - of what avail is the import of maxims?

29. Why resort to the wearing of the sacred thread of cotton to see the invisible thread - why resort to the wearing of the sacred thread of cotton?

30. That is the sacred thread wherein are strung all that are visible - that is the sacred thread.

31. Those who do not know of that thread, which cannot, if tried, be broken are simpletons - verily simpletons.

32. In that string all the worlds remain strung, as unto gems of a garland in a string - as unto gems of a garland in a string.

33. He who has known of that inner sacred thread, is the ever blissful, and the Brahmin.

34. Is any effort necessary to wear the sacred thread of cotton - is any effort necessary?

35. Why the necessity of wearing the Rudraksha beads to worship Rudra, of the nature chit (energy)- why the necessity of Rudraksha beads?

36. Why the smearing with ashes to see the mark on the forehead - why the smearing with ashes?

37. If salvation is had by smearing the body with ashes, the dog lies ever in the ash-heap-lies ever in the ash-heap.

38. Of what use is the tuft, fore and back, to him who has seen the root of hair - of what use is that tuft?

39. The freaks of those who have not known the real tuft, are indeed pitiable - are indeed pitiable.

40. None of them are real Sikhis (having tufts) who keep a tuft of hair on the forepart or hind part of the head - None of them are real Sikhis.

41. He is the real tufted, the blessed, who has the sikha or tuft of jnana, as flame is unto fire - He is the real tufted, the blessed.

42. What for is the matted hair for him who has seen the wonders of the Sushumna or central nerve - what for is the matted hair?

43. Of what use of beard and the tuft to him who reigns supreme, exulting in the Supreme - of what use is the beard?

44. Of what use is the complete shaving of the head to him who has seen the dance of kundalini in kulamarga (Sushumna) - of what use is the complete shaving?

45. Of what use is the deer-skin (to be seated upon) to exult in the ecstasy of the knowledge of one's own self - of what use is that deer-skin?

46. Of what use is the leopard's skin to see the equality in the leopard and the cat - of what use is the leopard's skin?

47. The dead body is said to be impure. How can the skin of that dead animal become pure? How can that become pure?

48. Those who wear the skin of animals, are indeed sinners that cause the death of those animals - those who wear the skin of animals.

49. Will one see the Atman by taking Kashaya, (ochreous robe), stick and the mendicants' bowl - will one see the Atman?

50. Is the ochreous robe necessary to get the mind absorbed without seeing the bliss with naked eyes - Is the ochreous robe necessary?

51. Of what use is the mendicants' wand to keep the eyes without winking in the target within - of what use is the mendicant's wand?

52. Of what use is the mendicant's wand to keep the mind rivetted in the ether with eyes closed - of what use is the mendicant's wand?

53. Can we see the One Supreme if we wear but a single cloth - can we see the One Supreme?

54. Can we see the One eternal even it we shamelessly remain naked without any dress - can we see the One eternal?

55. Is the Lord, a fool to be deluded by garb - is the Lord a fool?

56. Of what use are the diverse garbs for the illustrious man who is steady of mind - of what use are the diverse garbs?

57. The garb may help to feed the belly. The garb will not help to see the Full Supreme - will not help to see the Full Supreme.

58. Great indeed is the benefit to men by the garb of jnani - great indeed is the benefit to men.

59. Many are put to distress by the garb of the ignorant (without jnana) - many are put to distress.

60. Why the necessity of gross fire for him who has burnt down his sin in the fire on the forehead - why the necessity of gross fire?

61. Of what use is the slaughter of animals in sacrifices to unite the Cow of mind with the Lord (bliss) - of what use is the slaughter of animals in sacrifices?

62. Will the Bliss Supreme feed upon dead body, like foxes and dogs - will the Bliss Supreme feed upon?

63. Does the God beg of the sacrificial priests in the eager desire for meat - does the God beg?

64. Those who look upon all alike as unto themselves, will never to harm to others - will never do harm to others.

65. There is no merit like unto pity, no sin like unto doing harm - no sin like unto doing harm.

66. The man who kills the animal in sacrifice, without understanding what the real animal is that is to be slaughtered, is but like unto an animal, a sinner - like unto an animal, a sinner.

67. Of what use are the idols and the mystic circles (like Sreechakra etc.) to concentrate the mind in the triangle (trikona or Sushumna) - of what use is the mystic circle?

68. Of what use are the temples to worship the God of the temple of body - of what use are the temples?

69. Of what use are flowers to worship God when there is the flower of heart - of what use are flowers?

70. When there is the temple that is not built, why should people build temples - why should people build temples?

71. When there is the idol that is not installed, people instal idols - people instal idols.

72. When there is the circle that is not drawn, people draw mystic circles to worship God - people draw mystic circles.

73. Giving up the temple wherein dins the Yogic sound, without the beating of any drum, people suffer - giving up, people suffer.

74. It is verily that temple that is to be known, wherein burns the lamp eternally - It is verily that temple that is to be known.

75. In that temple shine for ever the luminaries of sun, moon and so forth - shine for ever in that temple.

76. In that temple sparkle lightning ether and the stars - in the temple sparkle.

77. In that temple are the five ethers, clouds and thunders - in that temple there are.

78. There are also the self resounding Vedic chanting and songs - There also the songs.

79. There are also the sounds of conch, harp, flute and

kettledrums, and poles for fireworks - there are also poles for fireworks.

80. In that temple abide divine sages, realised, released and all - in that temple abide.

81. If only that temple of the One supreme is entered, there will be eternal bliss, unalloyed - there will be bliss unalloyed.

82. What is the use of the earthly Gokarn to him who hears the Veda in his own Gokarna - of what use is the earthly Gokarn?

83. Of what use is the earthly Kaladi (the birth place of Sankaracharya to him who has seen the foot print (root) of Sat (existence) - of what use is the earthly Kaladi?

84. The ignorant runs out to the earthly Kaladi to roll in misery -runs out to the earthly Kaladi.

85. To see the All-pervading Supreme, should one go any where - should one go anywhere?

86. Will those be ever Aryans who go to Kasi to see the sun-will those be ever Aryans?

87. Will he, who has seen the temple of body ever roam about like a dog for salvation - will he who has seen the temple of body?

88. Should one go to the Himalayas to see the All-embracing Supreme that reigns in the heart - should one go to the Himalayas?

89. If one were to see in one's own temple of body the pole of fireworks, the Supreme lustre, will there be any unsteadiness of mind - will there be any unsteadiness of mind?

90. Of what use is the plunge in the holy waters to him who is immersed in the holy water of bliss - of what use is the plunge?

91. Why the bath in the Ganges and the like, to remove the dirt of the mind - why the bath?

92. The minds of those living by the holy waters, are seen to be impure - are seen to be impure.

93. The plunge in the waters, of the Ganges and the like, may conduce to remove the dirt of the body - the plunge in the holy waters may conduce.

94. Will the mind of the fishes living always in the water, become pure - will the mind become pure?

95. Will fasting conduce to any happiness except several diseases - will fasting conduce to any happiness?

96. Alas ! People deluded in the glamour of vows, roll in misery - roll in misery.

97. Why the necessity of rituals to remain exulting in ecstasy in the inward steadiness of mind - why the necessity of rituals?

98. Verily it is the ignorant that offer worship to the idols - offer worship to the idols.

99. Alas ! A great infatuation ! A great wonder ! Will the idol partake of the food offered as offering, will it speak - a great infatuation ! A great wonder !

100. When one exults in the path of the head (the Sushumna end) one will never wish to offer worship and the like - one will never wish.

101. Will any one who takes milk porridge, ever hanker after the rotten gruel - will ever hanker after?

102. The man deluded in ritualism, will never attain bliss eternal by birth - will never attain bliss by birth.

103. Are the postures of cock, lion and the like, necessary to attain the state of Hamsa (the realised) - are the postures of the lion and the like necessary?

104. Is the posture of lotus necessary to see the Power or Sakti in the thousand spoked lotus - is the posture of lotus necessary?

105. Is the posture of Siddhasana necessary to keep the mind steady in the spot of realisation - is the posture of Siddhasana necessary?

106. Is the posture of tortoise necessary to unite the mind unto the vital part - is the posture of tortoise necessary?

107. Why the necessity of Swastika posture, to keep the mind in itself - why the necessity of Swastika?

108. That is verily the right posture, wherein the mind remains always steady in bliss - that is verily the right posture.

109. Surely those postures that are lacking in it, are inferior- are inferior.

110. Should the tongue be cut to keep the mind in the Lord- should the tongue be cut?

111. That is indeed the sign Khechari wherein the mind moves in ether - that is Khechari Mudra.

112. Almost all go to ruin by taking up to rituals leading to misery - almost all go to ruin.

113. Enamoured of the extremely hot blazing fire, the moths seek their grave therein - seek their grave therein.

114. Will he, who knows the real truth, ever take to rituals like sacrifices and the like, for the sake of purity of the mind or salvation - will he ever take to?

115. People take to rituals, seeing the false Sastras - people take to rituals.

116. Jnana or knowledge will dawn within one, if it is meditated 'Who I am' Jnana will dawn.

117. None will then be deluded in rituals - bliss indeed bliss, bliss.

118. The man of knowledge will never say that the ignorant rituals are the stepping stone - the man of knowledge will never say.

119. To drink milk, should one first take liquor - should one first take liquor?

120. To drink water, should one first take toddy - should one first take toddy?

121. To eat food, should one first practise the taking of poison-should one first practise the taking of poison?

122. To attain spiritual knowledge, should one first take to the ignorant ritualistic practices - should one first take to the ignorant ritualistic practices?

123. To look at the light of the sun, should one first practise looking at the dense darkness - to look at the light of the sun?

124. To speak truth, should one practise daily the speaking of falsehood - should one practise daily?

125. Is it not, like unto these, that the practice of miserable rituals, is the first block against salvation - the practice of miserable rituals?

126. Even if the real meaning of the word 'mukti' is known, none will take up to miserable rituals - none will take up to miserable rituals.

127. Will the Vedantin who looks upon the world as unreal, go to temple - will he go to temple?

128. Will the Vedantin who knows Brahma to be himself, ever take up to rituals, and be miserable - will ever take up to rituals, and be miserable?

129. The Vedantin will never take to the miserable rituals of worship, vow and the like - will never take to the miserable rituals.

130. The knowledge about bliss is spoken of as jnana - is spoken of as jnana.

131. They esteem that as Yoga, whereby is had the union unto bliss - they esteem that as Yoga.

132. They speak of that as Mukti or salvation wherein on is released from misery - they speak of that as Mukti.

133. They condemn rituals since they lead to misery - they condemn rituals.

134. All ritualistic practices, whether performed in a spirit of disinterestedness or interestedly, are miserable - all are miserable.

135. To preserve the body, take to the necessary action without any delusion - without any delusion.

136. It is this body that is the ship to take one across the ocean of worldly existence - It is this body.

137. Without knowing the truth, millions and millions of people become prey unto death - become prey unto death.

138. Alas ! The vain glorious Acharyas and false texts lead people to misery - lead people to misery.

139. If the characteristic of mouna or silence is, not to speak, the dumb does not speak. Can he be a mouni - does not speak? Can he be a mouni?

140. Silence does not become of a jnani. It is becoming a child-it is becoming a child.

141. If the mind becomes absorbed in bliss, that becomes the highly esteemed mouna - becomes the highly esteemed mouna or silence.

142. Mouna or silence of the mind is really jnana, Yoga, and salvation - silence of the mind is really.

143. People suffer misery owing to condemnable practices, and never get united unto bliss - never get united unto bliss.

144. Why the necessity of rituals to enter the celestial abode of bliss - why the necessity of rituals?

145. What other ecstasy of joy is there is this world for him who exults in ecstasy in Dwadasanta - (the end of Sushumna) what other ecstasy of joy is there in this world?

146. Of what use is sovereignty to him who exults in the bliss of Rajayoga - of what use is sovereignty?

147. Of what use is the lordship of Gods to him, who has seen, in the dot within, the region of sun and the like - of what use is the lordship of Gods?

148. Is there any other covetable high position for him, who has attained the void - is there any other covetable high position.

149. People fall into misery, deluded in rank, status, name and the superiority of caste - people fall into misery.

150. He who sets high value on caste distinctions, is verily one who knows not his own caste - one who knows not his own caste.

151. He is indeed devoid of knowledge, who wards of another as of low caste - he is indeed devoid of knowledge.

152. Bliss is my caste, bliss is my father, bliss is my mother - bliss is my mother.

153. I am not another different. I am verily Ananda. Am I not the child of bliss - am I not the child of bliss?

154. Ananda is that Sakti or Power. That Sakti is my God. That Sakti is the All-God - that Sakti is the All-God.

155. We should all be united unto that Sakti of Ananda. We should all be united unto that caste of Ananda - we of the caste of bliss.

156. Bliss, indeed Bliss, Ananda, verily Anand. How shall I describe - what shall I say?

O mind ! Be united unto bliss. If you hanker after the worldly objects of pleasure, your lot will be misery - O mind ! Be united unto bliss.

1. Don't hanker in the least after earth or gold or woman. If you but always look into the ether, alas ! None can describe your bliss.

2. If you hanker after mystic powers, you will reap misery, but not bliss. Aim always at salvation. You should consider that as the virtuous action of merit.

3. Is it not on account of eager desire that you hanker after mystic powers? Desire is the seed of distress. If you entertain a little of it at least, you will suffer great misery.

4. Not only that. On account of that fond desire, you will

become a prey to all evils, like love, hatred and so forth. You will be led to the great fire of misery, and be burnt down to ashes.

5. Even though you are possessed of great wealth even though your friends and others be close by you, they are not able to prevent your death when it comes. Do not be attached to anything.

6. O mind ! If the world were to inflict harm on you, do not feel aggrieved thereby, and thus hate them in ignorance. Think of the One Supreme anon, and attain the bliss everlasting.

7. If your kith and kin were to forsake, do not be aggrieved thereby in the least, but rejoice extremely. Kith and kin and others are great bondages.

8. Be of cheer always and in all situations. Cheer is the supreme good. Alas ! Cheer is indeed bliss supreme, and that cheer is had through calmness.

9. Even if faced with great adversity, remain always undaunted and firm like a mountain. Even if death were near at hand, do not be perturbed, but remain shining like the moon.

10. O mind ! Who is there free from death? Who in the world is free from adversity? Sri Rama, Pandavas, Nala - are they insignificant figures? Did they not come by their death too?

11. How many did rule over this earth in the past? How many great men were there in the past? All of them are gone. What room then for any change or perturbation of mind?

12. Let there be prosperity or adversity. Let there be death, dotage and the like O mind ! Without any flinching whatsoever, face your days bravely.

13. O Mind, that is verily bravery, and that is how the brave have acted when faced with extreme joy or sorrow, it is but the cowards that are moved.

14. Never take to the company of the worldly. Never incur a little of sin at least. Do not run away to Kasi and other places. Know that real Kasi is at the end of the Sushumna nerve.

15. When the Lord is verily within the body some go out, seeking after Him, to all places. Do not run about like that. Look at the Lord who is always to be known, within yourself.

16. To see the sky, should one go to Kasi and other places? Do not be deluded seeing the mad pranks of the world, and meet your death in such running about. Be always steady.

17. O mind ! Don't be troubled. If you but remain in your own steadiness, you will always enjoy bliss supreme, and well never fall into the well of worldly existence.

18. What it the world praise you are respect you? O mind ! They will never affect you to take you to the region of bliss.

19. What is fame to you? What is affluence to you ! What of Kingdom? If your desires are to be destroyed, look at the Atman always, controlling all your desires.

20. O mind ! What of being a poet? What if you conquer the world by your lectures. If you should be free from distress, O mind ! Control your thoughts, and get yourself absorbed in sat (existence).

21. What if you live in the forest? O mind ! What if you be a judge presiding in a court of law? What if you be a king? All in vain, if you do not see the abode of Atman.

22. Whether the world praise you or abuse you, welcome them all in joy. Never be moved by anything O mind ! Remain always in your own steadiness.

23. Why, O mind ! any distress? Listen, you are verily the child of bliss. Give up the low worldly existence. Then O mind ! You can rightly reign in bliss.

24. O mind ! Do not be running about hither and thither, and be deluded and infatuated. Then, O mind ! You can always remain immersed in that bliss complete.

25. Come. O mind ! Don't run anywhere. Enter you soon your own home of bliss. Who then can be equal unto you in the world? Enough of your wandering.

26. O mind ! Don't run after the external objects. Go to the light within, and be always exulting in bliss. Don't waste your time in vain. O mind ! Give up all the evils of love, hatred and the like, completely.

27. O mind ! Love, hatred and the like will make you run, will take you to the well of worldly misery. Never keep company, O mind ! With love, hatred and the like. Be united unto bliss.

28. If, as you run after things not essential, you run after things that are essential, you can easily cross the ocean of worldly existence, and be immersed in the mid ocean of bliss.

29. To crush a flower, O mind, a little effort is needed. The

hand is to be moved. But to grasp the Supreme truth, you need not move at all.

30. No need of water, frankincense, flowers and the like, nor should you collect fruits, roots and the like, nor prepare any offering of food. Nor is there any need for men, or for a bath in water, nor for fasting. If you remain steady in your target of Atman, that indeed, O mind ! Is real worship?

31. There is no necessity, O mind ! Of Mulabandha and the like, nor any special time, nor the restraint of Prana the Vital breath. Give up your nature of unsteadiness, and get yourself absorbed in the goal of bliss. Then you come by yoga and jnana.

32. Whether walking or standing, whether lying or seated comfortably, keep yourself, O mind ! Always steadfast, without any break, in the goal in the Sushumna never.

33. The world wander about without knowing the path. If, on even knowing that path, you are to grope about, know you, O mind ! that you are indeed a greater food than the host of great fools.

34. Assuming the garb of the Sanyasin, O mind ! You too should not deceive others. Know that there is one God who will see the unrighteousness. Who can blind His eyes?

35. What difficulty is there to deceive the world? Smearing the whole body with ashes, keep mum like a dumb, and the world will praise you as a great mouni (one taken to the vow of silence).

36. By remaining firm with closed eyes in the posture Veerasana and the like, people will respect and worship you in great joy, as a brave great Yogi.

37. Keeping the fire kindled in front and seated close to it, people will bow down to you, O mind ! as a great Jnani, and will offer you milk and fruits as their offerings.

38. Installing idols, O mind ! and offering worship thereto, the world will praise you as a Jnani, and pay reverence to you as an Acharya, and give you presents of money.

39. When there is in yourself the thing to satisfy your hunger, alas ! Why should you, for the sake of earning money, take to a garb, and deceive the world?

40. If there is no sufficient money in your possession, you can take to manual labour and maintain your body. Should you resort to unbrighteous deeds? There is one to see everything.

41. Money earned by robbery or by illegal means, will never accompany you in your death. Then why should you take up to unrighteous deeds. Man should shun the ghost of desires.

42. If you entertain any desire, however small, for another's wealth, that is equal to theft. That is what the great seers have declared in Yoga Sastras. Who knows it?

43. If you cause any pain to beings, that is verily said to be equal to the killing of beings. Even in actually killing animals, people are not afraid of that truth.

44. If there is a chance to come by money, the wealthy and the learned too, will not hesitate to cut the throat of the victim with a knife. What wonder then that others resort to it !

45. Let all these be. O mind ! If truth is spoken, people, will take you to task. Enter you, through the path of the Sushumna nerve, your abode of bliss, and exult therein.

46. Which is superior, O mind ! Whether bliss infinite and full, or the worldly objects of pleasure that tend to pain and misery? Think of this but once a day, and then you will not fall into the well of worldly misery.

47. Do not hanker after respect from others, O mind ! When you become an object of respect, along with it comes that egotism. Don't feel angry, O mind ! When subjected to abuse. Abuse is like unto nectar to you.

48. O mind ! Don't believe the world, but keep faith in the string of the worlds (string where in all the worlds are strung up i.e., in bliss). Then all your misery will cease completely. Then is had salvation, and that is bliss eternal.

49. O mind ! that is verily the holy stage of life, since the realised reign supreme in that (bliss). It goes by the name of Siddhasana too. It is the cause for realisation and salvation.

50. That is your Asrama (holy stage) O mind ! Seek refuge in that Asrama. That is bliss eternal. O mind ! There is no other place for rest or refuge.

51. Some exult or pride in prosperity. Their mind does not move in the right path. Seeing always O mind the light within, may you go up soaring or dancing higher and higher.

52. Direct your inner vision to the root or sacred seat of the nose the (Anandasthana) then you can conquer even the mighty

Yama (God of death). You will see marvels in the third sacred eye in between the eye-brows and can plunge deep in the surging bliss.

53. O mind ! Listen always to the pealing sound of the bell (heard within). Listen to it with rapt attention without any faltering or failure in the least. That, the initial of Pranava (the mystic syllable Aum) will lead you safe to your abode of bliss.

54. O mind ! is not that your very experience. Then why should you indulge in composing poems? Does that Sakti impel you again to take up to that, in order to benefit the world?

Fifteen

Anandadarsamsam

(A Little Mirror To See The Eternal Bliss In Us)

1. युक्त्यानन्दानुभूत्याच मदुक्तंखराडयेतसुधीः।
श्रुत्वाचारैरयुक्तैर्मामाज्ञोप्तुमबलाप्यलम्।।

I would welcome criticisms from men of culture it they are based on reason and experience; but I give no consideration to wholesale condemnation merely based on Vedic texts and blind traditions. To fling at my face all the scriptures sanctioning caste-system, idol worship and observance of religious rites, and to say "These have been observed from time immemorial. Here is a man who contravenes them; he ought to be ostracised; etc." Is nothing heroic. For, even a mere woman (a weak and ignorant being) may do it. Those who would criticise me should demonstrate by facts and figures that the religious rites and ceremonies, and distinctions of race and religion are conducive to harmony, peace and happiness. Types of criticisms contrawise are mentioned in the third chapter.

2. समीक्ष्यसर्ववस्तु निस्वीकुर्वन्तीष्टवस्तुयत्।
असमीक्ष्यमतंकस्मात् संगृहन्तीनृपाअपि।।

Men as a rule accept things only after test, but how is it that even great rulers follow religion without any critical examination? If sovereigns demand that religions should establish their claims before they are accepted, that religion alone which is supported by reason and experience would survive. People as a rule follow their and rulers, where the latter are strict and critical with regard to religions, the former also refuse to accept any thing that does not stand the test of reason. This would create a spirit of tolerance, and persecution for differences of religion would be a thing unknown. Often has it happened that when some people, convinced of the truth of my teachings, chose to accept them and become my disciples, their orthodox kinsmen subjected them to social ostracisms, which, more often than not, obliged them to recant and return to the old fold with reluctant and disappointed hearts. On such occasions, I feel poignantly my inability to give them help or protection. Such things cannot happen if the heads of society are rational and inculcate rationalism in the members thereof. By this I should not be understood as advocating that those in power should force their opinions on persons under them. My only desire is that my teachings should be given a fair trial. In these days of religious strifes people should see whether my teachings contain truth, reason and experience which alone will lead them to a life of harmony and happiness. In almost all matters people do nothing without testing. The Government conducts elaborate examinations to recruit officers, who are to be in charge of the administration of the country. Even the man in the street carefully examines an article before he actually purchases it. No one buys gold without actually testing it on the touch-stone. Even the greatest devotee of God does not indiscriminately accept for his food every thing of His creations, but makes a careful selection from among them. For, do we not see that when he gets a piece of sugarcane he sucks in only the juice and throws away the rind and the fibre ? This instinctive law of selection operates even in the insect world. Offer a mixture of sand and sugar to the ant and it carefully selects and picks up only the particles of sugar in it leaving the grains of sand severely alone. Thus though the operation of this law of selection seems to be universal, but religion appears to be a forbidden ground to its application. When, even in trivial matters, we permit this laws to operate, it seems rather strange that we should taboo it from the one thing which is of vital importance to use - religion. The goal of every religion should be cessation of sorrow and misery and the realisation of supreme happiness. Hence all religions and teachers of religion should be judged by their capacity to guide people to that goal. Thus judged, all thinking men are sure to find the religion propounded by me satisfactory and acceptable to them; and, when they accept it, they shall realise the goal of supreme happiness. The pitiable position of the present day Hindus is due to their adherence to unreasonable religious rites and blind superstitious beliefs. It is evident that Hinduism has become degenerate on account of internecine strifes born of communal differences and idolatrous practices; and that the essence of Hindusim lies hidden in the meshes of false scriptures. To eradicate this evil and to resuscitate Hinduism which emphasises Nonviolence (**अहिंसा परमोधर्मः**) I have expounded the principle of Raja Yoga, and brought to light the central truth of Hinduism, and have criticised and condemned those false scriptures which enjoin upon the Hindus differences of caste and creed, idol worship, and observance of rites and ceremonies. I have also propounded that the whole world is one religion of bliss. My books have been in circulation in Kerala from 1069 M.E. onwards, and since then, the religion of Bliss has been spreading in Kerala; and, many associations (Ananda Samajams) and Communion Halls (Ananda Yoga salas) have sprung up in various parts of the country. To those who are lovers of Bliss let me state that for the first time in Kerala it was my books that successfully criticised idolatrous practices and thus resurrected Raja Yoga from beneath the false scriptures wherein it lay buried, and made it known even to the most ignorant in this country. My books have proclaimed to the world the religion of Bliss which quietens all the religious strifes and assures amity, peace and happiness. Have I not proved beyond doubt that those who are now being worshipped as incarnations of God have not been able to achieve this much? In fact, they were instrumental only to make people sink lower and lower in the pool of misery formed by caste distinctions and idolatrous practices. They are revered, and worshipped only because of the deep-rooted belief of the people in the traditions. In the scriptures we have been asked to look upon these men as divine incarnations, and their teachings as providing the only means for the attainment of material prosperity and realisation of heavenly happiness; and all acts to the contrary, we are told in the scriptures, are sure means to hell. Man longs for joy, but religion and its teachers give him only misery. We experience every day that human beings who ought to behave as members of a joint family, quarrel, fight and cut each other's throat, divided into hostile camps by differences of caste and creed. Why should those men who have destroyed peace among people by founding different religions, be praised? Why should those teachers, who prescribed the worship of images, observance of fasts, penances and austerities, exposures to sun and rain, wanderings from place to place, begging from door to door, and such other practices full of misery, and thus deprived man of real happiness, be revered? Persons, like myself, who are able to see with the eye of wisdom, know well that no one goes to heaven by giving money to these teachers or by making offerings to God, or by performing religious rites and ceremonies. If at all they go to heaven, that place would be worse than hell. That is what their own scriptures say:

"अतश्च संक्षेप मिमं श्रुणुध्वं नारायणः सर्व मिदं पुराणः।
ससर्गकाले च करोतिसंर्व संहारकाले च तदत्तिभूयः"।।

This is a stanza from the commentaries of Sree Sankaracharya on the Brahma Sutras. The meaning of this is, "Learn these that I state briefly. God creates this universe at the time of creation, and at the time of dissolution swallows the whole thing". Practically the very same opinion is held by Yogis, Aryasamajists, Brahmos, and various other Hindu Sects, as well as Christians and other religionists. Stories like those of Adam and Eve, the first two human creations of God whom He condemned to sin, and of the sacrifice of Jesus, the great devotee, demonstrate the mischievous nature of God. If God takes pleasure in destroying His own creations, in what plight would be those who go to heaven and be nearer Him? They may be compared to the moth lured into the fire or to the harmless deer which rushes into the dens of lions and tigers. Followers of creeds insisting on belief in God proclaim that He is an ocean of mercy. Does His mercy lie, then, in destroying His own children? These theistic teachers blow hot and cold in the same breath. They contradict this moment what they asserted vehemently only a moment ago. How can any one pin his faith to teachings teeming with such self-contradictions? Faith is good and necessary, but nothing has contributed to the turmoils and tribulations of this world as much as men's following of creeds and creedal teachers without exercising their faculty of discrimination. Nations quarrel, and wars break out between them; and after some fighting they make peace, and again live as friends;

but religious feuds continue with unabated fury and vigour though civilization appears to be advancing with rapid strides. It is for this reason that I urge that men should use their discrimination in accepting religions. Once we make up our minds to weigh and make a selection, it would dawn on us that the theories of incarnations and prophets are not entitled to credit. I have discussed this point already, and I shall elaborate it further.

God has no need to create religions like Vedism or to send to this world incarnations, sons and prophets, nor can He have the vanity to be worshipped. If God, as believers in Him declare, created the whole world by Will, and is Omnipotent and All-merciful, by the same Will can He make all men good and just, and worshipful of Him without resort to the tedious process of creating religions, undergoing incarnations, and sending down into this world sons and prophets.

As sugarcane is created sweet and moon cool, if man too had been created wise, kind, pious and full of virtues, he would have been all good and religious and prayerful, and he would have attained heaven as a matter of course. Sugarcane is never bitter and the moon's rays are never hot. Even so, man would never have been sinful, and there would have been no need for a hell to punish the wicked, no need for officers to weigh men's actions, and award joy and punishment in proportion to their virtues and sins. When God could have achieved this easily why should there be incarnations and prophets, and why should numerous men go about the country posing as teachers of religion enjoying upon men devotion to God?

4. We see man and woman loving each other and indulging in physical activities expressive of that love. They do not do so in obedience to any teaching of religious teachers or prophets sent down by God to instruct men in the science of love made by God. They do it under the dictates of the natural instinct in them. Even so, if love and worship of God is implanted by nature in human heart, every one would under promptings of that instinct love and worship God, even if teachers were to ask them not to do it. All the declamations of religious teachers against sexual life have not made men and women cease from indulging in it. On a consideration of the play of these natural instincts of men one is

driven to the conclusion that God has no need to create religions or to propagate them through incarnations, and He does not seem to posses the false pride that every-body should worship him. Why should He, therefore, incarnate Himself? Why should He create sons? Why should He send Prophets? Why should some people under the garb of religious teachers go about the world preaching worship of God?

5. If god is, as it is said, 'The All-merciful, all-powerful Father of all', He can make every creation of His attain salvation by simply blessing them. When he can save His creations so very easily, how can it be reasonably believed that he prescribed in scriptures as means of salvation the difficult and most painful practices of Hathayoga, such as cutting the parotid gland of the tongue, and stretching it into the skull, the pranayama which tires the lungs, the various postures such as 'Koormasana' which teachers be regarded as persons who have attained self-realisation and be praised?

6. If they are really men who have realised God, why should they contend that God is personal, impersonal, multi-personal and the creator and the destroyer of the universe; and thus contradict themselves and quarrel with one another like the four blind men of old who claimed to have realised the physical features of an elephant? No one has ever disputed that a goat is not a goat and an elephant is not an elephant. All are unanimous about their distinguishing features. If the teachers, as they claim to be, are people who have really realised God, why should their opinions about God differ? Therefore, they are not incarnations or sons of God or prophets, or persons who have realised God.

7. If, as some believe, God is impersonal, it follows that God is a being without qualities, and therefore impossible to be pleased by such things as worship and offerings. We do not see God investing the Hindus and other religionists, who worship Him day and night, with even the wisdom to cease quarrelling among themselves on account of religious differences. We find God impotent even to protect himself when robbers enter temples, break down the images and carry away all the jewels and treasure. The pathetic and agonising shrieks of poor fowls and goats which are butchered in lakhs in the worship of God have not been able to

move Him to put a stop to the merciless butchery perpetrated in His name. Men are guilty of various other cruel actions and sins also, and yet neither the impersonal nor the merciful personal God interferes to see that such things cease. The sinners are not punished and the pious are not protected. The fate should there be incarnations and prophets, and why should numerous men go about the country posing as teachers of religion enjoying upon men devotion to God?

8. We see man and woman loving each other and indulging in physical activities expressive of that love. They do not do so in obedience to any teaching of religious teachers or prophets sent down by God to instruct men in the science of love made by God. They do it under the dictates of the natural instinct in them. Even so, if love and worship of God is implanted by nature in human heart, every one would under promptings of that instinct love and worship God, even if teachers were to ask them not to do it. All the declamations of religious teachers against sexual life have not made men and women cease from indulging in it. On a consideration of the play of these natural instincts of men one is driven to the conclusion that God has no need to create religions or to propagate them through incarnations, and He does not seem to posses the false pride that everybody should worship Him. Why should He, therefore, incarnate Himself? Why should He create sons? Why should He send prophets? Why should some people under the garb of religious teachers go about the world preaching worship of God?

9. If God is, as it is said, 'The All-merciful, All-powerful Father of all', He can make every creation of His attain salvation by simply blessing them. When He can save His creations so very easily, how can it be reasonably believed that he prescribed in scriptures as means of salvation the difficult and most painful practices of Hathayoga, such as cutting the parotid gland of the tongue, and stretching it into the skull, the pranayama which tires the lungs, the various postures such as 'Koormasana' which teachers be regard as persons who have attained self-realisation and be praised?

10. If they are really men who have realised God, why should they contend the God is personal, impersonal, multi-personal and

the creator and the destroyer of the universe; and thus contradict themselves and quarrel with one another like the four blind men of old who claimed to have realised the physical features of an elephant? No one has ever disputed that a goat is not a goat and an elephant is not an elephant. All are unanimous about their distinguishing features. If the teachers, as they claim to be, are people who have really realised God, why should their opinions about God differ? Therefore, they are not incarnations or sons of God or prophets, or persons who have realised God.

11. If, as some believe, God is impersonal, it follows that God is a being without qualities, and therefore impossible to be pleased by such things as worship and offerings. We do not see God investing the Hindus and other religionists, who worship Him day and night, with even the wisdom to cease quarrelling among themselves on account of religious differences. We find God impotent even to protect himself when robbers enter temples, break down the images and carry away all the jewels and treasure. The pathetic and agonising shrieks of poor fowls and goats which are butchered in lakhs in the worship of God have not been able to move Him to put a stop to the merciless butchery perpetrated in His name. Men are guilty of various other cruel actions and sins also, and yet neither the impersonal nor the merciful personal God interferes to see that such things cease. The sinners are not punished and the pious are not protected. The fate of Jesus is an instance of the callousness of God towards his worshippers. In the face of these facts can it be reasonably advanced that God, be He personal or impersonal, created the Vedas and other scriptures for the benefit or salvation of man? Can it be believed that He incarnated himself and sent to this earth prophets to propagate the scriptures?

12. If we examine the belief that God is the creator. Preserver and Destroyer of the Universe, we find that really he is only a destroyer. The farmer sows that he may reap. Even so God creates so that he may destroy. If destruction is not the object, why should He create at all. Don't we see that even the greatest devotees of God die finally? Of the millions that pray for longevity, has God made a single man immortal? Therefore, how can we believe that God whose occupation is creation, preservation, and destruction,

to make scriptures the practice of which would put him out of job. If he is so good as spoken of he would not engage himself in creation at all. Birth and death, disease and poverty, all these have come in the wake of creation. How can anyone then believe that God made scriptures to give man salvation? It cannot also be believed that God would be pleased if men worship him for salvation as his object is to make men reap the fruits of creation, preservation and destruction. Even if men ask for Heaven or salvation God would not grant the request. Even if man manages to go to Heaven, God would kill him from there also.

3. "अत्रहिंसा स्वभावीशः सवर्गराज्येपि हिंसकः।
अधोप्यूर्द्धेपि सौधस्य दहनो दहनो यथा"।।

God who is destroyer in this world cannot be anything else in Heaven. Fire burns all the same whether it is downstairs or upstairs. Even as fire which burns on the ground floor cannot change its nature and become cold when it is in the second floor, God cannot shake of his destroying nature and make you happy even when you are in heaven nearer him.

4. "ओतोर्भीतः कश्चिदाखुर्बिलान्तरमयात्भ्रमात्।
बिलेशयेनभुक्तश्च स्वर्गयात्रा तथाभवेत्"।।

5. "असुराणांप्रपीडाच स्वर्गलोकेधिकाततः।
तत्तत्कालेदेवगणा अप्यटन्तिमहीमिमाम्"।।

Being afraid of a cat the mouse left its own hole and went into another, but unfortunately for it there was a snake therein which ate it up. Men's striving after Heaven is just like the attempted escape of the mouse into the latter hole. Frightened by the mewing of the cat the mouse left its hole and went into the other and got destroyed. Even so, distracted by the voices of religious teachers, men, forsaking the Heaven which is in their mind, go about seeking it somewhere else. Again, in Heaven the menace of Asuras (Demons) is intolerable. Even Gods take human form and wander on earth for fear of Asuras. Therefore Heaven is more miserable than Earth, for, we have not got here the danger of Asuras.

Once Gods who were wandering on Earth in human masks on account of the oppression by the Asuras approached Brihaspaty, their teacher, to seek a remedy; and he said:

"मन्त्रणाम् देवतायूयं तेपिदुःखैकभाजनम्।
जाताः स्वकालवशतः किंब्रवीमिप्रसाधनम्"।।

Devi Bhagavatam.

You are the deities whom men worship with mantras and in the cycle of time even you have been visited with sorrow and misery. What remedy, therefore, can I suggest to you !

Moreover:

6. अधः कृतानाम् संसर्ग नसहन्तेद्विजातयः।
तथामर्त्त्याश्च मर्त्त्यानाम् मर्त्यान् कुर्युरधस्ततः।।

Even as the Brahmins cannot tolerate any communion with non-Brahmins, the Gods cannot tolerate their mingling with human beings. Therefore, they are sure to push the men down from Heaven when the latter go there. That was what happened to poor Thrisankoo. Don't we find the natives of a country disliking the aliens therein, the white man hating the coloured people, and the high caste man lording it over the low caste man. If this is what happens among men themselves, is it a wonder that gods kick out the humanbeings who dare to enter heaven. Did not Indra, out of race prejudice, try to hinder the penance of Viswamitra and steal the horse of King Sagara which was dedicated for sacrifice (Yaga).

7. तीरभूमिर्यथानीरवासिन्यैमत्स्यजातये
तथैवभूमिवासिभ्यः स्वर्गलोकोपिदुःखदः।।

For these reasons, even as Earth is intolerable to the fish, which can live only in water, the Heaven is miserable for man who lives and has his being only on earth. The fish which live in the depths of the sea, the man manages to catch and eat. What would be their fate if they leave the sea and go ashore to men lured by their charm and beauty of their homes. None can go against nature without danger. Several teachers preached that there was nothing impossible for man and that even death could be conquered; but where are they? All dead and gone! The man cannot fight even a mosquito. It flies, but man can't. Those who cannot find their Heaven in their minds and do things to attain some external Heaven, only welter in sorrow.

The above discussion would show that the God who is the creator, preserver and destroyer would only ultimately destroy every one and that the Impersonal God is one who cannot do any thing, and that, therefore, it is of no use considering the meaning of the mantras and tantras and Vedas prescribed for the worship of that God.

8. "भेव्कों शब्दस्यभेकस्यकोर्त्थइत्यभिचिन्तनं।
यथातथैवमाक्षात्र्थमोङाक्राद्यर्थचिन्तनम्"।।

To enquire into the meaning of mantras, tantras and the Vedas for the purpose of attaining salvation is just like trying to find out the meaning of the croakings of the frog.

What the believers in God should say is as follows:-

9. भ्रान्तः पिशाचसृष्टयादि कर्त्तेत्युक्तिर्विशिष्यते।
दयादि गुणवानीशइत्युक्तिरसमञ्जसा।।

The being who creates now and destroys it immediately after is a lunatic and a devil. It is a misnomer to call him the merciful God. No father kills his own child; but God does. A lunatic does not know what he does and should do and so God is better described as a lunatic. Ye, religious teachers! the more one thinks of the destructive character of your God, the more is one tempted to run away from Him and His kingdom and seek protection at the hands of the devil.

Ye rulers and potentates! Can anybody pin his faith to the religions and religious teachers who have, by encouraging creedal and sectarian differences, destroyed the peace of the world? The great obstacles in the way of the progress and prosperity of the world are the religious teachers and religions. You punish in time those who commit theft robbery or murder and thus check those crimes. These crimes and criminals have not created so much struggle in this world as religions and religious teachers have done, but you, too, worship religions and religious teachers and thus enable religious strifes to stay on. Can it be believed that religious teachers who create quarrels and destroy peace and amity in the visible world are persons who have realized the truth and happiness of the Invisible? Be critical about religions, and then, you would be able to free yourself from the thraldom of religions and your land would be the real Kingdom of God.

Ye preachers of religions! from your own teachings I have shown that your God is a destroyer of his own children. Therefore, instead of instructing people to worship God, try to advise your God as follows:—

10. वृथापुत्रान् समुत्पाद्यमामारय जगत्पितः।
पितृधर्मः पुत्ररत्देत्यवधारय हेविभो।
11. त्वाम् दयावारिधिंलोक पितरं नीतिमत्तमम्।
वर्णयामो वयं सर्वेत्वन्तुहं सिसुतानिमान्।।
12. व्याघ्रादयः पिशाचाश्च स्त्रिह्यन्तिनिजसन्ततौ।
हन्त हन्त भ्वान् हन्ति सन्त्यजान्तककर्मते।।
13. क्रिस्तुं त्दमाशालिनं तंभक्तं पुत्रं भवान् पुरा।
बलिं चकार हत्वा हा कथं त्वं भक्तवत्सलः।।
14. दया समं नास्ति पुण्यं पापं हिंसासमं नहि।
सृष्टिसन्तानहननात् विरमत्वं जगत्पितः
15. यद्यस्तीच्छा सृष्टिकृत्ये सर्वानानन्दतुन्दिलान्।
चन्द्रवत् सृजहे तात! नन्दन्तुतवनन्दनाः।।
16. पुत्रमित्रादि मरणरोगादि परिपीडिताः।
रुदन्तस्त्वाम् समाहूय म्रियन्ते कोटि कोटयः
17. मार्ज्जारलीलामृतये मूषकाणाम् तथातव।
सृष्टिलीला पुत्रहत्यै लीलात्याज्यामहापितः।।
18. सृष्टिकर्ममहाकष्टं! मामासृज जगत्पितः।।
सुष्टिकृत्याद्विरक्तश्चेत् मोक्षः स्यादखिलस्यच।।

Thou, father of all, why should you create children and then destroy them? A father's duty is to protect his children. We praise you as just and merciful father and in return you visit us with death. Even the wild beasts look after their young ones, but you commit infanticide. You sacrificed the devoted and holy Jesus Christ. How can you claim to be the friend of the pious? There is no virtue greater than kindness and no sin greater than cruelty. Oh Father! cease killing your own children. If you cannot help creating, then create beings like the moon which cools and makes every one happy. Let each of your creation give similar happiness to every other. Diseased, and miserable, and bereaved, how many die crying out your name? The cat's play is death to the mice and your play is death to your children. Oh Father, give up this play. It is so tragic. If you give up creation, men and beast, all would attain salvation. If you abstain, the whole world becomes happy. It is creation that causes sorrow to all beings. If that ceases there is no sorrow. You are also relieved of the trouble of judging people and distributing rewards and punishments.

The religious teachers should speak to God in this wise. If a tree is watered at its base all the branches and leaves are refreshed. Even so, if God is improved the whole world is improved.

In the first chapter the religion of God is criticised and its defects exposed. It is also discussed therein how superstitious religions have spread in the world and how they can be destroyed. Besides, it is shown that it is only by high thinking and manliness that people can acquire wealth and respect. A portion of it may be epitomised here. Is it not by virtue of high thinking and manliness that the king of England has become also the Emperor of India? The Hindus who believed that Empire could be established by installing God's images and worshipping them have lost even the empire that they had. Is not this the result of want of thought and manliness? Are not the various inventions of the western people such as the telegraph, wireless, steamers, motor cars, photography, telephone, etc., things which even the so-called sons of God or prophets could not invent, the outcome of the development of mental power and individual self-respect among the people of the west. The so called prophets have only created various rites and rituals and worship of idols which destroy the intellect and self-respect of men and encourage ignorance, superstition and all kinds of strifes among men. The first chapter which deals with these things in detail would enable the readers to escape the misery resulting from religious worship and enjoy bliss.

11. The 2nd chapter entitled "Aananda Darsanam" shows that the Bliss is the supreme thing desired by all. All are born in bliss and therefore all belong to the religion of bliss. The theists, who fight among themselves on account of creedal differences, and the Atheists who deny God, want bliss alike. The child which is fed at its mother's breast does not know whether it is a Hindu, a Buddhist or a Christian or any other religionist. Neither does it want God. What it desires is only joy. We see from its actions that its religion is one of bliss. When it cries, the mother suckles and fondles it; and it is all joy. A moment's consideration will show us that all actions, good and bad, of all beings, have for their object the attainment of pleasure and not God. To secure pleasure men are prepared to scoff at God and do even wicked deeds. This

longing for pleasure inherent in every being is sufficient proof of their being followers of the religion of Bliss. Men call themselves Hindus, Christians or Mohammedans as they have been taught to do so from their very childhood. There is nothing in nature to mark out a person as a Hindu or a Christian or Mohammedan as the trunk distinguishes the elephant, the wings the bird, and the four legs a beast. But bliss exists in every being. All these things are explained elaborately in the second chapter. Those who read it will be able to cry out to the world as follows:—

19. आनन्दाज्जातोहं आनन्दोमेकुलंमतंजातिः।
आनन्दोमेसदनं, देशश्चानन्दएवममसत्यम्।।

I am born of bliss. Therefore I belong to the family of Bliss. My caste is bliss. My home is bliss. My country is bliss. As all men are born of bliss, to the whole world bliss is the religion, the caste and the home. Man would not cohabit with women if pain would be the outcome. It is because it results in pleasure that they couple. How could the baby and the family which is born of such bliss belong to a different caste or creed? An elephant can't be a goat; neither a goat an elephant. Try what we might; we can't change the essential nature of beings. Therefore, the divisions of men into Hindus, Christians, Musalmans, blacks, whites, etc., cannot really alter the essential unity of men as belonging to the one religion of bliss. This truth will only be confirmed if we think over the matter making our experience the basis.

20. नहिनहिकुलजातीमे, नमतं, सदनं ननामदेशादि,।
अहहानन्दादन्यत् श्रवणद्वारासमागतंबाल्यात्।।

I have no family or caste or religion or house or village or name. All these which are absent in the state of bliss have become attached to me as I have been hearing of them from my childhood. As my name cannot be found in my body or in my soul, my caste and religion also do not, in fact, exist. All the quarrels of all these years have been about things which do not really exist. Oh, the pity of it!

21. जातिमताश्रमकर्मसु नहिनहिकर्तव्यमस्तिमेकिञ्चित्।
कर्मणयधिकारोनभ्रष्टानां दृश्यतेलकुत्रापि।।

The duties enjoined upon castes and religions and positions (ashramas) do not bind me, for those who are out of caste have no duty or right to perform religious rites. If a Brahmin is put out of his caste, he is not allowed to participate in social and religious functions. The other Hindu sects also do similarly. Therefore, as I am from my birth outside the fold of these castes and religions, I am not entitled to perform the religious and other ceremonies. I am born of bliss and all those who are born of bliss need follow only the conduct of bliss. That is the only natural conduct, all others being artificial. In the second chapter, it is explained fully how the castes and religions have been responsible for the disintegration and internal quarrels of the Hindus. It is also explained that in matters religious it is the opinion of the wise and not of the majority that should be accepted. By understanding it, one will realize that all people are, in fact, followers of the religion of bliss and on that realization one will be able to free oneself from the pride of caste and religion and the strifes thereof. More than that, the realization of this truth will enable the world to get rid of the frightful religious wars and establish peace and good feeling among all the peoples of the world.

The third chapter describes the equanimity of mind which is otherwise known as Nirvana, Heaven, Salvation, the union of soul and God, Bliss, divinity, etc. To attain this state all that is needed is to control the mind. When the waves subside, they merge in the ocean. For this merger it is not at all necessary that the waves should know or contemplate the nature of the ocean. Even so, when the mind subsides that is bliss, that is God, that is Bramha. For the mind to attain this state why should it contemplate God. The mind can attain bliss without divine worship and religious ceremonies if only it can control itself. Every one knows that when the mind is absorbed in deep sleep no sorrow is felt. What would be the state then if the mind is absorbed in its real state of bliss! Only men like myself know it. It is that state which is called Heaven, Nirvana, etc. Persons who study this chapter in which is described the control of the mind as the only means of salvation would try to bring their minds under control and give up all worship of God and performance of religious rites. Very few in the world know the nature of mind. Some Vedantins regard it as a non-sentient thing, and thus leaving it to itself, they indulge in unconscionable acts. Here it is convincingly established that mind is soul and God, friend and enemy, in short, everything, and that in its control lies one's duty and virtue and that it is its disturbance that constitutes wrong and sin. Our ancient saints also have spoken the same thing. The Thaejobindo Upanishad says:

"मनएवजगत्संर्व मनवएमहारिपुः
मनएवहिसंसारो मनएवजगत्रयं
मनएवहिसंकल्पो मनएवहिजीवकः
मनएवहिचित्तश्च मनोहंकारएवच
मनएवहिभूमिश्च मनएवहितोयकम्
मनएवहितेजश्च मनएवमरुन्महान्
मनएवहिचाकाशं मनएवहिशब्दकं
स्पंर्शरूपंरसंगन्धंकोशाः पञ्चमनोभवाः
जाग्रस्वप्रसुषुप्यादि मनोमयमितीरितं
दिक्पालवसवोरुद्रा आदित्याश्चमनामयाः"।।
।।वा सि ष्ठं।।
"एकएवमनोदेवो ज्ञेयः सर्वार्त्थसिद्धिदः।
अन्यत्रविफलःक्लेशः सर्वेषांतज्जयंविना"।।

There is only one God worth knowing and that is the mind itself. That is the God which satisfies all desires. Without controlling this God, it is a waste to study the Vedas and Sastras which give information about God.

'वासनामनसोनान्या मनोहिपुरुषःस्मृतः'

Instinct is not distinct from mind. Mind is soul, Without caring for sayings like these of great teachers, people have followed men who taught rituals and ceremonies even as now many men follow ritualists ignoring my teachings. Many spend untold wealth in temples and sing praises of teachers who have established idols of ignorance. They keep silent over the religion of bliss which I have founded. It is in the Hindus that the misery brought about by religion has embodied. The atheists have not done a hundredth part of the harm, which believers in God have done to this world.

Kings, men of nobility and leaders of men, of what avail is the belief in religions which sanction differences of castes and creeds. By creating and encouraging eternal religious strifes it keeps us away from the happiness of peace and harmony. From observing the religious rules regarding penances, pilgrimages and worship of God, no benefit is derived. It only helps a man to deny himself the pleasures of this world and welter in the misery of action. What is the use of having faith in religions which teach that God creates, preserves and destroys for its result is destruction. Neither is it of any use that God is impersonal, for the contemplation of such a God is an impossibility. Therefore, the only means of universal happiness is to accept religion only after critical examination.

It is on account of want of clear thought that some say that to praise one's own work is to praise oneself. When a physician praises a medicine he has invented, men afflicted with diseases use that medicine and get relief. Even so when a wise saint founds religion universally beneficial and expounds its greatness, there will be people to study and follow it and get release from the religions in which they lie imprisoned now. Therefore, an author must be the first man to praise his work. If certain teachers could say that they were incarnations of God, born in this world for the punishment of the wicked and the protection of the good; that they were the sons of God deputed to proclaim the gospel to the people of the world, and cajole men into the prisons of their religions and castes, why not I proclaim the greatness of my work and that I am the person who has found out for the first time that the whole world belongs to the one religion of bliss, and laid down the means of attaining the kingdom of bliss by destroying religious rites and ceremonies born of ignorance. Nowadays, the so-called learned and great men have for the basis of their work, the customs and practices followed by innumerable people belonging to various religions from time immemorial. As I oppose that basis, they are trying to conceal the glory and greatness of the religion of bliss propounded for the first time by me in Kerala. If I praise my work that would help my religion to remove its screen and shine forth to the benefit of the whole world. An author should not praise his work if it is born of pride and if it tends to encourage ignorance and differences and destroy individuality. Neither should he make others praise it. It is praise of that type that makes differences of caste and creed persist in this world.

Ye men! when we desire joy why should we accept religions

which give pain. Just as we use medicines which expel disease and restore health, we should take only the religion which removes misery and ignorance and gives heavenly happiness.

22. **कारागृहबद्धान् नृन् मोक्तुंशक्तानृपादयोप्यत्र।**
मतकारागृहबद्धदण्डयन्तेहन्तकर्मठाचार्यैः।।

The teachers of religious sacrifices and ceremonies are able to entangle and enslave with their directions even emperors powerful enough to release hundreds of men cast into prison by others. What a pity! Millionaires who can relieve the poverty of many suffer starvation by the fastings and other austerities; and princes who live in palaces without suffering heat and cold are made to go on pilgrimages and stand extremes of weather. Sovereigns able to abolish slavery have themselves become slaves of idolatry. Even kings, who protect the innocent and the virtuous and punish the evildoer are harassed by the religious teachers. None has been able to escape the prison of religion. Men suffer because the religious teachers have made them believe that men go astray under the influence of 'Maya' (ignorance) or 'Kama' (*Venus) or Satan or devil and that to be free from sufferings they should worship God or believe in Christ etc. Let those who desire truth know that it is not Maya or Satan that lead men astray. The mind alone is the Satan or devil which influences men to run down the evil path. This fact is explained fully in the chapter entitled 'Manodarsana', but a few words will not be out of place here. When a man is being tried for rape in criminal court, if he pleads that it was Kama Deva, who was responsible for it and produces the Hindu scriptures in support of its would the Judge set him free? Similarly when a man is charged with theft or murder, it is of no avail to him ascribe it to the influence of Devil or Maya and exhibit Bible or Bhagavad Geeta in support of his statement. They will be punished in spite of such defence as the Judge knows that crimes are committed on account of the defects of the mind. Thus, men suffer believing things to which judicial officers, who are their own religionists, give no credit. Some hang themselves, some others die by shooting themselves. Can anybody say that it is Maya, Satan or Devil that hanged or shot them? Sometimes, many men die in great wars caused by the very kings who protect the people by punishing the wicked. Is this destruction also caused by Maya or Satan? No, Mind is responsible for it. It is the mind that is Maya, Satan or Devil. It is the great enemy. It is also the kind and merciful god, gives us salvation. And to we not see many men revered and respected on account of the greatness of their mind? It is on account of the development of mind that men like men are able to enjoy perfect bliss here and now. Lord Buddha, who by his non violence became the holiest and the most famous of religious teachers and who did not worship god attained 'Nirvana' and came to be himself worshipped afterwards. Is not this due to the greatness of his mind? Therefore, to attain salvation, it is enough if mind rests in its state of bliss as if in a deep sleep. To relieve the pain and fatigue of running, it is enough, if one sits down. Even so, to attain salvation one not change his religion; but it is sufficient if the mind is kept in its proper poise.

How can this be done?

23. श्रुत्वाद्दष्टानिपियान्तर्नादंज्योतिर्न्निजंरसं।
निश्चश्चलस्य मनसः सुस्थितिर्निमुक्तिरुच्यते।।

24. सुस्थितिर्मनसः स्वर्गो नरकस्तस्यदुस्थितिः।
नान्यत्रस्वर्गनरकौस्तश्चेत्तौदुःखदौनृणाम्।।

Meaning: It is that blissful state of the mind where it remains immersed in itself hearing its own voice, seeing its own light and enjoying its own sweetness; that we call salvation; that state is Heaven. The state of mind while in pain is Hell. There are no independent and ultramurdan Heaven or Hell and if there are, they only serve to give pain to humanity. This has already been stated in the stanzas from 3 to 7. This is the real truth, and it is, improper for teachers of religion to ask men to change their religion and thus convert them. No Christian doctor advises a lunatic that he will be cured if he converts himself to Christianity. No Aryasamajist doctor tells his patient that he should become a member of the Aryasamaj, and no Buddhist doctor says that he should be a Buddhist in order to be sane again. They give him medicine and cure him. Similarly, the religious teachers also should make religious fanatics mentally balanced by giving them knowledge without asking them to change their religion. If this were done, the religious strifes would be things of the past. A physician who treats a man for blindness tries to restore his eyesight. When the eye-sight is restored he walks along the right path without falling into pits or straying away. Similarly to improve people who are blind with ignorance, there is no need to ask them to change their religion. Let the teachers give the light of knowledge to their minds and then, they would not quarrel among themselves about the alleged inferiority or superiority of castes or creeds or change religions or involve themselves into sufferings caused by the performance of the rites and ceremonies prescribed by religions. They would then know that the whole world belongs to one and the same religion of bliss and that salvation is that blissful state of mind which is beyond the state of dream and deep sleep. They would then refrain from such things as the worship of God and idols and the observances of fastings which are all inconsistent with that knowledge. Instead of giving this real knowledge, why should men be asked to embrace Christianity, Buddhism or other religions, and religious confusion created in this world? Can it be contended that to see the sun, one should belong to any particular religion? No change of religion is necessary to relish the sugar as sweet, to appease hunger with food or to quench thirst with water. It is those who help people to remove the differences of religion and to enjoy happiness by getting absorbed in the bliss inherent in them that are the real saints and the benefactors of the world.

25. रोगच्छेदोवैद्यधर्मो नरोगोल्पादनंतथा;।
भ्रान्तिच्छेदोज्ञानिधर्मो नमतभ्रान्तिकर्तृता।।

Meaning: A physician should not create disease. His duty is to remove existing disease by administering medicines. Even so, the saints should not encourage fanaticism of religions but destroy it by teaching people the essence of their religion.

26. चिरस्थिरासत्यमतादिंसभ्रयात्
शिरस्थितानन्दमतं नजानते।
नरास्तुनानामत मानिनस्तत:
किंकुर्महेद्रव्यसहायवर्ज्जिता:।।

Meaning: The Hindus and followers of other religions are not able to appreciate this religion of bliss, which is not something extraneous but is really inherent in them, as they have been deluded by the religious scriptures, temples, churches, mosques, prayers, religious ceremonies, etc. created and believed in by men for long time past. It is on account of their ignorance that they boast that they are Hindus, Christians, Muhammedans, Buddhists, etc. If I have sufficient wealth and influence, I would distribute the books on the religion of bliss in all the languages in several countries, interview kings and emperors and demonstrate that the whole world belongs to one religion of bliss.

27. आनन्दवस्तुन्यखिलोत्तमांगगे
देहेखिलेभूतमयेच कुत्रवा,।
क्रिस्त्यादिचिहन्नंहिदृश्यतेक्कचित्
युद्धंमहद्धामतजातिभेदतः।।

Meaning: There is bliss inherent in every man. All human bodies consist of five elements. Where are the distinguishing caste marks of a Hindu or a Mohammedan or a Buddhist? Are they in the bliss or in the body? We don't find any such marks anywhere and, yet, alas! we find big strifes on account of religions and caste differences.

28. पुत्राभावोमहाभाग्यं दुष्पुत्रजननादपि।
मताभावोमहासौख्यं अयुक्तमतसंश्रयात्।।

Meaning: Better to have no son than to have a wicked one. Even so, happier would it be to have no religion than to rely on a religion which is not founded on reason. Wicked children cause misery, sorrow and material loss to their parents. Similarly, a religion which is unreasonable makes men quarrel and suffer privations on account of various rites and ceremonies. All know the sufferings of parents who have wicked children. The quarrels without reason or necessity engendered by religious differences from a long time past are also well-known. Therefore, I need not describe them here. I have dealt with them in detail in "Mokshapradeepam" and in my other works. I have done it for the welfare of the world and not to ridicule or condemn any religion or religious teachers. I need be taken to task for this only if I impose on religion and religious teachers, faults which they don't have. If a medical man discovers some wonderful medicine and explains its use, criticising the medicines and methods of treatment already in vogue, can anybody say that his idea is to ridicule and scorn the prevailing medical men and the medical system? If any body points out the defects in vegetables which we use for food, can it be said that he is defaming God by maligning his creation? Therefore the saint who points out the defects in various religions does not deserve any blame. The British Government, and under its influence the Indian Rajas also, have abolished the cruel practices of slavery, human sacrifice, sati, penalty of mutilation, and the oppression of the depressed. Would any body say that they have done these things to hold up to ridicule religions and religious teachers? No, they have done these things not out of malice, but for the benefit of the world. If such prince who are desirous of making the world happy, are made to understand the evils caused by religions, they would be able to help people out of the misery caused by religions and enable them to enjoy happiness. It is with that purpose that I have placed my works before the public from the year 1893 AD onwards pointing out the defects of religions. As a result of these publications, in religious matters, wonderful changes have happened in certain places in Kerala. He who desires and works for progress should welcome criticisms even from enemies and tell the critics that they are his real friends and teachers as they have helped him towards self purification through realisation of his fault. No one should break the mirror which reflects the dirt on one's face. Even so, we should not hate one who tells us our faults, though he be our enemy. If this be true, how can the saints who regard all equally, and work for the betterment of the whole world be taken to task if they criticise religions for their faults? If we blame them for it, how can we hope to come out of darkness into light and be happy? Therefore we should learn ourselves and teach others to welcome the man who shows us the defects of our religions. The differences of creeds are reinvigorated when we exhibit temper in religious discussions. We declare that all are high born, being born of bliss. But there are many who say that they are Brahmins, non-Brahmins, Nairs, etc., and organize sectarian associations like the Nair Samaj, the Ezhuva Samaj, etc. They desire higher status and wider union, but they are preventing both by admitting that they are lower people professing different creeds. This is really a great pity. Time has come for all to give up the thoughtlessness which is responsible for the differences of castes and creeds which divide people and also for the belief in rituals and ceremonials and in a

God who is the author of creation, preservation and destruction. Time has come to enjoy real bliss. It is the rulers of men who should move in this matter if the world has to be rid of this evil immediately and be made happy.

29. आलोचने! मनःशक्तेस्तवसाहाययवैभवात्।
अयुक्तमतमुक्तोस्मि युक्तोस्मिसुखितोस्मिच।।

किंच

30. अन्धीकृतजगत्सर्व मतश्चखण्डयंपुनः।
अवतारयमानन्द मतश्चसहजंनृणाम्।।

Meaning: Oh! Thought, you are the power of mind and with your help, I have freed myself free from unreasonable religions, and become blissful. I have also been able to vanquish the religions which have plunged the world into ignorance, and inaugurate the religion of bliss which is the natural religion for the world.

31. प्रकाशनंसूर्यधर्मो मद्धर्मश्चप्रकाश्नं।
द्दष्टेस्सर्व त्र सर्वेषांगोभिस्तं कृतवानहम्।।

32. आहल्दनंचन्द्रधर्मो मतेनाहाल्दनंमम।
धर्मस्तमेवकृतवानाहाल्दन्तांमतातुराः।।

Meaning: The duty of the sun is to give light. My duty also is to give light. The sun, by his rays, enables all beings to see with their eyes and I, with my words, enable the knowledge of truth, dormant in every being, to shine forth. Bliss exists hidden in the niches of the hearts of all beings, theists or atheists; therefore the religion of bliss is the truth. I do not advocate the differences of castes and creeds which exist neither in body nor in soul, for, if I do, I can't be truthful and see all equally. The moon gladdens men I, too, gladden men in matters religious. What I have propounded is that it is only by developing the power of thought, individuality and control of mind, that we can enjoy the world as we like and obtain bliss which is beyond senses. I have not enjoined differences of creeds and castes and rituals and made men quarrel among themselves and be miserable. Nor have I made men believe that God will grant all desires and thereby to ignore the need for mental control and to lose the four aims of man, viz, Dharma, religious merit; Artha-wealth; Kama-desires; and Moksha-salvation.

33. अस्तुवामास्तुवा तृप्तिनृणांसूर्यःप्रकाशते।
चन्द्रमाश्चतथासन्तः कुर्वीरन्जगतांहितम्।।

34. तस्मादयुक्तमतजमान्ध्यंघन्तुनृणांनृपाः।
सन्तापशान्तयस्सन्तुसन्तुष्यन्तुनरस्सदा।।

Meaning: The sun and the moon shine, no matter whether people like or dislike. The wise should do good to the world in a similar spirit. Let kings therefore exert themselves to remove the superstitions of the people caused by irrational religions. Let them be happy. Those princes who allow the people to continue in their superstitions, afraid of a popular agitation, are like the parents who spoil their children by allowing them to do as they like lest they should feel sorry and cry. It is the duty of a king to do what he thinks best for the people, even though people might rise against it.

"शिक्षारक्षाकरोयस्मात् राजाप्रत्यक्षदैवतं"।।

This sentence means that a king is the visible God who gives protection and punishment. It is only to these visible gods that we can appeal to save men from the evils of religions. It may be asked how people would like their religion and religious teachers to be criticised and punished. When religions are criticised, a few earnest truth-seekers would read those criticisms (critics) and see why they criticise beliefs followed by innumerable men from times immemorial, and thus they would come to understand the defects of their religions. Such men would be able to free themselves from those defects and enjoy bliss. Nothing is greater than the enjoyment of bliss and, if criticisms of religions and religious teachers would lead to it, they are certainly beneficial to the world. It is to benefit the world in this wise that saints like Vasishta condemned as beasts those people who spend their time in sacrifices, penances, pilgrimages, worship of idols, etc. They have said so, not because they are wicked or mad or drunk, but because they wanted to do good to the world. Therefore, criticisms made by seers like them should never be suppressed. The punishment given by kings are also beneficial to the world. Is it not a fact that the abolition of the cruel system of 'Sati' has been a great boon to humanity. If the Government had allowed people to do as they liked in obedience to the rules of Shastras which said that she who dies with her husband is the truly chaste (Sati) wife, even now many widows would have been compelled to mount the funeral pyre of their husbands. Is it not because of the orders of the Government that women are now able to educate themselves and live a life of freedom? When we consider all these things, we find that even the punishments and laws of kings are beneficial to humanity.

35. हितंयस्मात्नृणां धर्मस्सत्यपुण्यश्चतत्ततः।
मताक्षेपश्चदण्डश्च महान्धर्मोमहद्भितम्।।

Meaning: What gives happiness to people is virtue truth and meritorious act. Therefore, criticisms of unsound religion by the learned, and punishment of the wicked by kings are acts of great merit. By criticising religions, men, who quarrel among themselves on account of differences of castes and creeds, and who lead a life of sorrow and suffering, are enabled to unite themselves and to enjoy bliss. Punishments given by kings also help men to enjoy happiness. If kings do not provide for punishments the world will be miserable on account of the mischievous deeds of the wicked. It is punishment of the wicked that protects saints, people and kings alike. Therefore, it is proved beyond doubt that the penal codes of Governments and criticisms of religions by wise men are all for the good of mankind.

36. दण्डाभावेजगत्संर्व दुष्टशत्रुबलाधिकैः।
नित्यंखिन्देत्दणडएव सर्वरक्षाकरोमहान्।।

Meaning: If there is no system of punishment for misdeeds the world would be insufferable on account of the misdeeds of the wicked people. It is, therefore, the institution which guarantees protection to all. Wild beasts like tigers and lions are made to obey man in circus exhibitions, because they are afraid of punishments. But for the system of punishment, even the crowns would not be safe. It may be asked whether such penal systems are not violating the great principle of Non-Violence (Ahimsa), which enjoins that no being should be pained in any manner whatsoever. The answer to this question is that the real meaning of Non-Violence is not to cause sorrow to ourself or to any other being on account of one's desires and other defects of the mind. It does not mean the teaching of Christ:

Bless them that curse you and pray for them which

> despitefully use you. And unto him that smiteth thee on the one cheek, offer also the other, and him that taketh away thy cloak, forbid not to take they coat also.

If people take Non-Violence in this Christian sense, they would be in reality, malefactors to themselves and to others. If I tolerate a man who steals my wealth, I shall have to starve or beg in the streets. The wicked would victimise more and more such tolerant men, being sure that no harm would come to them at their hands. Thus such men of tolerance become a cause of misery to themselves and to others. Therefore it is beneficial to the world to get the evil-doers punished according to the law of the land.

If the wicked come to believe that if they rob the good men who live in non-violence no harm will happen to them, they will get emboldened to give them trouble. Therefore, it is beneficial to the world to resist the activities of the wicked and to get them punished by the state as the punishment is likely to improve the ways of such wicked men. It would be a blessing in disguise as such punishments are not inconsistent with the principle of non-violence. Even the God of the theists has, it seems devised hells for the punishments of misdoers. If that be so, the temporal rulers have to organise a system of punishments lest their countries should be tormented and ruined by the crimes of evil men. Even great revolts are suppressed by condign punishment. Considering these things it would appear that a system of penal justice constitutes the greatest protection to human society. Similarly, criticisms of unreasonable religions is the greatest help to people to save themselves from the conflict of religious beliefs and customs and to make them happy. That which enables men even while in this world to free themselves from the pain of ignorant actions is what we should call the true religion and the grand teaching and that which enables men to realise bliss is the most meritorious and virtuous action.

37. सार्वभौमानृपास्सर्वे जनाश्चसुखिनः सदा।
सन्त्वन्तर्मततत्वज्ञानिर्मत्सर हृदन्तराः।।

Meaning: May all the emperors, kings and people realise the religion inherent in them, i.e., the religion of bliss and be free from spite and hatred and be happy.

Apologia

1. Ye, who desire bliss! we are all born of bliss and therefore we all belong to the religion of bliss and to the community of bliss. None is regarded as low. There is no reason to think that I have done this out of malice.

2. How can it be said that in demonstrating that we all belong to the religion of bliss, so that our religious and communal quarrels might cease, I am prompted by malice?

3. If I tell people who, believing in the teachings of their religion and teachers, renounce all their wealth, go about begging, troubling all and sundry, and tormenting themselves with hunger and thirst, and subject themselves to great sufferings by pilgrimages, etc., that by such things God will not be pleased and only ignorance and sorrow will be increased, I do it so that they also may be enabled to realise bliss. Therefore, it cannot be said that it is malice that makes me do it.

4. It is for the good of the world that I say that God is made a devil when we say that he is the author of creation, preservation and destruction. When some children of a father scandalise him grievously, cannot another son ask them why they do so? Is there malice in it?

5. When I see the helpless animals being killed I feel as though I am myself being killed, and so it is that I have criticised the practice of animal sacrifice. It is not on account of any ill-will towards those who eat flesh but on account of the softness of my heart. All religions say that we ought to be kind.

6. I find many people suffering due to idleness and thoughtlessness. For their redemption, I say, that for all the means of attaining desires is to develop thought, personality and control of mind. In this also there is no malice.

7. As men are following the opinion that the majority has been holding for a long time careless of the opinion of the great, they are in a confusion as regards their castes, religion and duty. In order to clear that confusion I tell them that in matters religious they should follow not the majority but the substantial men. Herein also there is no malice.

8. Several persons put on the garbs of saints thinking that

thereby they can fill their stomachs and command respect without effort. Thinking that they can attain salvation if they only renounce everything that they have, some rich men give up all their wealth and some educated men all their University degrees and go about begging and preaching, assuming attractive names like Paramahamsa, Sanyasi, Ananda, etc, and spend their time in living in caves and worshipping idols and indulging in similar other ignorant practices. Newspapers sing the praises of such men and the masses are encouraged in their ignorance and superstitions. To remedy this evil I say that a teacher should be accepted only after a critical examination. How can it be said that I am malicious in this.

9. Innumerable men believe that certain sayings found in the works of some learned men, are the sayings of God and of great sages and therefore they should be obeyed blindly. Believing thus, they perform all things prescribed in unreasonable and false works and suffer in this world. To save such men I have proved that God has no need to create scriptures or to come into this world as incarnations and that religions should be critically examined before their acceptance. I have no malicious motives in this.

10. We find generally that even some great men dislike persons who criticise them. Sometimes they even file complaints against them in courts. I have shown that this is a bad habit and that the one who points out to us our defects even though he be our enemy we should regard him as our teacher and thank him for it. Men become improved because the parents correct their children, the teachers their pupils, and the kings their subjects. Those who correct us, even if they ridicule us should be regarded as our saviours. From this point of view if I point out the defects of the existing religions none has any reason to complain against me on account of it.

11. Certain places in Kerala have become they cynosure of all eyes. As I have made it possible for the educated and the uneducated equally to enjoy the spiritual bliss which in former times, even emperors and renowned religious teachers could not get, but only a few Yogis could realise, can it be said that this state of things, unprecedented in the history of the world, has been brought about by me out of malice?

12. Religious missionaries adopt all sorts of tactics to get converts and thus create quarrels among people. This is certainly improper. A doctor restores eye-sight to a blind man and thus helps him to walk without falling down. Similarly, all that the religious teachers do is to remove ignorance and give knowledge. Then the people will give up their differences and live in peace. That is what I do. I do not ask people to change their religion and thus create quarrels at home or abroad. I give instructions only to those who come to me admiring my works. Therefore I cannot have any evil motive for my action.

13. That the spiritual enjoyment is to be realised in this world before we die even as the worldly bliss is enjoyed here and that for this, we should keep the mind in its own inherent blissful state, is what I preach. I cannot possibly have any bad intention in doing this.

14. The Theeya community proclaims through its press that men should have only one caste, one religion and one God but in action they go counter to that principle and build separate temples to different Gods and worship different images. In Travancore, Cochin and Malabar they have established big temples and organised image worship. They have done this, following the teaching of the ritualistic Hindu teachers who are responsible for the innumerable divisions and the fall of Hindus. When they are asked to reconcile their practice with their principle of one caste, one religion and one God, they don't give any answer. Some of them are embracing Buddhism, some Christianity, some the Arya Samaj, some the Brahma Samaj, and some Islam. If they know truly to which religion and caste they belong, why should they seek all these religions. Suppose that when they are in the witness box in a court, they are asked what their caste or religion is, and they reply "one caste, one religion" would it convey any meaning? The white men are called as white men and the black as black men. None says about the colour of a person as one colour because all can see the colour of the body. Similarly when we are able to understand the real nature of man all will have to proclaim that all belong to the one religion of bliss.

I have given above the essence of the religion of bliss. None has any reason to denounce this religion. If one is to attack it one will have to contend as follows. "All are not born of bliss, some are born of sorrow." "Therefore it is necessary that people should follow the teachings of certain religious teachers and to renounce and starve and suffer. God is really the destroyer of His own creation. The dumb creatures can be killed. We need not be kind to them. We don't require thought, personality and control of mind. We should worship God for the attainment of our desires. In matters religious we should follow the opinion of the majority. We are to follow the teachers blindly and not critically. We should not test them by reason and experience. Conversion is proper and even if it creates quarrels, it does not matter. We should have bliss only after death and not before it." In fact this is the kind of criticism of which some people indulge. Such criticisms tend only to destroy the peace and harmony in the World. Litigation agents create quarrels between the managers and members of families, drag them to courts and thus impoverish and destroy them. Similarly, the protagonists of different religions create dissensions among the people of the world who ought to be like the members of a family, and cause troubles and wars and misery.

To avoid these things criticism of religions is necessary. It is want of thought that makes men regard such criticisms as insult to religions and religious teachers. We don't think because we have been hardened in our differences of religion and in belief in the scriptures and Gods from time immemorial. Those persons who are accustomed to criticisms based on reason and experience will acknowledge that my criticisms are prompted by the desire for the welfare of the world.

The knowledge and bliss which some persons educated and illiterate in Kerala have got from my works, is something which the worshippers of God have not been able to get even from God. The religion of bliss is capable of putting a stop to all religious quarrels and establishing peace and harmony amongst the people of the world. My works would prove these facts. This pamphlet is only a summary of them.

If some people can create divisions amongst men and deprive them of the great joy arising from harmony and peace why cannot we unify people and restore to them the blessings of peace and unity? Men afflicted with dangerous diseases subject themselves to surgical operations knowing that such operations do them good, and consequently enjoy good health. Similarly, those who know that the religion of bliss which contains criticisms of other religions will help a man to escape from the trammels of religions and free themselves from the troubles caused by religions accept it and enjoy bliss. To prevent the spread of this religion without understanding the great benefits caused by religious criticisms is to prevent a patient from being treated in the best manner possible, and that would be a great misfortune to the world. There is no religion which can stand comparison with the religion of Bliss in bringing about the good of Mankind.

38. वयमानन्दात्जातास्सर्वे वयमानन्दात्जीवामश्च।
वयमानन्दंवाञ्छामश्च त्यजतानन्दविरोधिमतानि।।

Meaning: We are born of bliss; we all live in bliss and we always desire bliss. Therefore give up religions hostile to it.

39. ईश्वरदूषकदुःखविधायक शाश्वतसुखहरमतगुरुवचनम्।।
त्यजत, जनाहेभवतानन्दा वयमानन्दावयमानन्दाः।।

Meaning: Avoid the teachings of religious teachers who scandalise God and cause misery to people by destroying their sense of happiness. Be blissful.

40. मित्थ्याजातिमतादि भ्रामितमर्त्यसमूहव्यसननिवृत्यै।
सत्यानन्दमतंमयिशंसति दुष्टविचारःकथमिहशन्क्यः।।

Meaning: I have propounded this religion to save those people who are suffering enmeshed in the meaningless and the baseless differences of caste and religion. Therefore I have no ill-motive in this.

41. मतकर्त्तृणामपमन्ताहं नहिनहिदुष्टविचारश्चमम।
हितवचनादिहसर्वजनानां कुतुकचिकीर्षुःकुतुकचिकीर्षुः।।

Meaning: I am not a scoffer of the founders of religions. I want to please all by telling them what is to their good.

42. वैद्यस्तिष्टेद्राज्ये तद्वद्योगीकुयी हिवनगमनम्।
वन्यानांहरिहरिणादीनां वैद्यज्ञानेकरणीयेकिं।।

Meaning: The spiritual man should remain in the world even as a doctor does and not in a forest. It is not the beasts of the forests that require instructions in such matters. Men having spiritual knowledge should live amongst people and try to give the world unity and peace by removing their ignorance. I ask whether a doctor is needed in a forest without men or in a town full of them.

43. आर्यसमाजोब्रह्मसमाजः क्रिस्तुर्हिन्तुर्बौद्धंजैनम्।
इतिनानामतकलहमतीनां दुःखं दुःखं दुःखं दुःखम्।।

Meaning: Nothing but sorrow and misery awaits those who fight among themselves as Aryas, Brahmos, Christians, Hindus, etc.

44. जननिवहस्सुखमिच्छतिसततं जनयतिदुःखंमतमहहात्र।
व्रतभिक्षाटनपूजादिभ्यः शतविधदुःखंहतसुखजातम्।।

Meaning: People want happiness. But religions ask them to do worship, begging, pilgrimages etc., which all cause sorrow.

45. पृच्छत पृच्छत गुरुवर्यानिदमिच्छत्स्वस्मास्वनिशंसौख्यं।
यच्छथदुःखंकस्मात्कृत्यैः कृच्छ्रैस्तुच्छैर्व्रतपूजाद्यैः।।

Meaning: Ye me! ask your religious teachers why, to men, who want happiness, they prescribe penances and silly worship of images, and give pain?

46. विप्रोदितमतभागंकृत्वा स्वीकृतवन्तःकतिपयभागान्।
उपनयनादिक्रियययाबद्धा उपविप्राशाबहवः किल्ष्टाः।।

Meaning: Many men are being put to great troubles and unhappiness on account of their adopting, and therefore bound by, certain portions of the religious teachings of the Brahmins such as the worship of images, the wearing of the sacread thread the recitation of Mantras, etc.

47. बीये एम्मे प्रभृतिपरीक्षा बिरुदधराअपि मतविश्वासात्।
प्रतिमार्चादिषुकृतमतयस्ते प्रतिभाहीनाःप्रतिभाषन्ते।।

Meaning: Even persons who have acquired high university degrees, with blind faith in their religions, follow practices like image worship and speak illogical things in defence of them. I have dwelt on this aspect in the third chapter.

48. नहिजातिमतेजात्याचारो मतकृत्यं ममनहिनहिकिंचित्।
अविकृतजातिमताचारोहं अहमानन्दोह्यहमानन्दः।।

Meaning: I am free from all the perversions of castes and creeds. I am bliss; I am bliss.

49. निजमानन्दमतमेकंतत् सकलजनानांसत्यंसत्यं।
इतिजानन्तः सुखभाजस्ते नहिनहिदुःखंमतभेदेन।।

Meaning: They are happy-who realise that for all the one in-born religion is the religion of bliss. The differences in religion do not affect them.

50. शक्तिस्सत्या नित्यानन्दा मस्तकमद्ध्येह्यस्तिचकास्ति।
तत्रन्यस्तेचित्तेस्वस्थे हस्तेमुक्तिर्हस्तेमुक्तिः।।

Meaning: In the head of every one there is energy indestructible and blissful in its nature. When the mind is made to merge itself in it salvation is attained.

51. मणिनादादीन्श्रुत्वाश्रुत्वा मणिदीपादीन्दृष्टादृष्टा।
महितानन्दंपीत्वापीत्वा भवतानन्दाहेहेमर्त्त्याः।।

Meaning: Oh Men! Be happy by listening to various sounds, seeing various lights and enjoying the indestructible bliss. I have proved that the world have become pervasive on account of false scriptures which have made men to take their God, religion and caste. In my Mokshapradeepa I have dealt with these false scriptures. I close my pamphlet with the following couplet.

इदंपापमिदंपुण्यमिति विम्यतिकर्मठाः।
दृष्टाकैतवशास्त्राणि वाग्डंभघटितानिवै।।

इति 'शिवज्ञानदीपिका'।।

Men of world are frightened by the false scripture composed by men who boast about their control over words into believing that some thing is sin and that some other thing is virtue and, therefore, into doing what the composers want them to do !

Sixteen

Ananda Matha Parasyam

(The proclamation of the religion of bliss)

O, ye aspirants after Bliss! There are at present many noble and eminent men who found schools and colleges, establish institutions for the study of Sanskrit, Medicine, Music and Dancing, build operas and theatres, and introduce various other reforms, all conducive to worldly happiness. Innumerable too are the religious teachers at the present day, who intensify the hold of ritualism in society by encouraging the building of temples, worship of idols and the like, which are but conducive to the development of ignorance and misery. But none are seen hitherto, neither men of affluence and influence, nor of power, nor those world celebrities who shine with the honorific titles of Acharya, Yogi. Jnani. and so forth, to have made any attempt at the dissemination of Ananda Yoga or the Yoga of Bliss, which wards off all religious misery and grants eternal bliss both to the high and the low. The reason for their indifference or neglect is to be sought in their want of experience of the bliss of Rajayoga, and this want of experience is in its turn to be traced to the fact that Rajayoga has become extinct in the world, enveloped as it is with false texts. As it has thus become extinct, it is said in Devi Bhagawata that there is no yoga on earth (Na yogah prithivithlay) To cite textual authority to show that yoga has been kept hidden by false texts, I quote the following from Sivajnana Deepika:

Pragopyamewa Kalyani! Yogamanandasanjayam I
Mohadibhirapathreshu Upadeshta naradhamha II
Capostheethi cirasthasya Spudathyeva sahasrasah I
Ithi sanjimthya machhapam Sanakadya maharshaya II
Aadinadha dayassarve, Bahirgamabhiya dhiya I
Gopayanthi smathanmoolam Vyaja sastrischa thaih kritaih II

This means: "O Blessed ! The Yoga, the repository of bliss, has to be kept well hidden. That base fellow of a man who imparts it to the unworthy, will incur my curse that his head will burst into a thousand pieces. Thus thinking and fearing my curse, the sages like Sanaka and others and the Yogis like Aadinatha and so forth, have kept it hidden with their own false texts, lest it should gain publicity in the world".

Placing implicit faith in those false texts, which are therein said to be revealed by Siva, or Vishnu or Venerable Seers, and thus giving themselves up to the observance of ritualistic practices like idol worship, vows, fasts pilgrimages, sacrifices and so on, and being unable to bring out true Rajayoga from out the closet of false texts, Hindus do groan under the misery of the evil practices of caste distinctions and the ritualistic practices of idol worship and the like. It is to ward off this misery and to bring relief that I have composed the Siddha works, like Mokshapradeepa and so forth, wherein I have criticised those false texts, proving that caste distinctions, idol worship, vows, fasts, pilgrimages, sacrifices and similar rituals, are all but obstacles to the attainment of salvation, wherein I have shown that there are not the several distinctions of castes and creeds but all are of the one caste, creed, and practice of bliss, and have thus lifted up the Yoga of bliss from the hidden abyss, holding aloft the banner of the virtue of non-injury. By so doing, it has become clear that all religious works that have seen the light of the world hitherto are not conducive to the welfare of mankind. On the other hand, my works have enabled many to discard these religious works, to get themselves liberated from their misery, and to exult in the deep ecstasy of bliss supreme, and saved many a helpless fowl and goat from the pain of slaughter. Further, they have been instrumental to bring into existence in the world a superior and supreme religion, the religion of Ananda or Bliss. To prove:

1. Those seekers after truth who have gone through my Siddha works of Mokshapradeepa and so forth have entirely given up the ritualistic practices of idol worship and the like and the recitation of works like Bhagawat Gita and others. Many an Anandasamajam or assembly of bliss has sprung up in several places, like Cannanore, Walluvanad, Shertally and others. Many a

Yogasala or Communion hall has been established, wherein the Siddha works of Mokshapradeepa and others are recited, and lectures delivered on the topic. A great institution, the Ananda Mahasabha, has been set up which proclaims, "We of the human race are not of the different castes known as Nambudris, Nayars. Ezhuvas, and so on, nor are we of the different religions that go by the names of Hinduism, Buddhism, Christianity, Brahmo Samaj, Arya samaj so forth, nor are we of the different countries to exult in the pride of being a native of the soil or alien. All of us are of the one caste of Ananda, of the one religion of Ananda and of the one country of Ananda". Thus they proclaim and exult in that ecstasy. Even those eminent ones who have attained world celebrity as Acharya, Swami, World Preceptor, and so on, have not been able to bring such ecstasy to men, nor into existence even a single Communion hall of bliss or Yogasala. As such, when ritualists hold the field and form a powerful section, when by the overpowering influence of their lectures on ritualism, even those who were not used to wear the sacred thread hitherto, are talking up to the ignorant ritualistic practices of wearing the sacred thread, building temples, installing idols therein and so forth, when the Missions like Sri Ramakrishna Paramahamsa and the Theosophical Society are given up to preach aloud about ritualism as to tighten its hold on society, when Ritualists, Yogins and Vedantins are indulging and exulting in their criticism about me and my Siddha works, were the Vedas, Sastras and the like of Hinduism and other religions, ever able to produce that effect which my Siddha works like Mokshapradeepa and others have been able to produce by bringing existence at present several Communion halls of Anandayoga of an unheard of type, and by establishing the religion of Ananda? What is required at the present day is one religion of Ananda, which would bring under its fold the several religionists now ranged under hostile camps on the score of the difference of religion, and the atheists who negate the existence of God, which would keep them in amity and harmony and would rouse in them that deep ecstasy of bliss supreme. Did ever the Vedas, Sastras and the like of Hinduism or any other religion, produce the effect which my Siddha works like Anandasutra, Mokshapradeepa and others have been able to produce and introduce in the world the religion of Ananda? No. To prove, please listen to the following extracts of correspondence.

2. "Before we got down the Siddha works of Mokshapradeepa and others, we were used to get down several religious works, and go through them. During those days we were admiring and paying great respect and regard to those works and their authors. All such admiration, respect and regard began to wane within us, after we began to go through the Siddha works Mokshapradeepa and others got down for our library. The reading of Bhagawat Gita had the effect not only of intensifying an outlook of inequality and fostering a passionate favour for ritualism, but also of bringing home to us that the meditation of the Impersonal, attributeless Brahma, the necessary factor for the attainment of salvation, could be had only after great difficulty, and that too for the select few. It was with the help of Mokshapradeepa that we were enabled to have an outlook of equality, to destroy our fervour for ritualism and to come to realise that the meditation of the attributeless Brahma, so very necessary for salvation, is within the easy grasp of even the veriest Chandala who is eager after salvation".

14-1-'01 P.A. Anandan

3. "If in ancient days Sri Krishna or any of the gods who are known to the world as `The Father of the universe, The seat of mercy, Omniscience, the Bestower of desired objects of the devotees and so forth, had written any work as unto what has been graciously done by your noble self, the followers of Hinduism would never have taken up to injury nor to ritualism, thereby installing and worshipping idols of stone and wood, and thus be tossed about in the ocean of worldly bondage to their great misery".

A.S.

4. "Owing to the excessive pride of superiority complex, some scholars of yore have introduced false texts. I salute unto your noble self who have exposed the same in all their nakedness, so as to be looked down upon even by the ignorant striplings".

15th Karkitakam 1087 P.K.K.

When even the great were confounded, not being able to detect the false texts interspersed in the authoritative texts of Bhagawat Gita and the like, was any work in Hinduism ever able to detect the same, except the Siddha works which have enabled even a stripling to detect them?

5. "Here in Trivandrum there is a temple dedicated to Bhadrakali in a place called Aattukal, and here in this temple there is a ceremony, called Kuruthi, wherein are slaughtered about a hundred goats and five times that number of fowls. We were not able by our lectures and preachings to put a stop to this horrible practice. It was at such a juncture that a man of the locality happened to come into possession of a copy of Mokshapradeepa. Why more on the topic? The men of the locality have in one voice resolved that the horrible practice should cease for ever from the ensuing ceremony in the month of Kumbhom. What greater proof is necessary to show how much power Mokshapradeepa wields to dispel the darkness of ignorance?"

7th Dhanu 1088. K.C. Kesava Pillay.

6. "Were the Vedas and other works of Hinduism or any other religion, other than the Siddha works of Mokshapradeepa and so forth ever able to put a stop to the horrible practice of the aforesaid Kuruthi and save the innocent helpless goats and fowls from their pitiable horrible slaughter? Thus, many are the acts of injury that have been put a stop to."

7. "O Lord of Yogins! Overpowered as we are with our nature of dull inertia, groping in the darkness of ignorance without the power of discrimination as to what is proper and improper, we, your dependents, have become filled with the ecstasy of bliss on account of the rays of the shining moon of Rajayaga, the result of your inwards compassion toward all beings."

R.P. and Others.

8. "Since no work has been powerful enough hitherto to relieve men and innocent beings of their misery, it is within our experience that your Sidha works on Ananda are more powerful than the Vedas, Sastras and the like of Hinduism.

O noble self of great mercy! How many have ceased from

doing harm in these days, seeing the evils of injury described by your noble self. If thus pondered over the several reliefs to injury rendered by your noble self, who else other than your noble soul of deep compassion is entitled to be addressed as the protector of the virtue of non-injury and as the Ocean of Mercy?

O Lord of Yogins! Since you have wafted away the cloud of ritualism with the force of the wind of reason, and brought to full view the moon of Rajayoga, many in these days are exulting in the ecstasy of bliss. Every seeker after truth cannot but admit if he were to go through Ananda Sopana (the Ladder of Bliss) which contains the several extracts of correspondence sent from various quarters to your noble self, that this is not the Iron age, but the age of Bliss. Therefore who else other than your noble self is worthy to be styled as the Incarnation of the moon of Rajayoga and as the Founder of the religion of Ananda?

O King of yogins! Is it not with the aid of your Siddha works and your grace that we are fortunate to soar at large in the ethereal region of chit (intelligence), seated in the aerial car of Ananda Vimana, without becoming a prey to the demon of ritualism? But for your noble self, how would we have been fortunate, dull-witted as we are, to experience that deep ecstasy of bliss, not possible even for great kings, great pandits or for even the wealthy lords? Is it not your noble soul that has detected the deceitfulness of the demon of ritualism and beheaded him with the sword of knowledge? By doing so, how many are saved from the dire miseries, physical fatigue and loss of wealth, due to their observance of vows and fasts, pilgrimages, idol worship and the like practices of ritualism and pass their days happily in the enjoyment of wholesome food? Not even Rama and others who destroyed the demon Ravana and other wicked ones, were able to accomplish anything like this. As such, which noble soul other than your noble self is entitled to be addressed as the destroyer of the demon of ritualism?

O Supreme teacher! Any seeker after truth, if he were but to go through your Ananda Vimana (the aerial car to bliss) and take a panoramic view, can see for himself that the Incarnations, the Acharyas of ritualism and their occult powers, and the false texts that are interspersed in Bhagavat Gita and the like works, are rooted out and flown down by the torrential force of your argumentation, just as the rising and rushing flood of a river uproots the trees on its banks and takes them down the river. By the force of your bombs of experience, reason and authoritative texts, thrown down by you from your Ananda Vimana the fortress of idols built up by those wise who make playful ridiculous gestures at you seeing you illustrious works, and their gods have been reduced to ashes. They have no god now but to elect a new god or appoint a president to that place. What else in the world other than your noble works on Ananda has become the real ladder to take even an atheist to the mansion of final beatitude?

O noble soul, the ocean of knowledge! Yours alone are the illustrious works that conduce to liberate the distracted fallen mother India from the grip of the leprosy of caste distinctions, of the paralysis of inequality, and the cataract of ignorance and of the evil ghost of ritualism, and raise her to her glorious pedestal, illuminated with the power of Rajayoga. Some among the Hindus denounce you just as they denounced that immaculate soul, Buddha, acknowledged by those very Hindus as the Incarnation of Vishnu. The reason for this has to be traced to your extraordinary merits and excellence..., deep knowledge, your compassion, vow of non-injury, and your unflinching courage to denounce the unrighteous and unholy ritualism and so forth".

13th Chingom 1092. The Anandasamajams

It is on account of liberating men from the miseries of religious rituals, and pointing out to them the glorious state of bliss and keeping them contented, that many have praised and do praise your noble soul and the Siddha works in ecstasy. Men in their worldly bondage are by nature subject to miseries like disease, poverty, premature death, loss of beloved objects, and persons like sons, friends and relations, and to mutual strifes, fond hopes, and so forth. It is in addition to these that religions increase their miseries, just unto oil poured on burning fire. To explain. The various creeds and religions like Saivaism, Vaishnavism, Saktam, Brahma Samajam and the like allied branches of Hinduism, the religion of Christianity and others, do enjoin that God is to be pleased for mental purity, for relief from misery and for the attainment of bliss. In implicit obedience to those injunctions, people take to the recital of the names of God, to the muttering of the mantras of Gayatri and the like a million times, to the worship of idols with various offerings, to the performance of homas and sacrifices and to the offering of oblations, and so forth. Further, in the same implicit faith they take to fasts in accordance with their rigorous vows, and to meditation. They wander forth in pilgrimages exposed to scorching heat and biting cold, pouring rain and falling dew. They prostrate and supplicate in bitter tears that they may be given their daily bread and that they may be cured of all their diseases, poverty and all other miseries. They vow many an offering of gift and perform various deeds to gain the favour of God. Yet not gaining any relief to their miseries, they fail to gain the knowledge about their self, and fall down from their inherent bliss within, and suffer extreme misery. It is thus that religions add to the miseries of men in addition to their natural miseries of worldly existence. Since our Siddha works do convincingly prove to the world that God is never of a type to be pleased by any kind of word, much less by the ritualistic practices of ignorance, people are liberated from their fond and passionate fervour of ritualism and heave a deep sigh of relief. Since those very works do convincingly prove that there is no means other than Yoga to get one united unto bliss and that the whole world is of the one religion of bliss, they have helped many a people to exult in the ecstasy of bliss and to introduce the religion of Ananda into the world. Have the Vedas, Sastras and the like of Hinduism or any other religion produced any effect similar to that achieved by our Siddha works? In order to understand fully to extraordinary proof adduced to show that God is not of a type to please or to be pleased, is impersonal without any attributes whatsoever, one should go through the works of Ananda Vimana, Anandaadarsa and Vigraharadhanakhandana (criticism of idol-worship). Since this is but a short treatise, I shall pick out but one fact from them and prove that the propitiatory rituals of God are all in vain.

O Ye advocates of religion! Since you and your religions advocate that God is the Creator, Protector and Destroyer, it becomes clear on the strength of your own tenet that God is a wicked being, really fastidious, and all your rituals to gain His favour are of no avail. To explain. It turns out that creation, protection and destruction are the natural functions of God.

How can God give up those His natural functions? A farmer sows the seeds, protects the crops and eventually harvests them, Will he show any mercy in the harvesting of the crops? No. Since God's cultivation is of the nature of creation, protection and destruction. He cannot but destroy you, however fervently you pray or bitterly cry out to be saved of such destruction. The dealer in flesh rears up goats and fowls; eventually he slaughters them, feeds upon them and trades in their flesh too. However bitterly the fowls and goats may cry out in agony, does he spare them out of mercy without slaughtering them? No. Likewise God also has no go to show any mercy and save them from destruction, for, what you advocate is that destruction also is the natural function of God. Will God give up that duty even if you entreat Him to desist from that duty of destruction? Will the sun ever desist from emitting heat, and keep everything cool even if he is entreated, saluted or worshipped not to do so? Will fire however much we may attempt to propitiate it with hymns of praise and worship and entreaty, every cease to burn us and keep us cool? Fire burns the very hand of its votary who consecrates and maintains the sacred fire and worships it daily. If he were to touch fire, overcome with excessive devotion to his favourite deity with the soothing words 'He is my own God of Fire, my beloved deity', he is sure to have his fingers burnt. If he approaches that fire too close, that fire will reduce that devotee to ashes. None can stop or alter the course of nature. As such, all your ritualistic practices of prayer and the like to desist God from his natural duty of destruction and bless you with His favour are of no avail. Look at the life of Jesus Christ. He was a great devotee of God, who ever prayed unto him, "O creator, O creator" What a noble and virtuous soul was he who ever preached about God and made many others too to sing his praise and pray unto Him? How supremely moral he was ! Such a Christ was caught hold of by his enemies who spat him in his face, smote him on his cheeks, laughed at him, set a vessel of vinegar mixed with gall before him to drink, tied him to the cross, nailed him on the breast and crucified him. Unable to bear the agony, he cried out in a loud voice saying. 'My God, my God! Why has thou forsaken me' and yielded up the ghost. God did not give him any relief whatsoever. Where was the mercy of the Creator then? If God is of a type of be pleased at His devotees, He ought to have showered His mercy on Christ. But Christ was not blessed by God even with the insight to know whether he had been accepted or not by God. If he had really known, would he have cried aloud saying, 'O my God! Why has thou forsaken me?' When such is the state of Christ himself, what is the lot of those who believe that belief in Christ would ensure the grace of God and open the gate of Paradise for them? Surely their lot is that of pitiable Arjuna who, in the sincere belief in the words of Bhagawat Gita, the teachings of Sri Krishna, was ever devoted to the performance of action in a spirit disinterestedness, yet without gaining that knowledge of self, was afraid of the impending advent of Kali, the presiding deity of the Iron age, fled the country out of that fear, and perished on the way. The words of Christians that God created Christ and offered him in sacrifice to redeem mankind of their original sin, do not turn out to be a satisfactory explanation, but turns out only to a blasphemy that God is wicked beings, who curses His own created children and kills by crucifying in the cross. These people preach that He is All-Powerful and is the seat of mercy! What is not the Omnipotent capable of accomplishing! Adam and Eve, the first creation, had become sinners and become the object of His curse. Could He not absolve them of their sins by blessing them? Is it the characteristic of that One who is the seat of mercy, to curse His own created children and destroy them? Is it reasonable to think that He would show that mercy towards those heartless cruel, who kill and feed upon the innocent goats and fowls without showing His mercy towards them, in spite of hearing their piteous groans shaking their legs when they are slaughtered by men and of seeing their last agonies of death, unable to put up with the pain of their last moments? Is there anything more foolish than the thought that God would show His mercy towards those men who indulge more in the taste of the flesh and blood of the innocent beings like goats and fowls than in the sentiment of compassion and extreme devotional love to God? The Vedas, Sastras and the like proclaim that there is no virtue equal to pity and no sin equal to injury, and all religions enjoin on the virtue of pity. As such, if men give up this noble virtue of pity and indulge in doing harm to innocent beings, and if there is a God who would show His mercy towards them, who is there in the world more wicked than such a God? There is not a God who is thus partial towards men. If there is, to which religionist Has he shown such a mercy or has shown His favour? We see among those, who propitiate God in extreme devotion, many a calamity like fell disease, dire poverty, premature death, loss of beloved sons, friends, wife and the like, which are not the lot of even those ignorant who do not propitiate any God at all. Is this the grace of Gods towards His devotees? What religions teach is that they will be saved and blessed with happiness in heaven. Is it not bless His devotees with any happiness here in this world, will bless them with the same in heaven? Have those religionists been witness at any time to the fact that God had blessed any one thus? Is it not reasonable and proper that He should bless them here in this world? Should not one be fed when one is hungry? Should not one be given relief when one is afflicted with misery? O Ye men! If God is, as you advocate, the creator, protector and destroyer, then it has been shown here that He could not be pleased at you in any way and grant you salvation. By granting you salvation, God runs the risk of a great loss and a dereliction of His own inherent duty. To explain. If God is pleased and grant salvation to beings, His cultivation in the form of creation, protection and destruction would entirely fail, and He will fail in the discharge of His natural duty too. Without seeds how will the farmer sow? How will he reap the harvest? If all beings are granted salvation, how can creation continue? How can there be destruction? As seeds to the farmer, is not the aggregate of lives,... the aggregate of lives should gradually get dwindled, and the cultivation of crops in the form of worldly life must have come to an end long long ago. According to the tenets of your religion, there is no scope too for any increase in the primeval aggregate of lives. The following facts and authorities would show that when the aggregate of lives gets dwindled in consequence of its individual constituents gradually getting salvation, there is no chance to make up the deficit by the creation of new lives. It is the very water that rises up to the sky as vapour owing to the heat of the sun that comes down as rain. The very water that falls as rain over mountains and plains, flows through streams and rivers and enters the ocean. Again in season, the same process continues. To make up the deficit of the water evaporated as vapour, no new supply of water is resorted to. If the water that has risen up above as vapour were not to come down as rain, oceans, lakes and wells would have all dried up long ago. That it does not so happen even after the lapse of a long period of time is due to the fact that water, thus gone up as vapour, comes down in due course as rain. Likewise, lives or souls also are going up and coming down, and thus it is that the ocean of worldly existence continues to exist for ever. If, on the other hand, it is argued that the deficit caused by the gradual emancipation of the constituent individual souls, is made up by the creation of fresh souls, and thus it is that the ocean of worldly existence ever remains unaffected, without any change, this very argument strikes at the root of the scriptural text which says

"Boothagrama sa evayam
bhuthwa bhuthwa praleeyathe"

which means that the same original aggregate of lives come and go revolvingly. Further it is contradictory to the scriptural text *"Aho nithya shaswathoyam puranha:"*, which means that the soul is upborn constant eternal and indestructible. Further, the above argument necessitates the creation of new heavens and abodes of salvation too. If not, will not the earlier emancipated and the later ones, get gradually crowded in the existing heaven, exposed to the unpleasant impact of daily increasing rush? So many are the souls that were and are being given passports to heaven by the various religions in the course of time. This is but what is revealed by these very religions too. Many are the ways enjoined in religions whereby many souls are liberated in a moment. Yet God's work of creation, protection and destruction, has not in the least been affected by it. As we think over this state of nature on the strength of experience, those religions which advocate that by the grace of God or of His Incarnations or of His sons, if any, many can be and have been emancipated, lose their very stand, and the nature of the Vedas which say *Na sa punaravarthathe na sa punaravarthathe* which means that the emancipated do not take birth again, is exposed in all its naked reality. O Ye Founders of religions! As we proceed to comment upon the tenet that God is the creator, protector and destroyer, it becomes clear that God is heartless and is the seat of all evil virtues, who teases His own created children, that He is of a type fastidious in all ways, that He is despicable, ever bent upon doing base and wicked actions, which would not be resorted to even by the wild beasts like lions and tigers or by the wicked demons and ghosts, and as such, He ought to be punished by the united governments of the world, since He destroys all His children, as any government would punish a father who destroys his own children. O Ye Founders of religions! It was indeed harsh and rash of you to have made your God such a being. As such, have you any justification to lay down the several rituals to gain the favour of God, or to perform or to have them performed? Can you with any reason describe that your God is the seat of mercy, the friend of the distressed and the bestower of the desired objects of His devotees, and so forth? Is there any greater mistake or inconsistency than saying that God is the seat of all vices and also at the same time that He is the seat of all virtues, as one would blow hot and cold at the same breath, when one says that fire is hot and at the same time cold too? Were the Vedas and the like of Hinduism or of any other religion ever capable of producing those uncommon powers of knowledge and reason and so forth, as have been produced by our Sidha works of Anandavimana and others, to introduce into the world the religion of Ananda which detects and points out to the world this absurd inconsistency, weans them off from the several ritualistic practices of misery, and keeps them ever in the rapture of ecstasy born of Yoga? O Ye Aspirants after bliss! Those religions which advocate that Iswara (God, known as Brahma) is the Seat of mercy, Friend of the distressed. Bestower of the desired objects of His devotees, the Creator, Protector and Destroyer of the universe, and so forth, are of a nature wafted away like chaff and the light cotton, when the wind of reason blows over them. If these religions, which are reduced to ashes like rags or moths in the fire of the knowledge of experience, are believed in, neither man has, not had he, at any time any chance to experience real knowledge, mental steadfastness or bliss supreme, but his lot is only to fall a victim to fear, to get deluded and lead a miserable life, engaged in the performance of several ritualistic practices. If, on the other hand, they had a chance to experience the same, people embracing the one religion of Hinduism, would never go down, fighting on the score of caste distinctions. They would neither be quarrelling on the score of the distinctions of Saivaism. Vaishnavaism and so forth installing several idols of stone and the like, without knowing the idol of bliss supreme. They would neither be seduced by the glamour of the muttering of mantras, like Gayatri, nor by the Tantric modes of worship, and so on. Nor would the worshippers of God wrangle on the score of the distinctions of religion, without knowing that the whole world is of the one religion of Ananda. Nor would they describe in glowing terms, that heaven would, be had after death, without giving expression to the experience of bliss or salvation, while alive here in this world. For the sake of alleviation of misery and the attainment of desired objects, they would never cry out to a God any pray unto Him, as children cry out to their father. In spite of such profuse shedding of tears, God, their Father, has not blessed them with anything, not even with the knowledge that His children should not take to quarrel and that there is neither any distinction of caste or creed, nor has He stopped their crying. On the other hand the delusion of religion and the crying out to God, are daily on the increase in the world. Alas! Are ignorance, calamity and tears, the result of propitiation of God? Hence neither traditional customs nor textual authorities should ever be accepted as guides to salvation, on the belief that they are enjoined by the Vedas, or they are created, by God, or they are approved by all, or that they have been practised from time immemorial by the followers of all religions, and none has a dissenting voice in the matter. If they are found to go against experience and reason, they are to be discarded as unto the outer rind and joint of the sugar cane, supposed to be created by God. Then alone bliss can be realised. This is the gist of the religion of Ananda. That salvation consists in the control of the mind, and that is within one's own power and not dependent upon God, is the cardinal tenet of the religion of Ananda. What we require is a religion which is capable of imparting real courage to keep oneself steady and unflinching, without any wavering or retracing a single step, even though the entire universe might be ranged against us, and which, with such aid, is capable wiping out entirely all ignorance, ritualism and all evil unworthy religions. The religion of Ananda is such an unassailable religion. It is a religion that brings ecstasy of bliss to all theists and atheists, young and old, man and woman. I have slightly alluded to the extraordinary knowledge and bliss, that are experienced nowadays by several persons in several places, owing to the help of our Siddha publications. How can I describe them in detail in this short treatise? Listen to one thing more. Coming to know of the glory of Yoga through our Siddha works, many a person who has not known anything of Yoga, has now begun to express in words and writings that they are adepts in Yoga. Some section of the people, who asserted boldly on the absolute necessity of the distinctions of castes and idol-worship, have begun to write in paper and journals that they are to be given up, quoting in support of their new view, the very reasons set forth by me in my Siddha works like Mokshapradeepa and others. They argue too on the strength of those very reasons. Some have taken up to interdining. Some cite the very reasons, advanced in Mokshapradeepa and other works, to prove the existence of false texts in Hindu religious treatises. Further a reputed acharya of a major section, who had built several temples at immense cost, installed idols therein and encouraged idol worship, has written in the issue of the paper *Samadarsi* of Trivandrum dated 6.6.1918, as follows: "Temples are not to be built. People are losing their faith in temples. They may have to repent that they have wasted vast sums in the construction of temples. Times have undergone such a change".

O Ye intelligent! Think over why it is that times have thus changed. Was time white in olden days, and now turned black? Are we think it had no legs and hands formerly and it was poor, but it has hands and legs at present and has grown excessively aggressive? What is the underlying idea of the above statement that times have undergone such a change. Listen to me. I shall explain.

Owing to the rapidly increasing circulation of our Siddha works which denounce the distinction of castes and creeds and ritualistic practices of idol-worship and so forth, and expound the Yoga of bliss and the religion of Ananda, some have, in absolute disgust, thrown overboard all rituals like idol-worship, the distinctions of castes and creeds, and so forth. They have begun to criticise the evils of those ritualistic practices *in extenso*. Since they get the chance to experience the ecstasy of Yogic bliss, they proclaim in all joy that this is not the Iron age, but verily the age of Ananda or bliss absolute. They extol our Siddha works and the ways chalked out therein. They demolish temples, and put up in their place Ananda Yogasalas or communion halls of Yogic bliss. They set up Anandasamajams, and convene meetings. They proclaim that there is no God higher than Bliss, and that the whole world is of the one religion of Ananda. Thus has risen up in Kerala a religions awakening, not seen anywhere else in the world. That is the reason why it was published in *Samadarsi* that times have undergone such a change. Never at any time before the advent of our Siddha works like Mokshapradeepa and others, has arisen in Kerala such a religious awakening as to give expression to the idea that times have changed, that money spent on the construction of temples has become a waste, nor has arisen that dawn of courage and peculiar knowledge to criticise the existence of the distinctions of castes and creeds and the ritualistic practices of idol-worship and the like, to encourage interdining, to describe the bliss of yoga, and to expose that there are false texts in Hinduism. If, on the other hand, there had been such an awakening earlier, before the advent of these works in 1894 AD, there would have come into existence several publications in the forms of lectures, pamphlets, and books, criticising the distinctions of castes and creeds and the ritualistic practices of idol-worship and so forth. Interdining would have become an accomplished fact in society. False texts of Hinduism would have been detected and exposed to the public and denounced, and Rajayoga or Anandayoga would have been disseminated. There would have been no room to denounce me and my Siddha works like Mokshapradeepa and others on their advent into the world. Even now many a man of blind implicit faith in immemorial customs, out of false pride, of jealousy and envy, does indulge in uttering and reporting falsehoods and in several other questionable devices to misinterpret me and my Sidha works to the public. Seeing this practice and thinking that thereby those who do not know me and who have not the chance to go through my Siddha works, may misunderstand me and my works, and thus be deprived of their chance to attain that peculiar knowledge and bliss absolute, which can be had by going through those works. I have brought out this booklet. On going through my Siddha works like Mokshapradeepa and so forth, not only those aspirants after bliss absolute, but even schoolboys will be able to understand the cardinal truths of religion and be armed with the powers of reason, courage and intellect to destroy the creeds of the advocates of religion. If the works on the religion of Ananda happen to be prescribed as text books in schools and colleges, or if they happen to be translated into other languages, or if the rich and highly placed in society happen to taste a little of bliss of Rajayoga, the followers of all religions will turn out to be of the one religion of Ananda. If fact we are all of the religion of Ananda or bliss. Hence it is that both the theists and the atheists, who wrangle about God in diverse ways, do aspire alike for bliss. To attain bliss and to be relieved of misery, other religions enjoin the propitiation of God, while the religion of Ananda refutes it. This will be clear from what has been stated hitherto and what is to be set forth below.

O Ye aspirants after bliss! It is only when the physical body comes in contact with water that it is relieved of heat and becomes cool. None would be relieved of heat nor would feel cool by the mere muttering of the words 'water, water', nor by praising water and praying unto it, nor by worshipping, prostrating before and meditating on water. Likewise, neither relief from misery nor the attainment of bliss can be had by the mere recitation of God's names, by the muttering of mantras and prayers, by prostration, worship, meditation and so forth. Bliss and relief of misery can be really had only when the mind is united unto its own real nature. Giving up that path of Rajayoga, all attempts to win the grace of God by the propitiatory rites of prayer and so on, are of no use. If there is a God who would be pleased, all our prayers and the like would have borne their fruit. There is no such God. Therefore get the mind absorbed, and united unto bliss. Then only will misery cease. When the mind is absorbed in deed sleep, no religionist feels any sort of misery. I shall further prove that without advising the path of Rajayoga whereby all could easily absorb their mind, it was not right and proper to have advised to take to the propitiation of God. When the eye is cured of the disease of cataract, it sees of its own accord the light of the sun. Is it right to advise to propitiate the sun by prayers and so forth? Likewise, to wash away the impurities of the mind and to experience the inherent light within one self, it is enough if one is advised to keep the mind absorbed by due control. Without advising thus, but advising them chiefly to propitiate God, people have misunderstood that only by propitiation of God the mind could be got under control and man could be relieved of all misery, and not otherwise. Thus instead of controlling and getting the mind absorbed unto itself, they attempt to win over God by propitiating Him through prayers and other similar practices. They do not remove the impurities of the mind like desire and so forth. When faced with failure and misery, they cry out aloud to God in prayers and tears, like unto children crying aloud to their parents. Not only the foolish ignorant, but even the intelligent wise, do not realise that the path to the relief of misery lay in the conquest of the mind. Therefore to remove darkness and to gain sun's light, the eye has to be treated and cured of its disease. There is no use in attempting to please the sun by prayers, prostrations and so forth. Likewise, to be relieved of misery and to experience bliss, one is not to attempt to please God by prayers or offerings of porridge and so on. One should treat the mind and improve it. That is real propitiation of God. There is no God who would be pleased through prayers and the like. These are the several tenets of the religion of Ananda. Even by the few facts briefly alluded to herein, it will be clear that God is not of a type to be pleased in any way. If this is not enough to convince you, go through the Siddha works of Ananda Vimana and others. Then it will be clear to you that God is impersonal without any attributes and is not liable to any change or modification. Nor is He partial to bless in accordance with the prayers and the like offered to Him. It will further become clear that those religions which describe God as the seat of all virtues like mercy and so forth, as the bestower of all desired objects, as the destroyer of the universe and so on, and, thus instilling fear and hope in men, enjoin them to propitiate God, do but make them slaves of ignorance and miserable ritualism, lead them astray from real truth, deprive them of their own manliness and thoughtfulness, and make them blind implicit believers. It is by so doing that these unreasonable religions hold their sway and retain an honourable place in the society of blind believers. If the leaders of Kerala set out to reform religion, accepting but what stands the test of experience and reason by whomsoever, high or low, it may be said, it will become clear that Kerala will earn the name of being the eye of knowledge, not only of India, but of the entire world, and that the Siddha works are the supreme Vedas that would help men to be relieved of their misery of worldly life, and of the greater misery of being slaves to religions.

Prose Translation of the Verses

1. Seeing that Gita has enjoined the performance of action in a spirit of disinterestedness, you should not get deluded and give up the easy path of Rajayoga. If so given up, you will not attain the bliss absolute, but will perish like Arjuna who perished on the way. Discard therefore the delusion of ritualism.

2. The wicked enemies of Jesus Christ caught hold of him, spat him in his face, smote him on his cheeks and gave him for drink vinegar mixed with gall. Did God help him vet?

3. They reviled at him in derision saying, 'you say you are the son of God. Let God release you from the cross'. Even then did God show any mercy unto him?

4. 'If you perform any miracle, your words cannot fail, and we shall believe in them and in you'. Even though the leaders of Pharaohs did address him thus, did God show even a little of mercy to Jesus?

5. If we think of the fact that God was heartless and did not show any mercy at all unto Jesus, though he was nailed to the cross and though he cried aloud in distress, 'O my God, my God, Hast thou forsaken me', will that God, the creator of the universe, be imbued with mercy towards the believers in Jesus?

6. O Men! God has no son, nor has He any mercy or love towards His devotees, nor is He in the habit of bestowing their desired objects. That is verily the supreme Rajayoga which teaches that the mind should be cleansed of its impurities of desire, infatuation, pride and so forth, and that it should be got absorbed unto itself within.

7. Neither for the atheists who negate the existence of God, nor for the theists who postulate His existence and believe that even stone is their God, their is anything equal to the religion of Ananda that will help to take one to the stronghold of bliss. This will be clear if the Siddha works like Ananda Vimana are gone through.

"Manasachalanam dukkham thallayo Moksha ochhyathe
Nathah: paratharow Swargamokshou thow Mathakalpithov".

"The motion or unsteadiness of the mind is misery while its absorption is salvation. Other than this, there is neither heaven nor salvation. That there are such heaven and salvation is but the speculation of religion. Even if such exist they are of no use to us too".

He who goes through this booklet of Anandamata parasya, will not get deluded in the several religions like Hinduism, Christianity, the creeds of Sri Ramakrishna Mission, of Brahmo Samaj, Arya Samaj. Vedanta, Yoga Visishtadwaita and so forth. Why? For, all these religions and creeds enjoin Herculean efforts to win over God. God will never be pleased by rituals of prayer, muttering mantras or by the Tantric modes of worship, charms and other practices. I have proved in this work that He will but destroy His own devotees all alike, and those ritualistic practices of prayer and so forth do but conduce to increase ignorance and misery. Unlike these religions, Buddhism does not help to increase ignorance and misery born of the propitiation of the personal God of attributes. Verily it is a religion of pure knowledge, but that lacks in that Yoga of Ananda which helps all to attain Nirvana or salvation. Since the eight-fold path enjoined therein is highly conducive to create a version to worldly pleasures and instil a spirit of renunciation, one acting up to that will not be affected by the miseries of worldly life. But it is not sufficiently powerful to lead one to experience completely that bliss absolute. Without knowing the real truth about Rajayoga, shrouded as it is by false texts, and that of Vedanta, many do even at the present day publish many a book with the titles of Rajayoga, Hamsayoga, Vedanta Rahasya and so forth. Some among them have employed therein their perverted skill by stating that Brahmanandaswami Sivayogi has but caught hold of the one aspect, viz, meditation at the centre of the eyebrows, has given up the breathing processes of Pranayama and the like and, by misinterpreting Yoga, leads people astray. But it has become quite evident that they have not been able to bring out true Rajayoga from out of the closet of false texts, since unlike my Siddha works, they have not been of any use to society but to delude people into the practice of Pranayama, Mantras and Tantras. They have but further turned out, in the eyes of seekers after truth, only as accords of evidence to prove that they revile at me out of their blind superstitious faith and of that passion of jealousy and envy towards me. O Ye seekers after truth! The intrinsic merit or excellence of Acharyas and religious works is to be decided by the single test whether the teachings and practices of religions and religious teachers are conducive to the relief of misery and to the attainment of bliss supreme, and not on the opinion of the majority. Why? Because all of us are verily desirous of being relieved of misery and of exulting in bliss. The majority test is not to be applied in the matter of salvation. Are not mutual wranglings and degeneration the result that Hindus have reaped and do reap on account of their majority view of caste distinctions and ritualistic practices like idol-worship and so forth? Likewise the majority view in other religions too brings on but evils in other ways. A majority party is of real help in the construction of buildings, bridges and so forth. One is not able single-handed to carry timber, tiles, stones, bricks and so on to the place of construction and to construct it. The help of many, even of elephants is required. Only the view of the significant party of truth, though it be of minority, is to be accepted in the matter of salvation.

Ajnanadukhapagamah
Swanandapthischa yena sah
Sa saronyasthu Nissaro
Mathagrandho Vishopamah

(Anandadarsa)

"That is the real religious work of significance by which the misery of ignorance is removed and the attainment of bliss within is had. All other religious works are insignificant and are like unto poison". The gist is that those religions which are not able to take one to the experience of bliss absolute while alive here in this world, but lead them to the performance of ritualistic practices of prayers, Mantras, and Tantras in the belief that heaven could be had after death or in another life, are all like unto poison.

Brahmanandaswami Sivayogi.

Index